FEAR ITSELF
BLACK PANTHER
THE MAN WITHOUT FEAR

WRITER
DAVID LISS

ARTISTS
JEFTE PALO (ISSUES #519-520)
FRANCESCO FRANCAVILLA (ISSUES #521-524)

COLORISTS
JEAN-FRANCOIS BEAULIEU (ISSUES #519-520)
FRANCESCO FRANCAVILLA (ISSUES #521-524)

COVER ARTISTS
SIMONE BIANCHI WITH SIMONE PERUZZI (ISSUES #519-520)
PATRICK ZIRCHER WITH ANDY TROY (ISSUES #521-523)
FRANCESCO FRANCAVILLA (ISSUE #524)

LETTERER
VC'S JOE CARAMAGNA

ASSISTANT EDITORS
JOHN DENNING & JON MOISAN

EDITOR
BILL ROSEMANN

MATT MURDOCK (A.K.A. THE VIGILANTE CALLED DAREDEVIL) HAS LEFT THE NEW YORK CITY NEIGHBORHOOD KNOWN AS HELL'S KITCHEN IN THE CARE OF HIS LONGTIME ALLY T'CHALLA, THE FORMER BLACK PANTHER AND KING OF WAKANDA. AFTER STEPPING DOWN FROM HIS RULE AND SUFFERING THE LOSS OF POWERS ONCE GRANTED TO HIM BY THE PANTHER GOD, T'CHALLA SEEKS TO REDISCOVER HIMSELF ON THE STREETS OF MANHATTAN, REFUSING THE HELP OF HIS MANY FRIENDS AND FAMILY.

RECENTLY, T'CHALLA TOOK DOWN THE RISING CRIMELORD VLAD DINU, THOUGH MANY INNOCENTS ON BOTH SIDES WERE HURT IN THE CONFLICT. TYING UP LOOSE ENDS, T'CHALLA NOW SEARCHES FOR HIS FORMER EMPLOYEE BRIAN, WHO WAS LEFT WANDERING THE STREETS AFTER BEING LOBOTOMIZED AND ALTERED BY A ROGUE SUPER-POWERS EXPERIMENT, UNAWARE THAT THE SCIENTIST INVOLVED HAS ALREADY HIRED KRAVEN THE HUNTER TO FIND BRIAN FIRST...

COLLECTION EDITOR: CORY LEVINE • ASSISTANT EDITORS: ALEX STARBUCK & NELSON RIBEIRO
EDITORS, SPECIAL PROJECTS: JENNIFER GRÜNWALD & MARK D. BEAZLEY • SENIOR EDITOR, SPECIAL PROJECTS: JEFF YOUNGQUIST
SENIOR VICE PRESIDENT OF SALES: DAVID GABRIEL • SVP OF BRAND PLANNING & COMMUNICATIONS: MICHAEL PASCIULLO
BOOK DESIGN: JEFF POWELL

EDITOR IN CHIEF: AXEL ALONSO • CHIEF CREATIVE OFFICER: JOE QUESADA
PUBLISHER: DAN BUCKLEY • EXECUTIVE PRODUCER: ALAN FINE

BLACK PANTHER: THE MAN WITHOUT FEAR — FEAR ITSELF. Contains material originally published in magazine form as BLACK PANTHER: THE MAN WITHOUT FEAR #519-523 and BLACK PANTHER: THE MOST DANGEROUS MAN ALIVE #524. First printing 2012. ISBN# 978-0-7851-5206-4. Published by MARVEL WORLDWIDE, INC., a subsidiary of MARVEL ENTERTAINMENT, LLC. OFFICE OF PUBLICATION: 135 West 50th Street, New York, NY 10020. Copyright © 2011 and 2012 Marvel Characters, Inc. All rights reserved. $16.99 per copy in the U.S. and $18.99 in Canada (GST #R127032852); Canadian Agreement #40668537. All characters featured in this issue and the distinctive names and likenesses thereof, and all related indicia are trademarks of Marvel Characters, Inc. No similarity between any of the names, characters, persons, and/ or institutions in this magazine with those of any living or dead person or institution is intended, and any such similarity which may exist is purely coincidental. **Printed in the U.S.A.** ALAN FINE, EVP - Office of the President, Marvel Worldwide, Inc. and EVP & CMO Marvel Characters B.V.; DAN BUCKLEY, Publisher & President - Print, Animation & Digital Divisions; JOE QUESADA, Chief Creative Officer; TOM BREVOORT, SVP of Publishing; DAVID BOGART, SVP of Operations & Procurement, Publishing; RUWAN JAYATILLEKE, SVP & Associate Publisher, Publishing; C.B. CEBULSKI, SVP of Creator & Content Development; DAVID GABRIEL,.SVP of Publishing Sales & Circulation; MICHAEL PASCIULLO, SVP of Brand Planning & Communications; JIM O'KEEFE, VP of Operations & Logistics; DAN CARR, Executive Director of Publishing Technology; SUSAN CRESPI, Editorial Operations Manager; ALEX MORALES, Publishing Operations Manager; STAN LEE, Chairman Emeritus. For information regarding advertising in Marvel Comics or on Marvel.com, please contact Niza Disla, Director of Marvel Partnerships, at ndisla@marvel.com. For Marvel subscription inquiries, please call 800-217-9158. **Manufactured between 8/8/2012 and 9/10/2012 by R.R. DONNELLEY, INC., SALEM, VA, USA.**

10 9 8 7 6 5 4 3 2 1

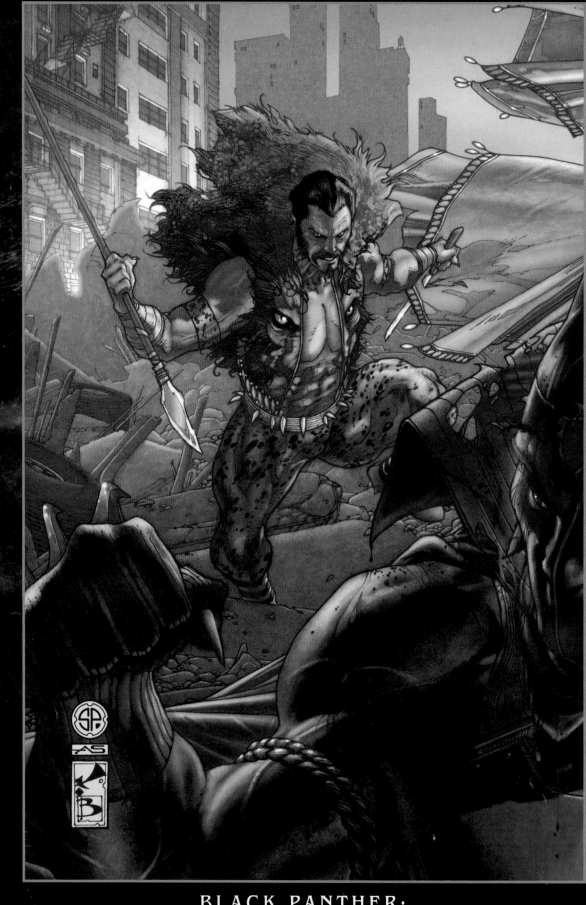

BLACK PANTHER:
THE MAN WITHOUT FEAR #519

ORORO IQADI T'CHALLA, A.K.A. THE MUTANT X-MAN KNOWN AS STORM.

I CAN SEE HOW **TIRED** YOU ARE, MY LOVE. YOU HAVE ONLY JUST DEFEATED THIS VLAD. YOU NEED TO **REST.**

I DON'T HAVE THAT OPTION.

BRIAN IS OUT THERE SOMEWHERE. IF I HADN'T HIRED HIM TO WORK AT THE DINER, NONE OF THIS WOULD HAVE HAPPENED.

I THOUGHT VLAD KILLED HIM, BUT HE'S STILL **ALIVE, CONFUSED** AND **DANGEROUS.** HE HAS INCREDIBLE POWERS HE DOESN'T UNDERSTAND.

I'VE GOT TO FIND BRIAN BEFORE HE HURTS HIMSELF OR OTHERS.

THEN LET ME HELP YOU THIS **ONE** TIME. I CAN HAVE PIXIE **TELEPORT** ME TO NEW YORK.

ORORO, THIS IS SOMETHING I MUST DO--

ALONE.

⹂SIGH⹂

HEARING THAT **NEVER** GETS TIRESOME.

THAT'S GOOD TO KNOW, BECAUSE YOU ARE LIKELY TO KEEP HEARING IT.

I CANNOT TEST MYSELF IF I HAVE ONE OF THE WORLD'S MOST **POWERFUL** BEINGS BY MY SIDE.

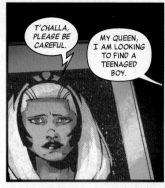

T'CHALLA, PLEASE BE CAREFUL.

MY QUEEN, I AM LOOKING TO FIND A TEENAGED BOY.

HOW **DANGEROUS** CAN IT BE?

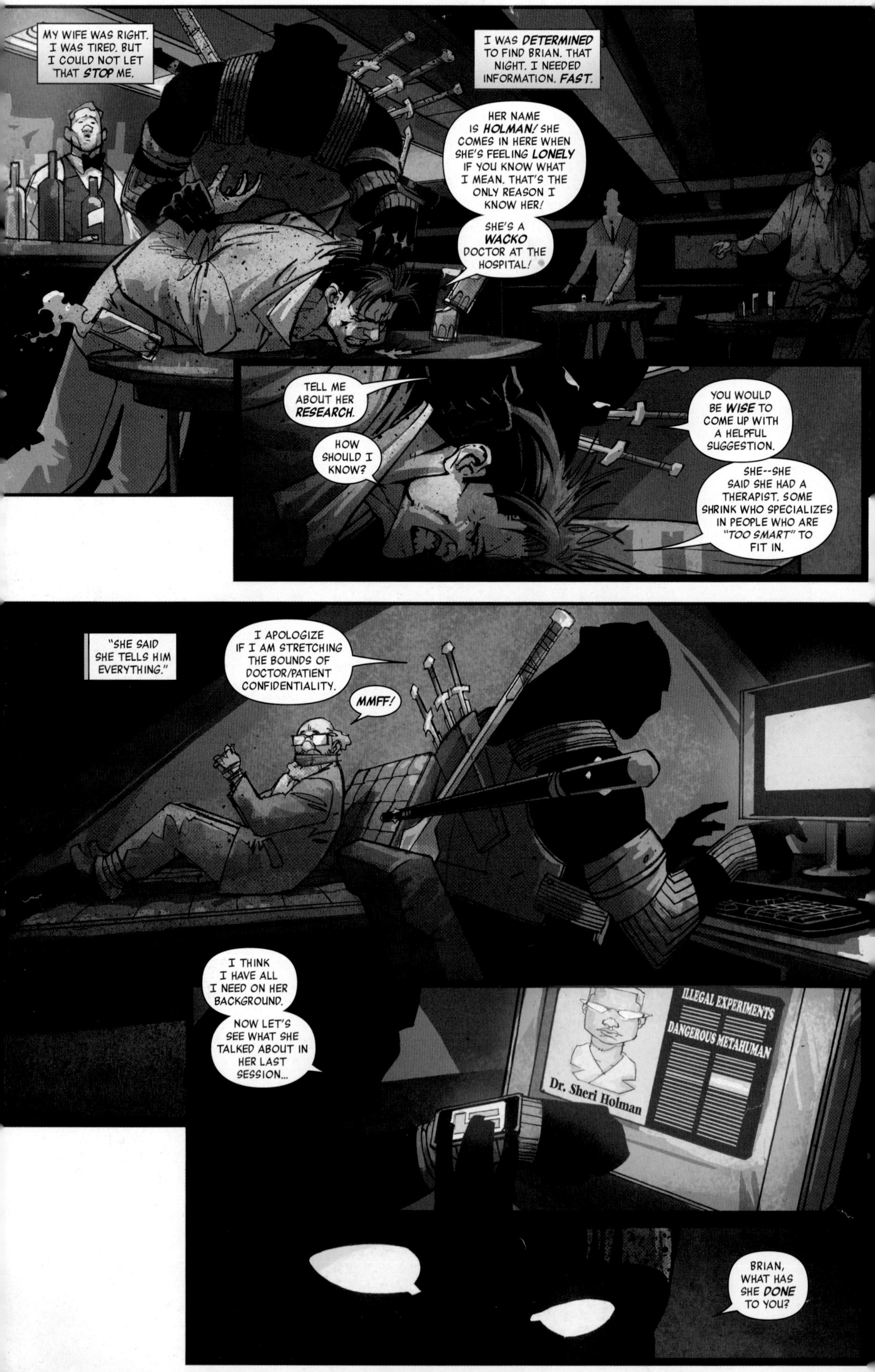
MY WIFE WAS RIGHT. I WAS TIRED. BUT I COULD NOT LET THAT STOP ME.
I WAS DETERMINED TO FIND BRIAN. THAT NIGHT. I NEEDED INFORMATION. FAST.
HER NAME IS HOLMAN! SHE COMES IN HERE WHEN SHE'S FEELING LONELY IF YOU KNOW WHAT I MEAN. THAT'S THE ONLY REASON I KNOW HER!
SHE'S A WACKO DOCTOR AT THE HOSPITAL!
TELL ME ABOUT HER RESEARCH.
HOW SHOULD I KNOW?
YOU WOULD BE WISE TO COME UP WITH A HELPFUL SUGGESTION.
SHE--SHE SAID SHE HAD A THERAPIST. SOME SHRINK WHO SPECIALIZES IN PEOPLE WHO ARE "TOO SMART" TO FIT IN.
"SHE SAID SHE TELLS HIM EVERYTHING."
I APOLOGIZE IF I AM STRETCHING THE BOUNDS OF DOCTOR/PATIENT CONFIDENTIALITY.
MMFF!
I THINK I HAVE ALL I NEED ON HER BACKGROUND.
NOW LET'S SEE WHAT SHE TALKED ABOUT IN HER LAST SESSION...
ILLEGAL EXPERIMENTS
DANGEROUS METAHUMAN
Dr. Sheri Holman
BRIAN, WHAT HAS SHE DONE TO YOU?

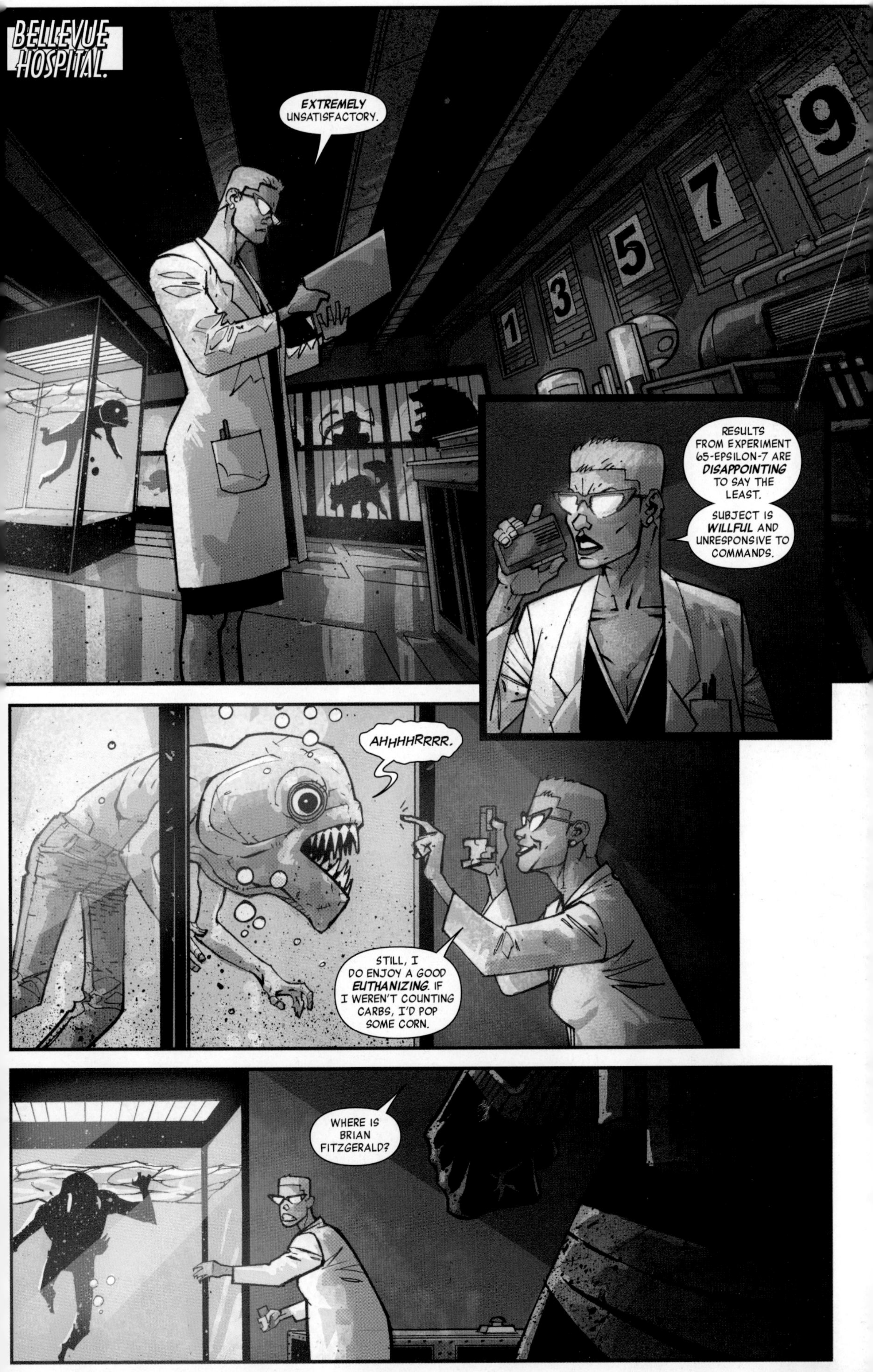
BELLEVUE HOSPITAL.
EXTREMELY UNSATISFACTORY.
1
3
5
7
9
RESULTS FROM EXPERIMENT 65-EPSILON-7 ARE DISAPPOINTING TO SAY THE LEAST.
SUBJECT IS WILLFUL AND UNRESPONSIVE TO COMMANDS.
AHHHHRRRR.
STILL, I DO ENJOY A GOOD EUTHANIZING. IF I WEREN'T COUNTING CARBS, I'D POP SOME CORN.
WHERE IS BRIAN FITZGERALD?

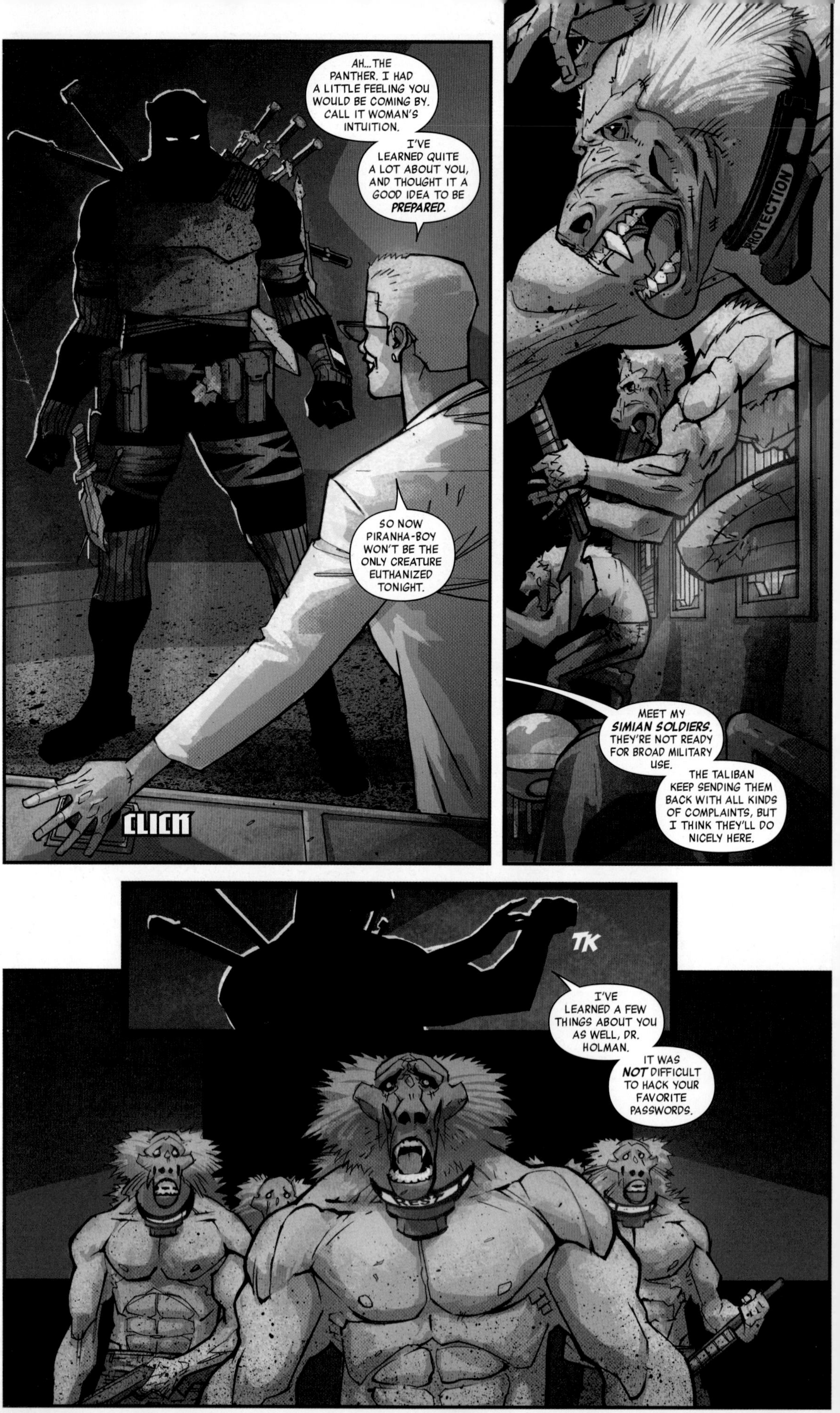
AH... THE PANTHER. I HAD A LITTLE FEELING YOU WOULD BE COMING BY. CALL IT WOMAN'S INTUITION.
I'VE LEARNED QUITE A LOT ABOUT YOU, AND THOUGHT IT A GOOD IDEA TO BE PREPARED.
SO NOW PIRANHA-BOY WON'T BE THE ONLY CREATURE EUTHANIZED TONIGHT.
CLICK
PROTECTION
MEET MY SIMIAN SOLDIERS. THEY'RE NOT READY FOR BROAD MILITARY USE.
THE TALIBAN KEEP SENDING THEM BACK WITH ALL KINDS OF COMPLAINTS, BUT I THINK THEY'LL DO NICELY HERE.
TK
I'VE LEARNED A FEW THINGS ABOUT YOU AS WELL, DR. HOLMAN.
IT WAS NOT DIFFICULT TO HACK YOUR FAVORITE PASSWORDS.

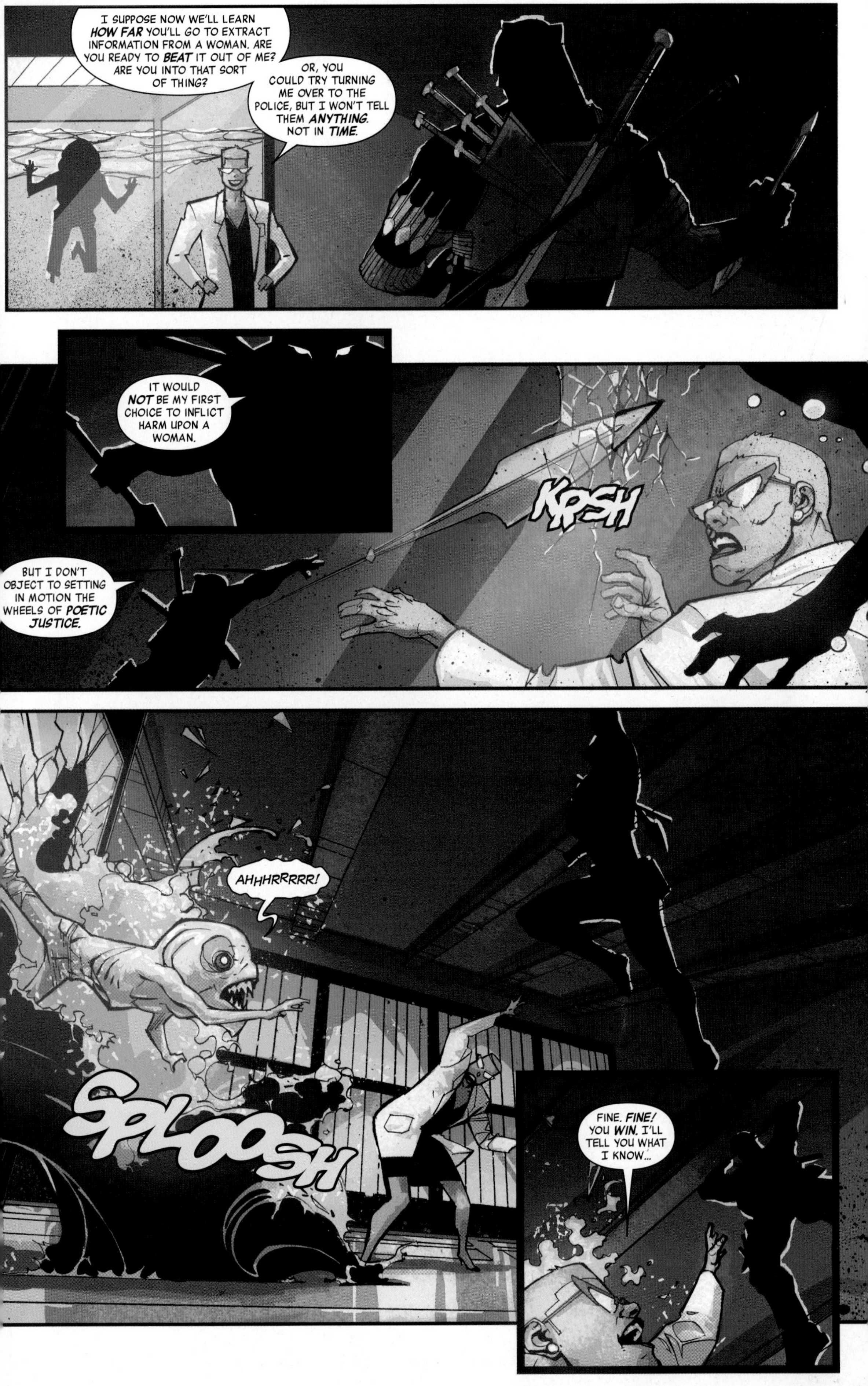
I SUPPOSE NOW WE'LL LEARN HOW FAR YOU'LL GO TO EXTRACT INFORMATION FROM A WOMAN. ARE YOU READY TO BEAT IT OUT OF ME? ARE YOU INTO THAT SORT OF THING?
OR, YOU COULD TRY TURNING ME OVER TO THE POLICE, BUT I WON'T TELL THEM ANYTHING. NOT IN TIME.
IT WOULD NOT BE MY FIRST CHOICE TO INFLICT HARM UPON A WOMAN.
BUT I DON'T OBJECT TO SETTING IN MOTION THE WHEELS OF POETIC JUSTICE.
KRSH
AHHHRRRRR!
SPLOOSH
FINE. FINE! YOU WIN. I'LL TELL YOU WHAT I KNOW...

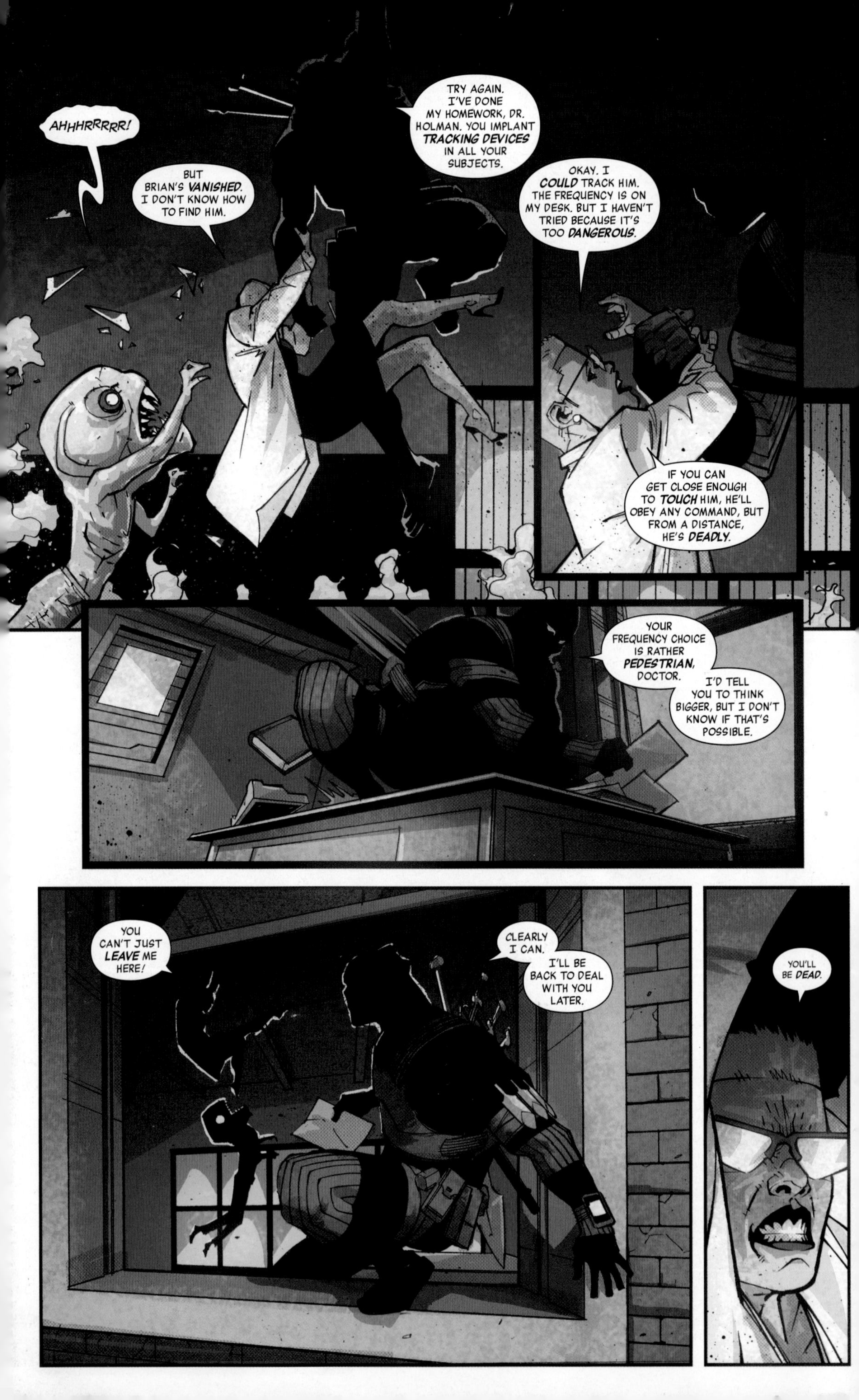
AHHHRRRRR!
BUT BRIAN'S VANISHED. I DON'T KNOW HOW TO FIND HIM.
TRY AGAIN. I'VE DONE MY HOMEWORK, DR. HOLMAN. YOU IMPLANT TRACKING DEVICES IN ALL YOUR SUBJECTS.
OKAY. I COULD TRACK HIM. THE FREQUENCY IS ON MY DESK. BUT I HAVEN'T TRIED BECAUSE IT'S TOO DANGEROUS.
IF YOU CAN GET CLOSE ENOUGH TO TOUCH HIM, HE'LL OBEY ANY COMMAND, BUT FROM A DISTANCE, HE'S DEADLY.
YOUR FREQUENCY CHOICE IS RATHER PEDESTRIAN, DOCTOR.
I'D TELL YOU TO THINK BIGGER, BUT I DON'T KNOW IF THAT'S POSSIBLE.
YOU CAN'T JUST LEAVE ME HERE!
CLEARLY I CAN.
I'LL BE BACK TO DEAL WITH YOU LATER.
YOU'LL BE DEAD.

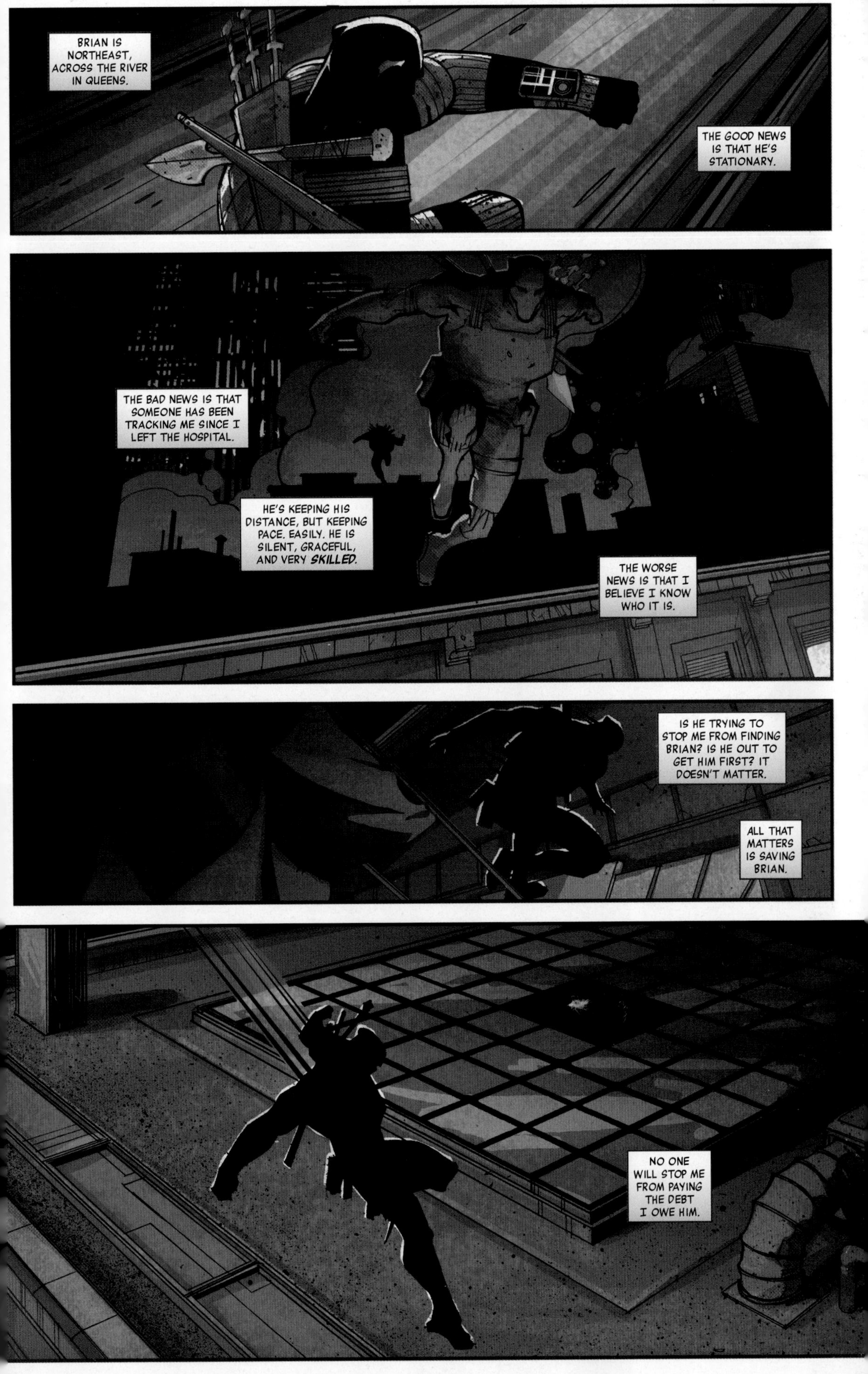
BRIAN IS NORTHEAST, ACROSS THE RIVER IN QUEENS.
THE GOOD NEWS IS THAT HE'S STATIONARY.
THE BAD NEWS IS THAT SOMEONE HAS BEEN TRACKING ME SINCE I LEFT THE HOSPITAL.
HE'S KEEPING HIS DISTANCE, BUT KEEPING PACE. EASILY. HE IS SILENT, GRACEFUL, AND VERY *SKILLED*.
THE WORSE NEWS IS THAT I BELIEVE I KNOW WHO IT IS.
IS HE TRYING TO STOP ME FROM FINDING BRIAN? IS HE OUT TO GET HIM FIRST? IT DOESN'T MATTER.
ALL THAT MATTERS IS SAVING BRIAN.
NO ONE WILL STOP ME FROM PAYING THE DEBT I OWE HIM.

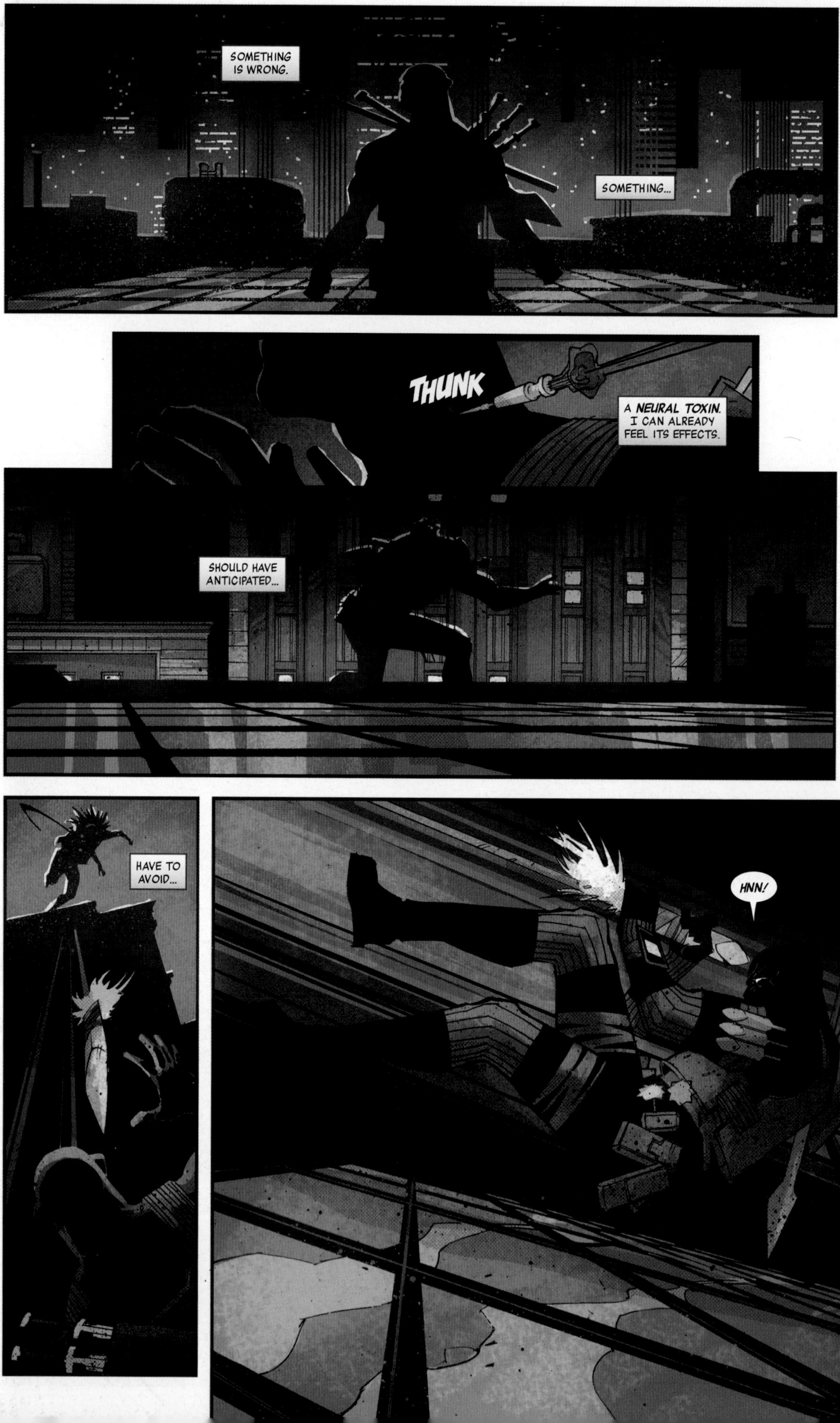
SOMETHING IS WRONG.
SOMETHING...
THUNK
A NEURAL TOXIN. I CAN ALREADY FEEL ITS EFFECTS.
SHOULD HAVE ANTICIPATED...
HAVE TO AVOID...
HNN!

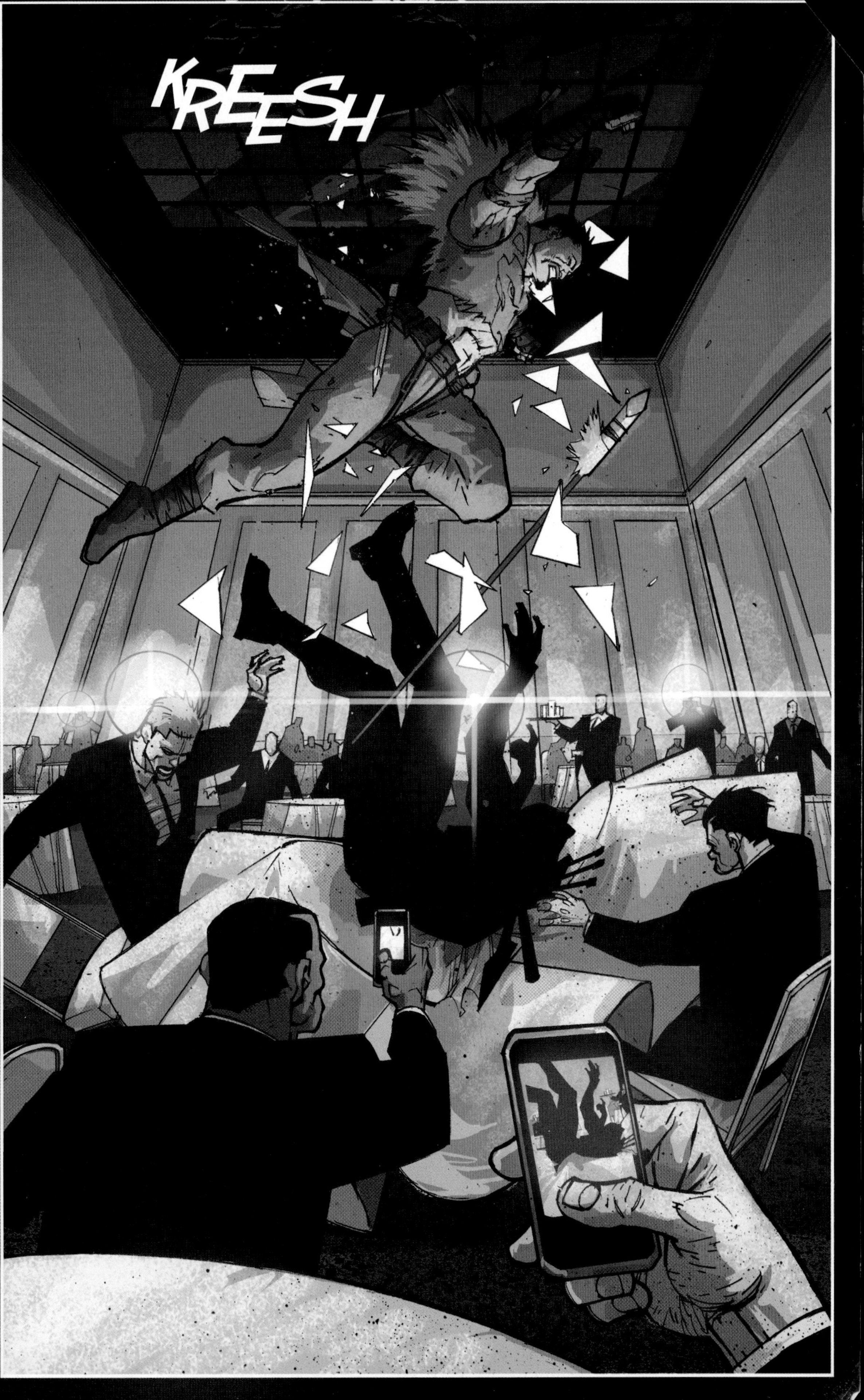
KREESH

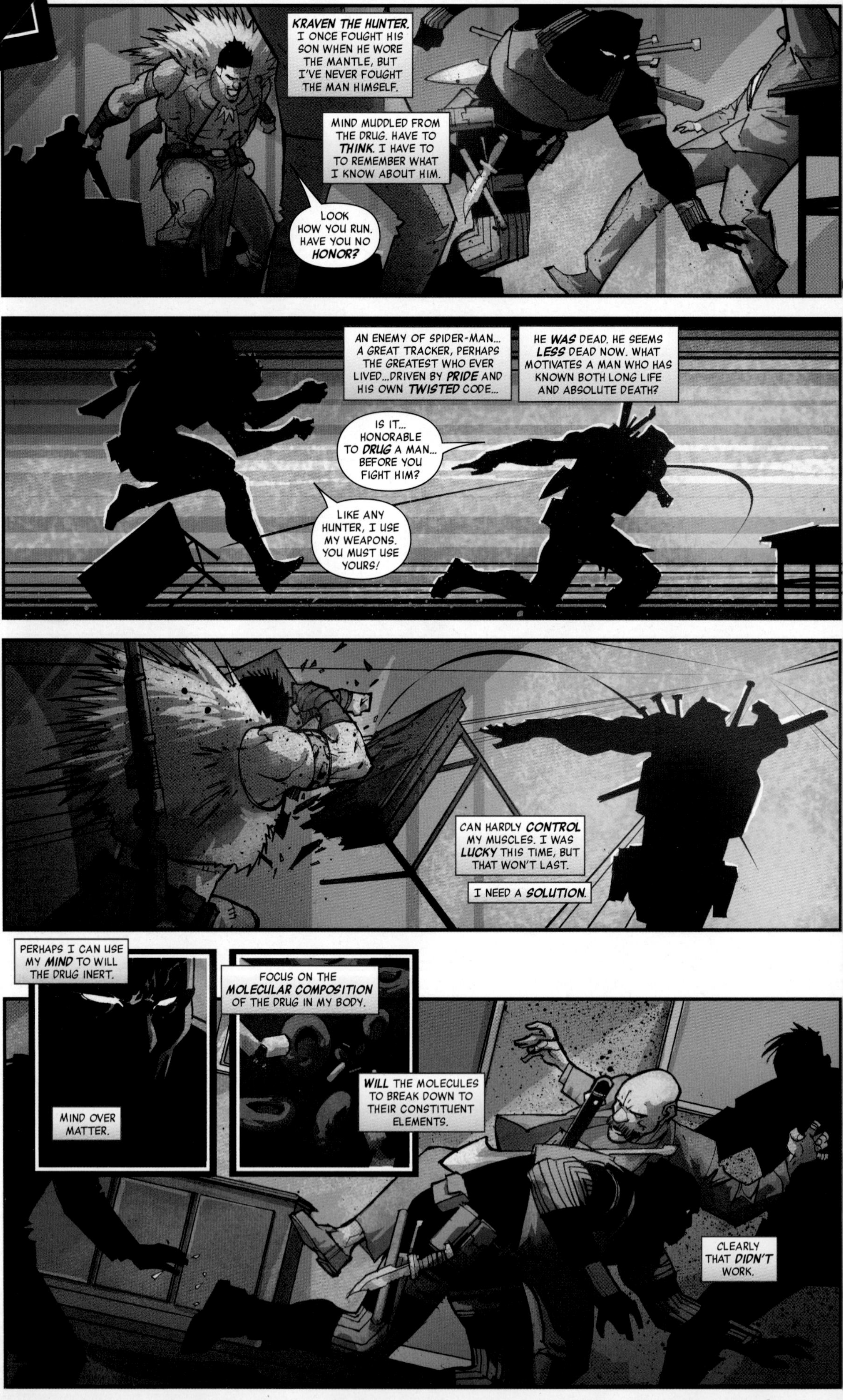
KRAVEN THE HUNTER. I ONCE FOUGHT HIS SON WHEN HE WORE THE MANTLE, BUT I'VE NEVER FOUGHT THE MAN HIMSELF.
MIND MUDDLED FROM THE DRUG. HAVE TO THINK. I HAVE TO TO REMEMBER WHAT I KNOW ABOUT HIM.
LOOK HOW YOU RUN. HAVE YOU NO HONOR?
AN ENEMY OF SPIDER-MAN... A GREAT TRACKER, PERHAPS THE GREATEST WHO EVER LIVED...DRIVEN BY PRIDE AND HIS OWN TWISTED CODE...
HE WAS DEAD. HE SEEMS LESS DEAD NOW. WHAT MOTIVATES A MAN WHO HAS KNOWN BOTH LONG LIFE AND ABSOLUTE DEATH?
IS IT... HONORABLE TO DRUG A MAN... BEFORE YOU FIGHT HIM?
LIKE ANY HUNTER, I USE MY WEAPONS. YOU MUST USE YOURS!
CAN HARDLY CONTROL MY MUSCLES. I WAS LUCKY THIS TIME, BUT THAT WON'T LAST.
I NEED A SOLUTION.
PERHAPS I CAN USE MY MIND TO WILL THE DRUG INERT.
MIND OVER MATTER.
FOCUS ON THE MOLECULAR COMPOSITION OF THE DRUG IN MY BODY.
WILL THE MOLECULES TO BREAK DOWN TO THEIR CONSTITUENT ELEMENTS.
CLEARLY THAT DIDN'T WORK.

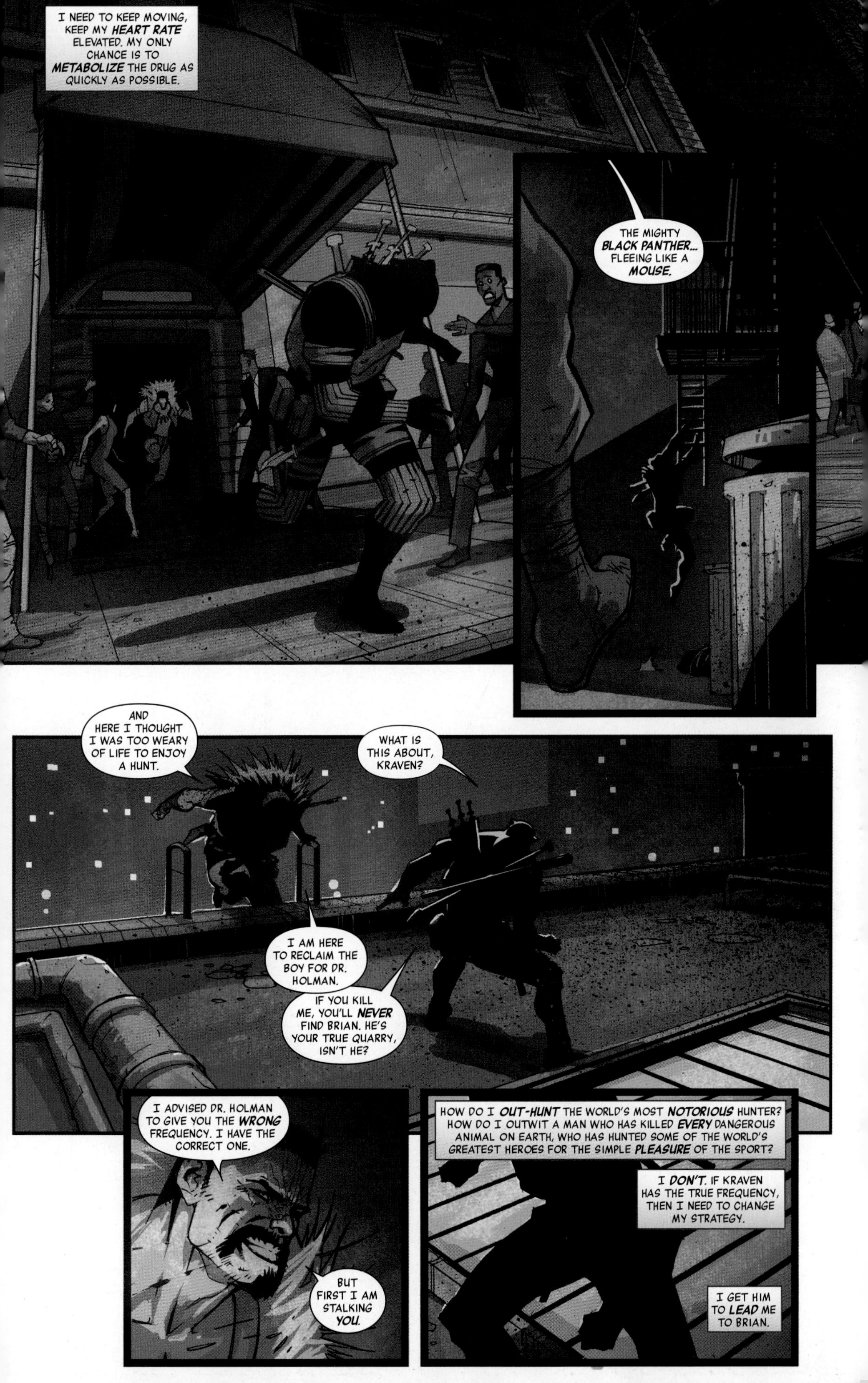
I NEED TO KEEP MOVING, KEEP MY HEART RATE ELEVATED. MY ONLY CHANCE IS TO METABOLIZE THE DRUG AS QUICKLY AS POSSIBLE.
THE MIGHTY BLACK PANTHER... FLEEING LIKE A MOUSE.
AND HERE I THOUGHT I WAS TOO WEARY OF LIFE TO ENJOY A HUNT.
WHAT IS THIS ABOUT, KRAVEN?
I AM HERE TO RECLAIM THE BOY FOR DR. HOLMAN.
IF YOU KILL ME, YOU'LL NEVER FIND BRIAN. HE'S YOUR TRUE QUARRY, ISN'T HE?
I ADVISED DR. HOLMAN TO GIVE YOU THE WRONG FREQUENCY. I HAVE THE CORRECT ONE.
BUT FIRST I AM STALKING YOU.
HOW DO I OUT-HUNT THE WORLD'S MOST NOTORIOUS HUNTER? HOW DO I OUTWIT A MAN WHO HAS KILLED EVERY DANGEROUS ANIMAL ON EARTH, WHO HAS HUNTED SOME OF THE WORLD'S GREATEST HEROES FOR THE SIMPLE PLEASURE OF THE SPORT?
I DON'T. IF KRAVEN HAS THE TRUE FREQUENCY, THEN I NEED TO CHANGE MY STRATEGY.
I GET HIM TO LEAD ME TO BRIAN.

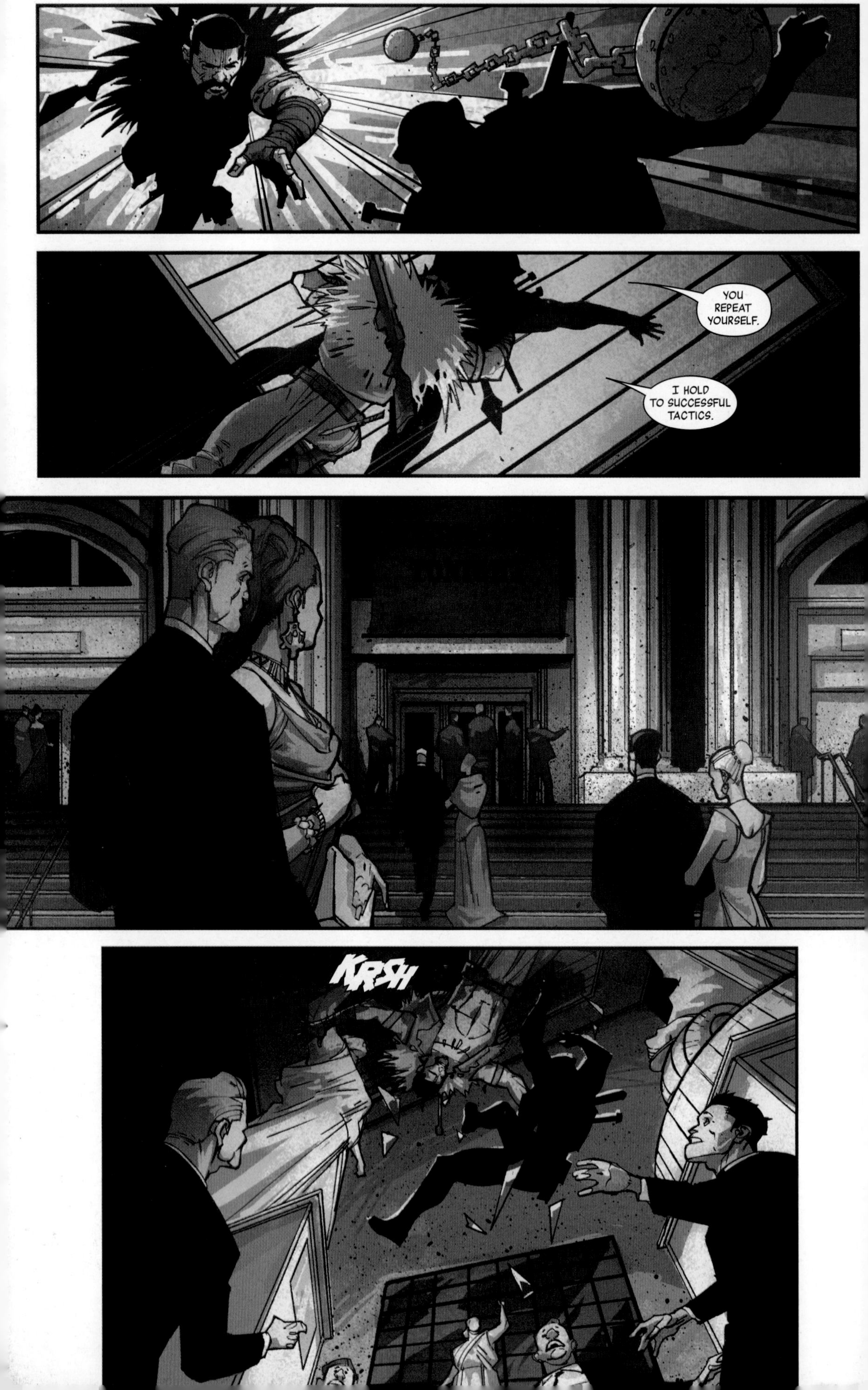
YOU REPEAT YOURSELF.
I HOLD TO SUCCESSFUL TACTICS.
KRSH

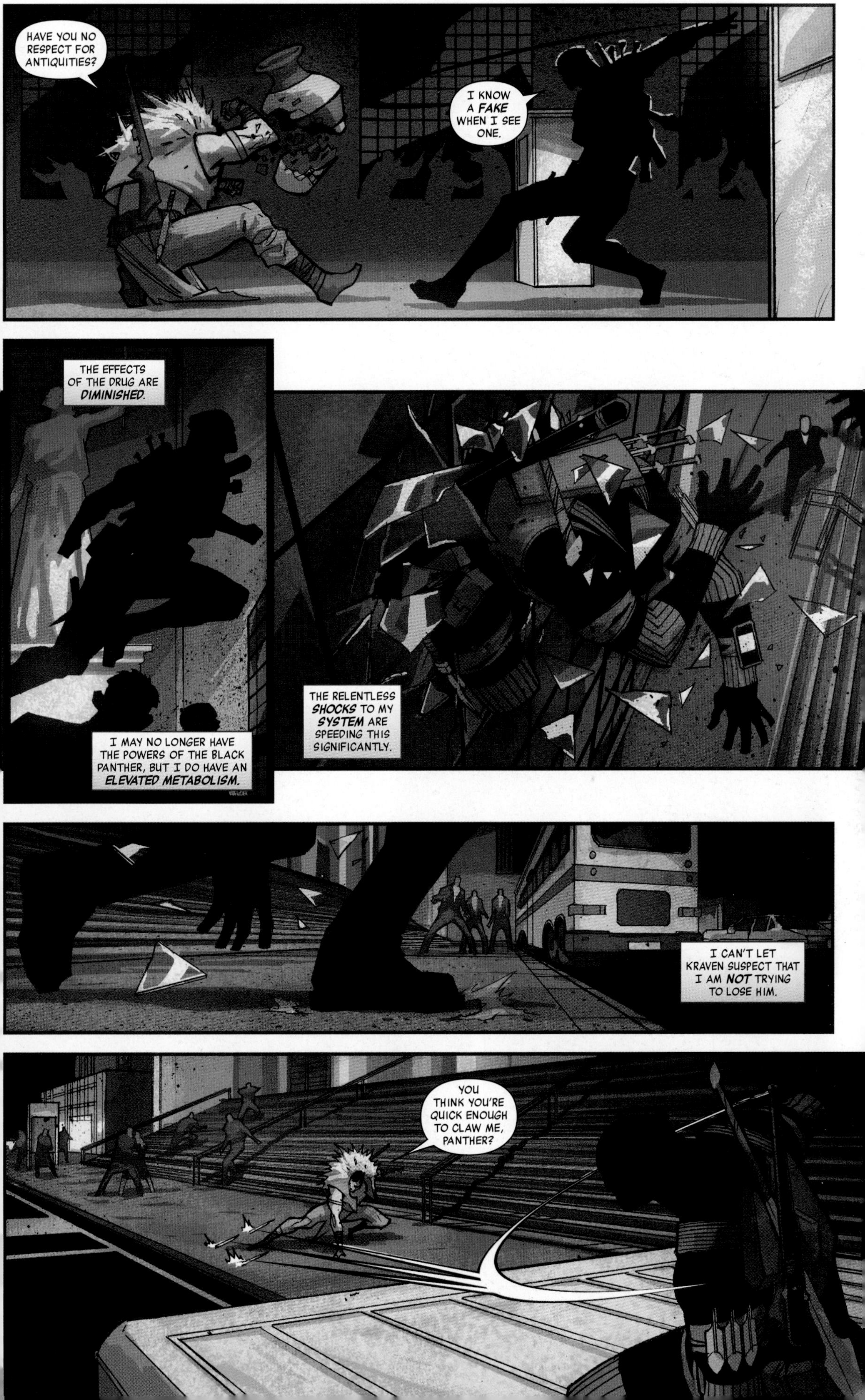
HAVE YOU NO RESPECT FOR ANTIQUITIES?
I KNOW A FAKE WHEN I SEE ONE.
THE EFFECTS OF THE DRUG ARE DIMINISHED.
I MAY NO LONGER HAVE THE POWERS OF THE BLACK PANTHER, BUT I DO HAVE AN ELEVATED METABOLISM.
THE RELENTLESS SHOCKS TO MY SYSTEM ARE SPEEDING THIS SIGNIFICANTLY.
I CAN'T LET KRAVEN SUSPECT THAT I AM NOT TRYING TO LOSE HIM.
YOU THINK YOU'RE QUICK ENOUGH TO CLAW ME, PANTHER?

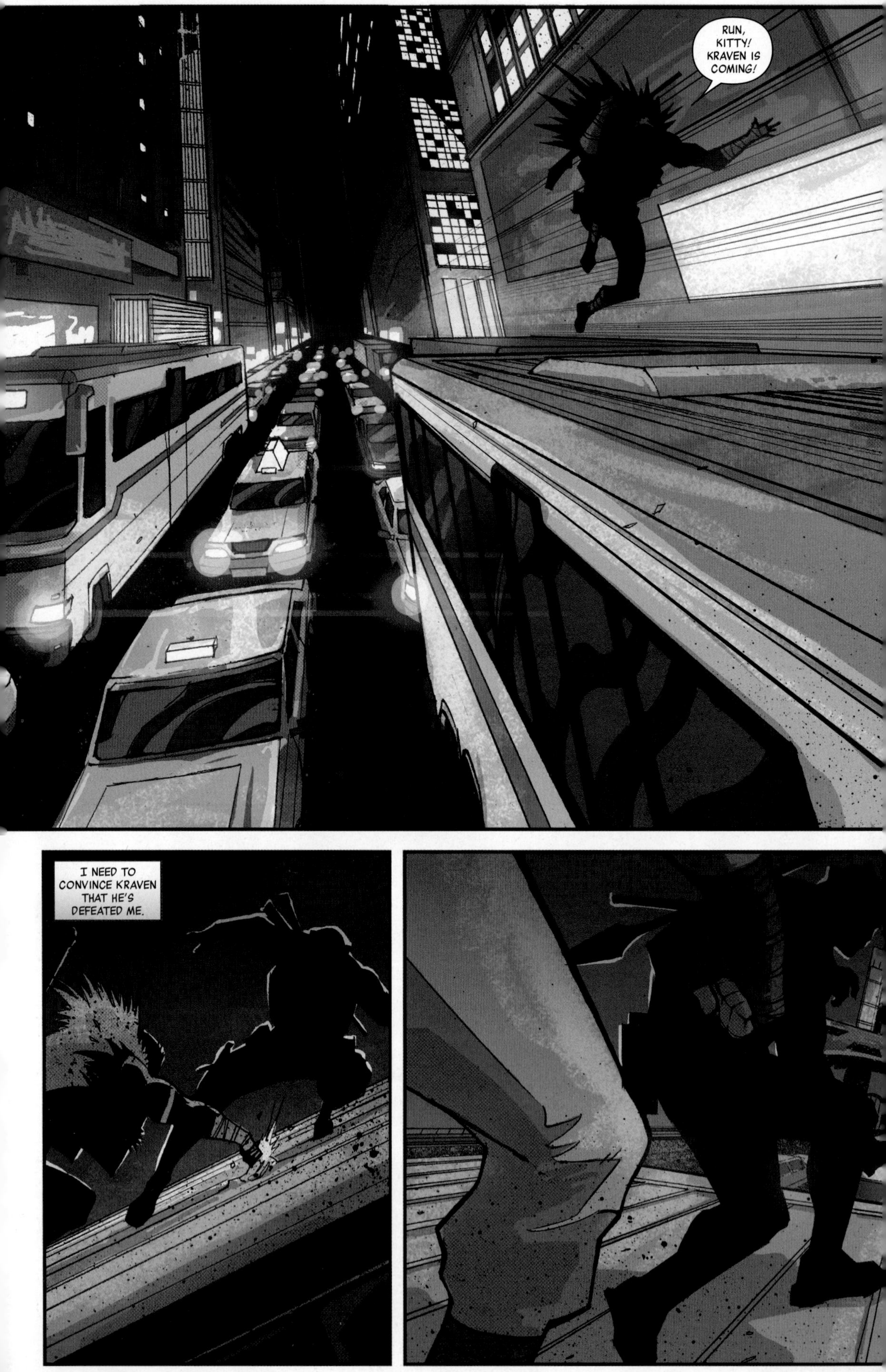
RUN, KITTY! KRAVEN IS COMING!
I NEED TO CONVINCE KRAVEN THAT HE'S DEFEATED ME.

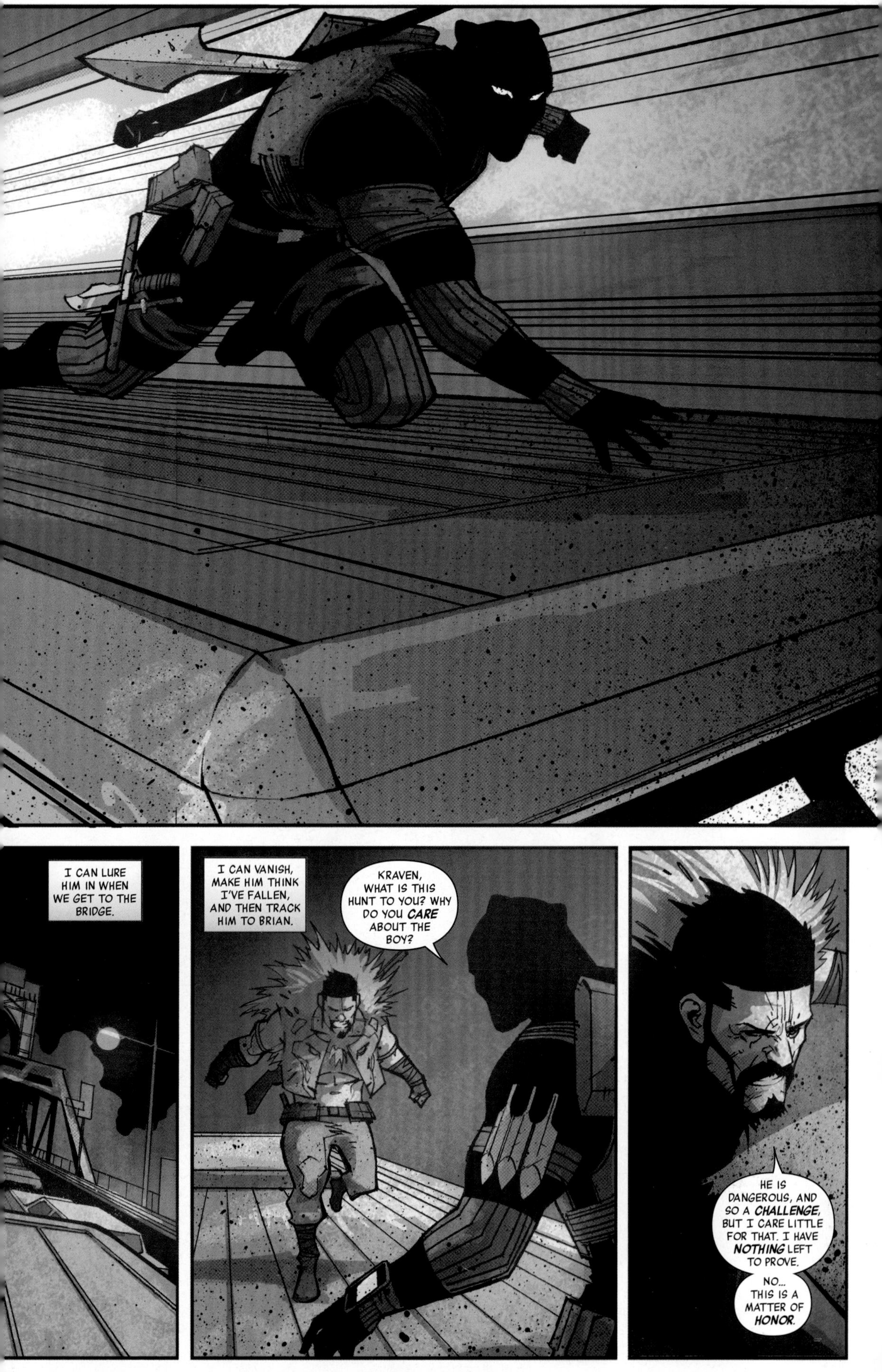
I CAN LURE HIM IN WHEN WE GET TO THE BRIDGE.
I CAN VANISH, MAKE HIM THINK I'VE FALLEN, AND THEN TRACK HIM TO BRIAN.
KRAVEN, WHAT IS THIS HUNT TO YOU? WHY DO YOU CARE ABOUT THE BOY?
HE IS DANGEROUS, AND SO A CHALLENGE, BUT I CARE LITTLE FOR THAT. I HAVE NOTHING LEFT TO PROVE.
NO... THIS IS A MATTER OF HONOR.

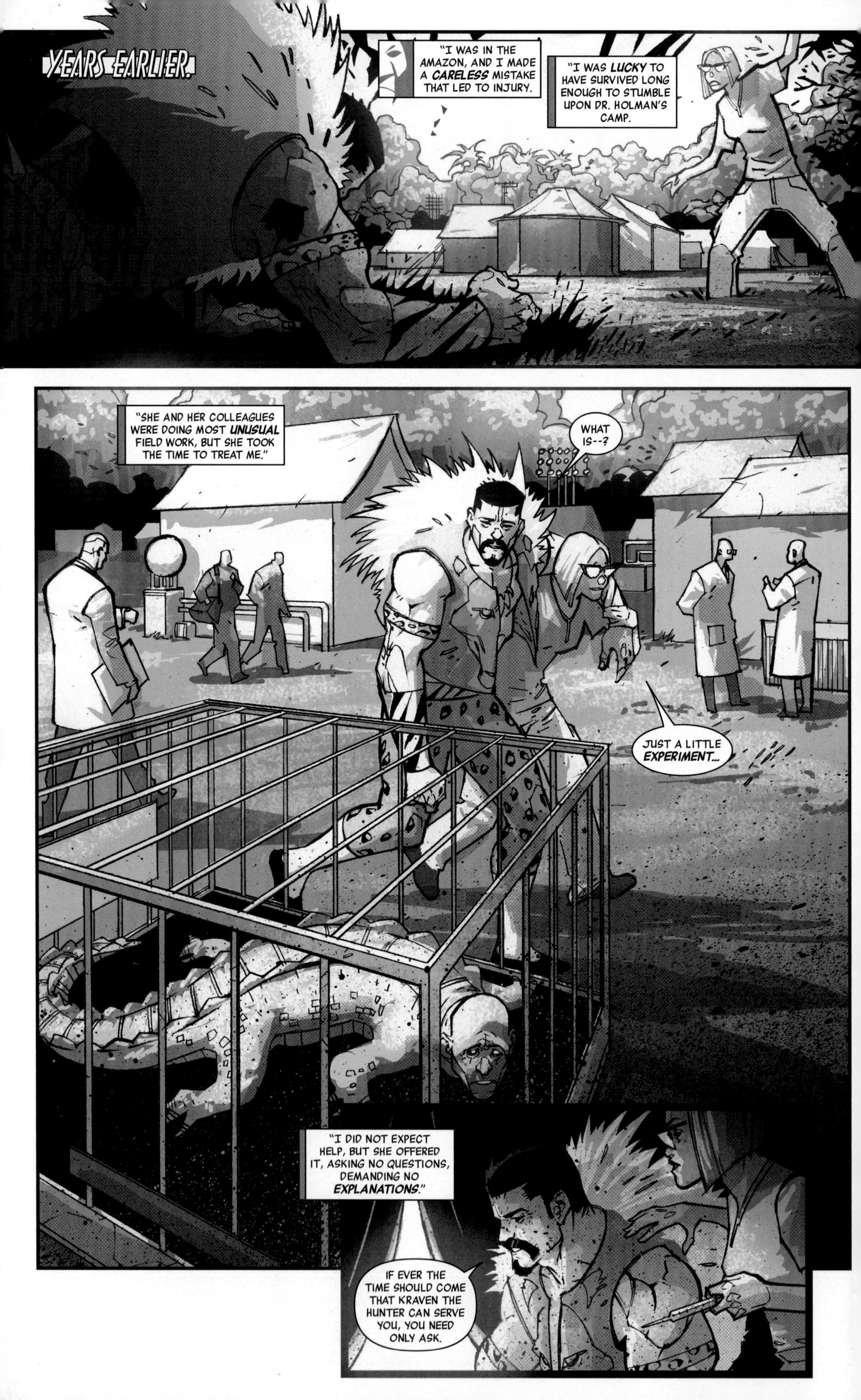
YEARS EARLIER.
"I WAS IN THE AMAZON, AND I MADE A CARELESS MISTAKE THAT LED TO INJURY.
"I WAS LUCKY TO HAVE SURVIVED LONG ENOUGH TO STUMBLE UPON DR. HOLMAN'S CAMP.
"SHE AND HER COLLEAGUES WERE DOING MOST UNUSUAL FIELD WORK, BUT SHE TOOK THE TIME TO TREAT ME."
WHAT IS--?
JUST A LITTLE EXPERIMENT...
"I DID NOT EXPECT HELP, BUT SHE OFFERED IT, ASKING NO QUESTIONS, DEMANDING NO EXPLANATIONS."
IF EVER THE TIME SHOULD COME THAT KRAVEN THE HUNTER CAN SERVE YOU, YOU NEED ONLY ASK.

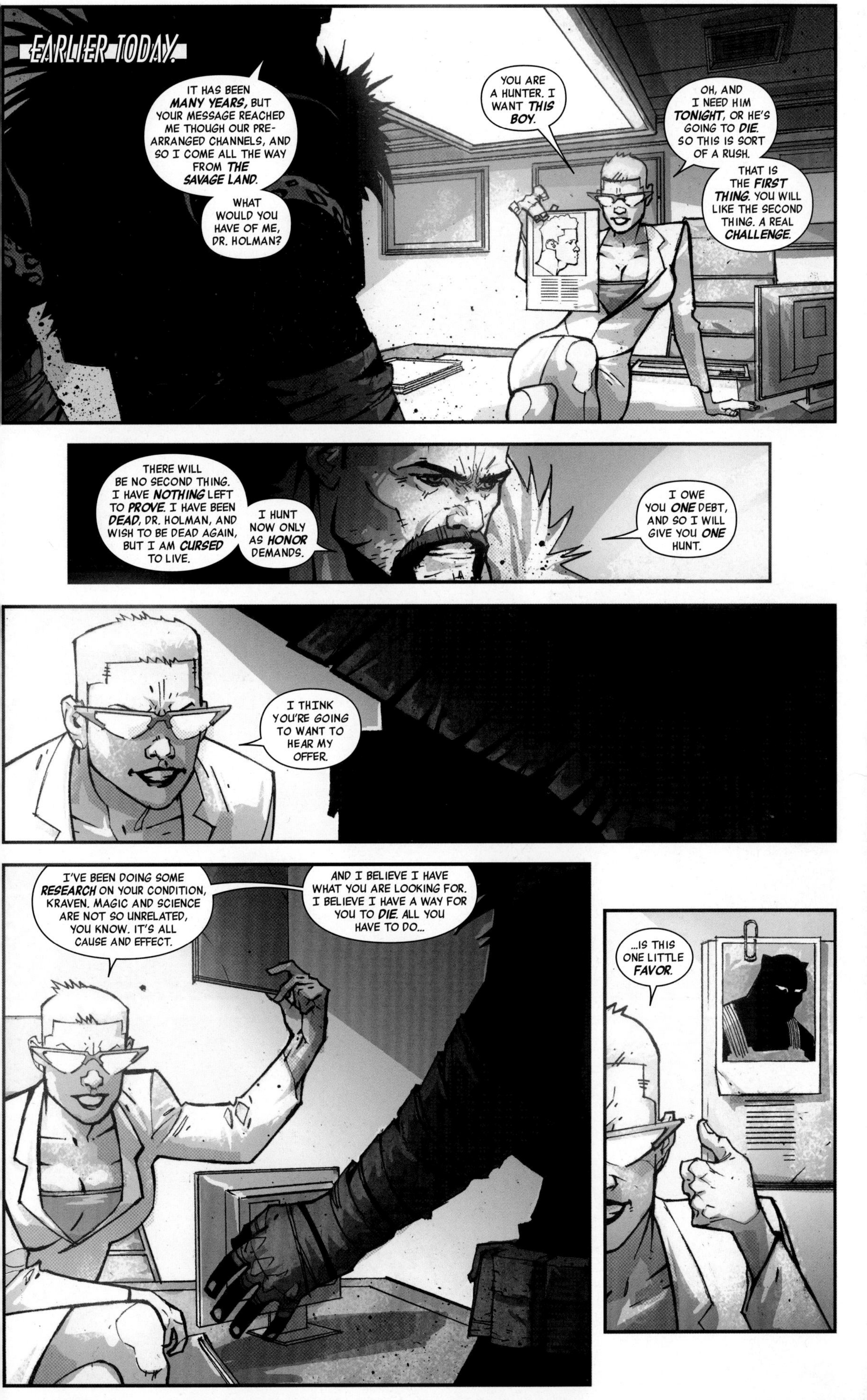
EARLIER TODAY.
IT HAS BEEN MANY YEARS, BUT YOUR MESSAGE REACHED ME THOUGH OUR PRE-ARRANGED CHANNELS, AND SO I COME ALL THE WAY FROM THE SAVAGE LAND.
WHAT WOULD YOU HAVE OF ME, DR. HOLMAN?
YOU ARE A HUNTER. I WANT THIS BOY.
OH, AND I NEED HIM TONIGHT, OR HE'S GOING TO DIE. SO THIS IS SORT OF A RUSH.
THAT IS THE FIRST THING. YOU WILL LIKE THE SECOND THING. A REAL CHALLENGE.
THERE WILL BE NO SECOND THING. I HAVE NOTHING LEFT TO PROVE. I HAVE BEEN DEAD, DR. HOLMAN, AND WISH TO BE DEAD AGAIN, BUT I AM CURSED TO LIVE.
I HUNT NOW ONLY AS HONOR DEMANDS.
I OWE YOU ONE DEBT, AND SO I WILL GIVE YOU ONE HUNT.
I THINK YOU'RE GOING TO WANT TO HEAR MY OFFER.
I'VE BEEN DOING SOME RESEARCH ON YOUR CONDITION, KRAVEN. MAGIC AND SCIENCE ARE NOT SO UNRELATED, YOU KNOW. IT'S ALL CAUSE AND EFFECT.
AND I BELIEVE I HAVE WHAT YOU ARE LOOKING FOR. I BELIEVE I HAVE A WAY FOR YOU TO DIE. ALL YOU HAVE TO DO...
...IS THIS ONE LITTLE FAVOR.

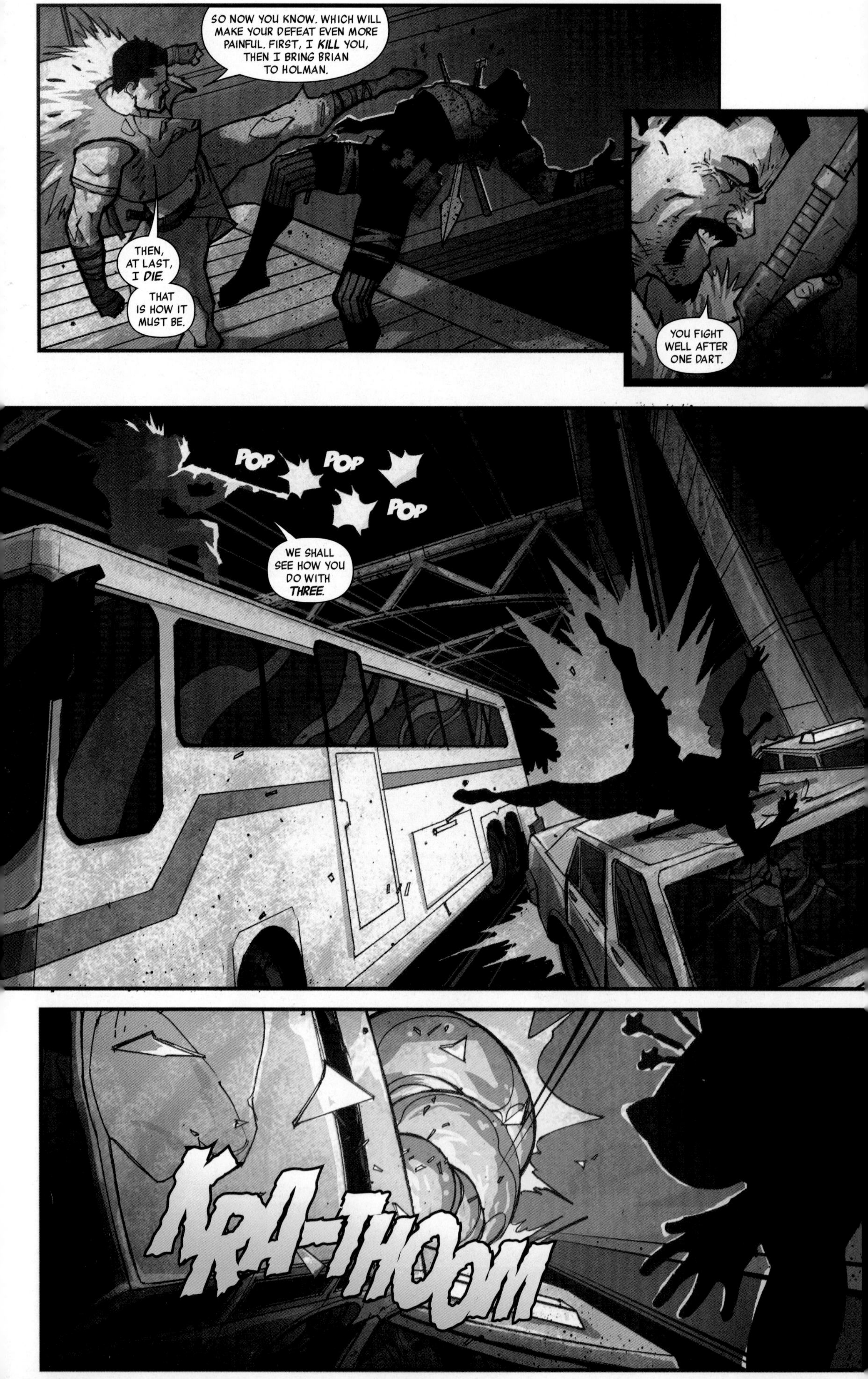
SO NOW YOU KNOW. WHICH WILL MAKE YOUR DEFEAT EVEN MORE PAINFUL. FIRST, I KILL YOU, THEN I BRING BRIAN TO HOLMAN.
THEN, AT LAST, I DIE.
THAT IS HOW IT MUST BE.
YOU FIGHT WELL AFTER ONE DART.
POP
POP
POP
WE SHALL SEE HOW YOU DO WITH THREE.
KRA-THOOM

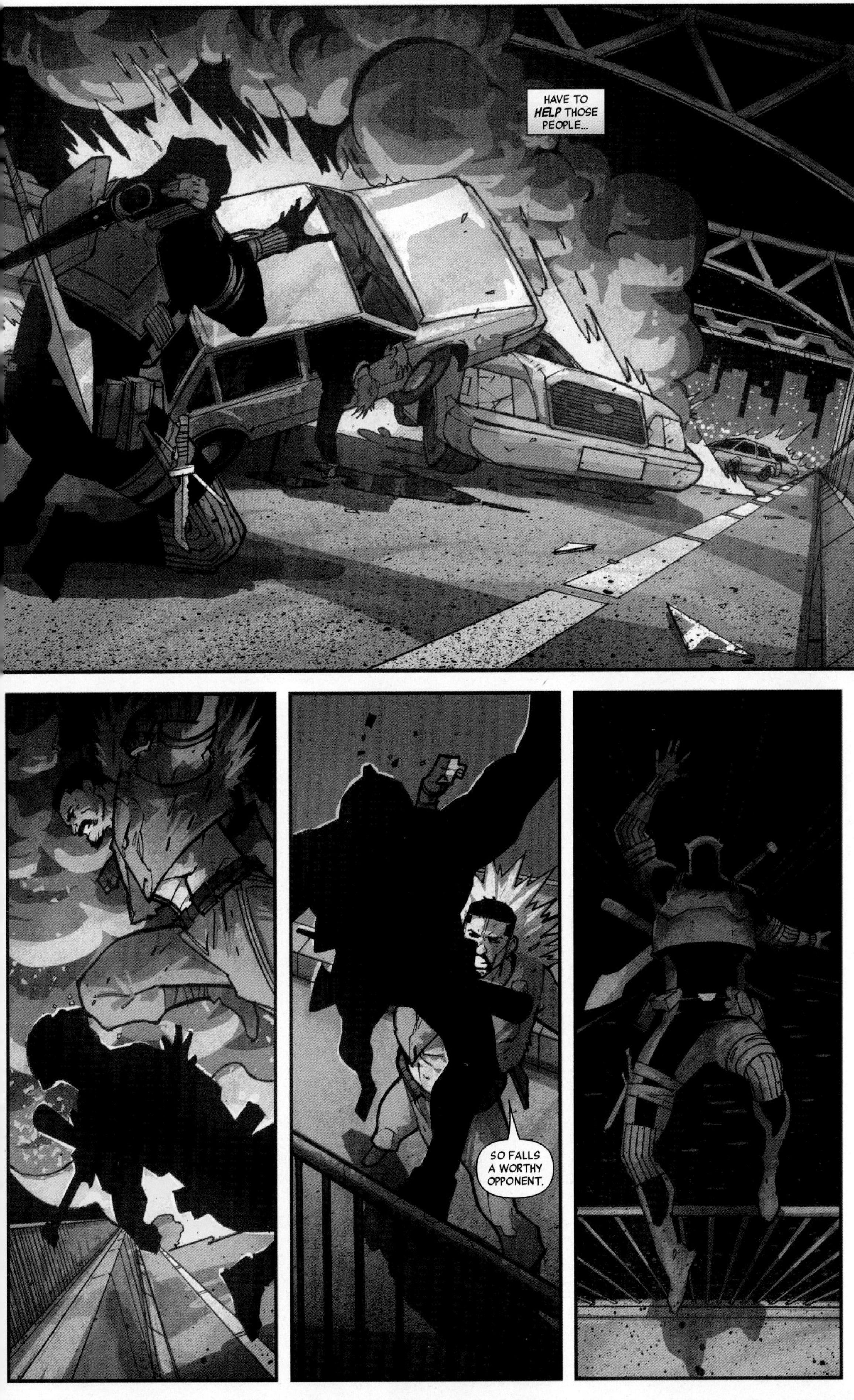
HAVE TO HELP THOSE PEOPLE...
SO FALLS A WORTHY OPPONENT.

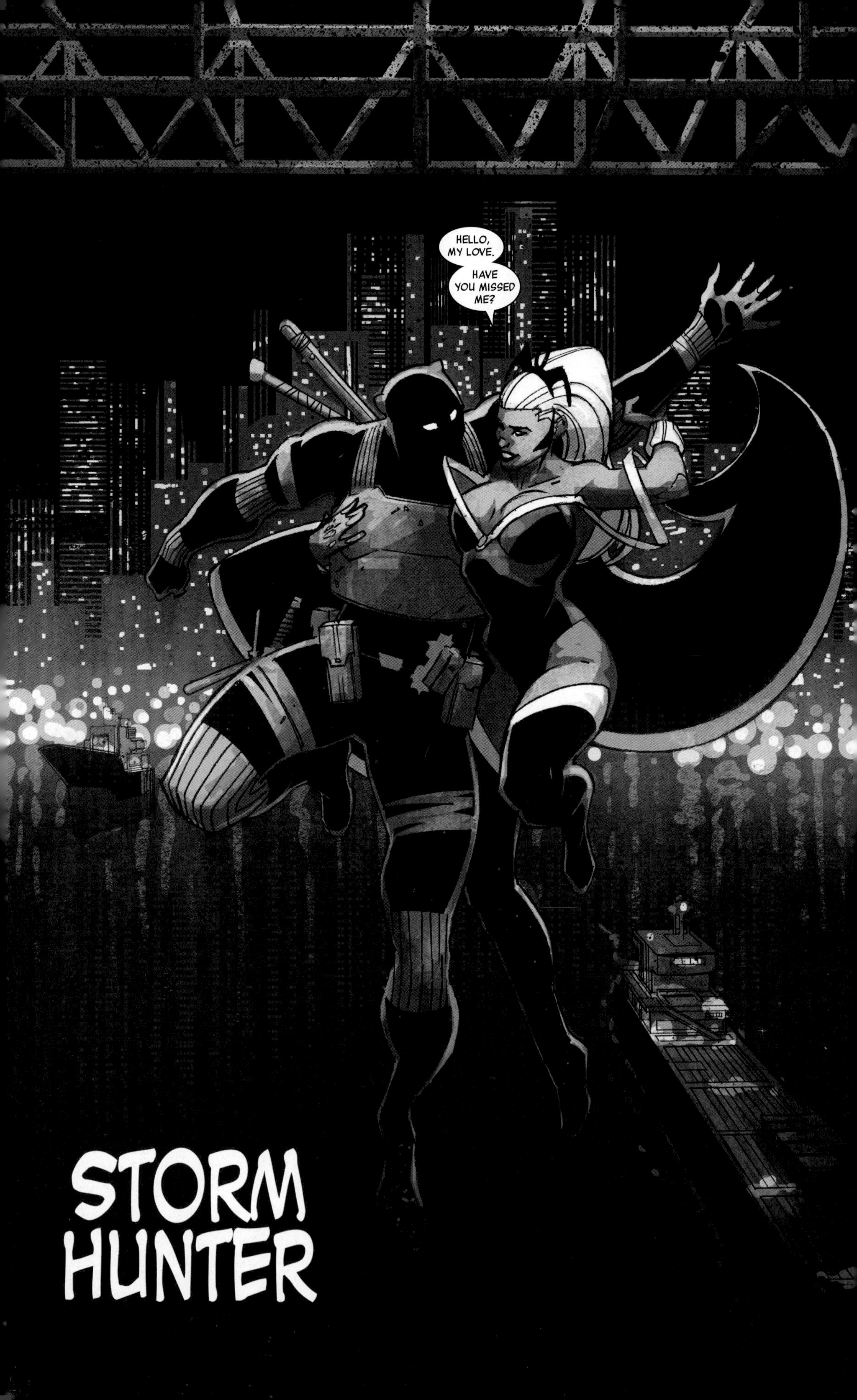
HELLO, MY LOVE.
HAVE YOU MISSED ME?
STORM HUNTER

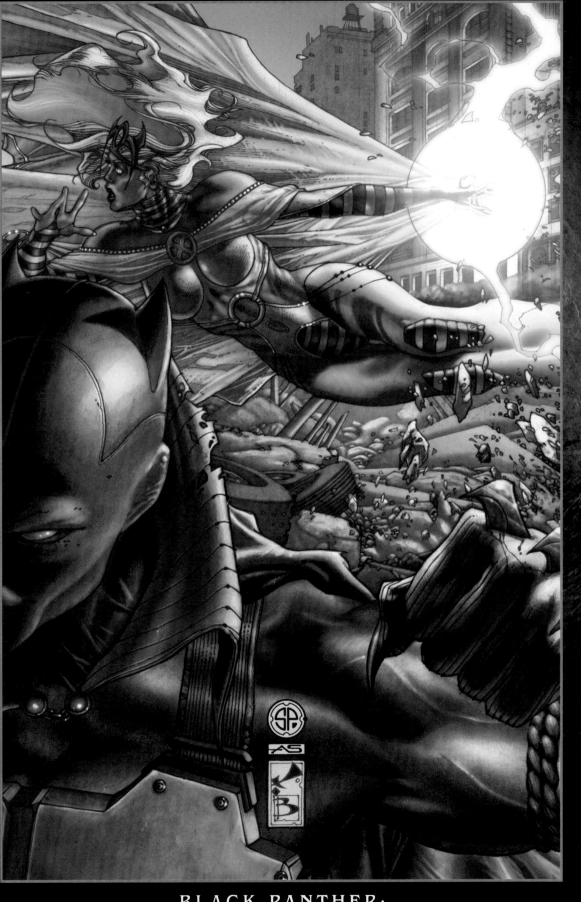

BLACK PANTHER:
THE MAN WITHOUT FEAR #520

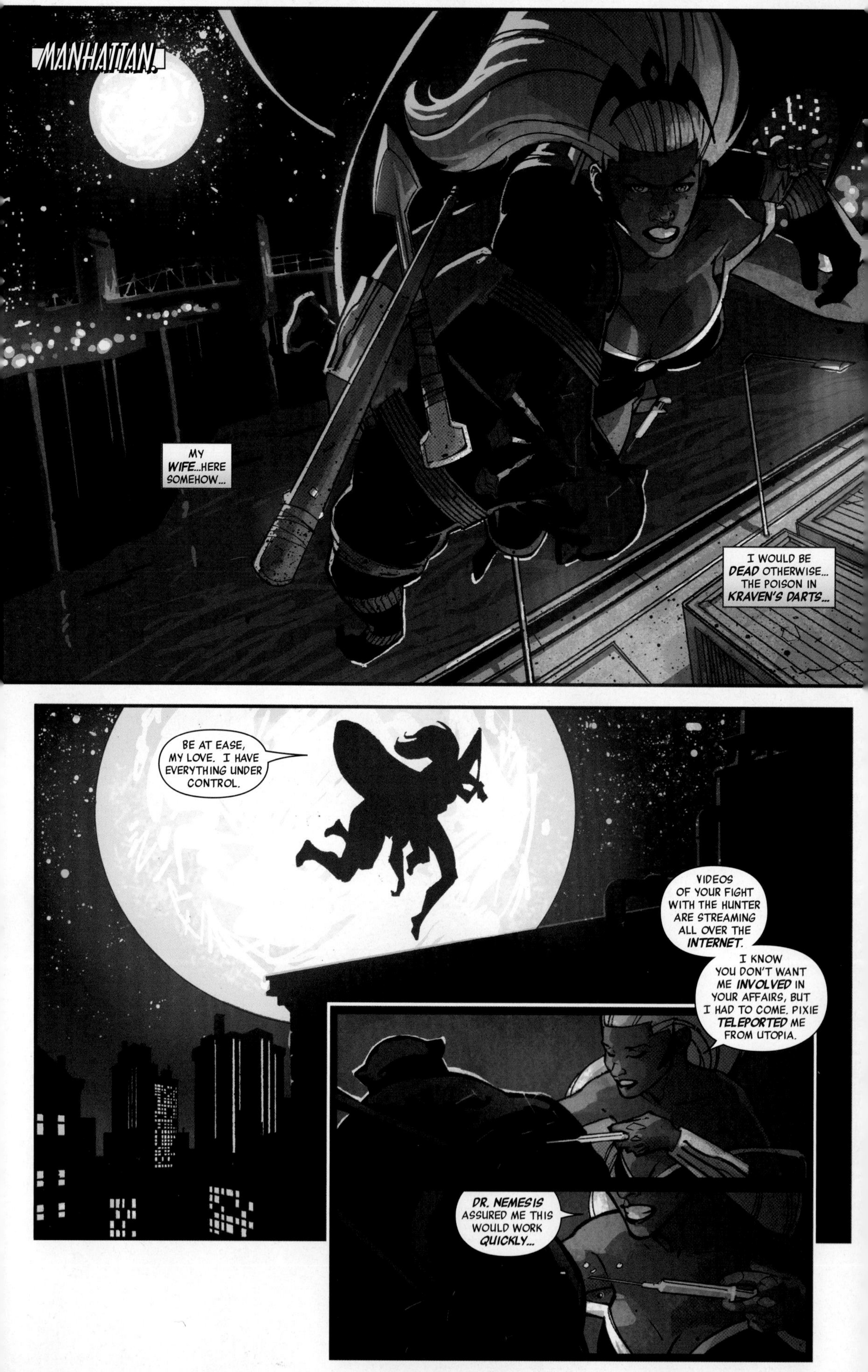
MANHATTAN.
MY WIFE...HERE SOMEHOW...
I WOULD BE DEAD OTHERWISE... THE POISON IN KRAVEN'S DARTS...
BE AT EASE, MY LOVE. I HAVE EVERYTHING UNDER CONTROL.
VIDEOS OF YOUR FIGHT WITH THE HUNTER ARE STREAMING ALL OVER THE INTERNET.
I KNOW YOU DON'T WANT ME INVOLVED IN YOUR AFFAIRS, BUT I HAD TO COME. PIXIE TELEPORTED ME FROM UTOPIA.
DR. NEMESIS ASSURED ME THIS WOULD WORK QUICKLY...

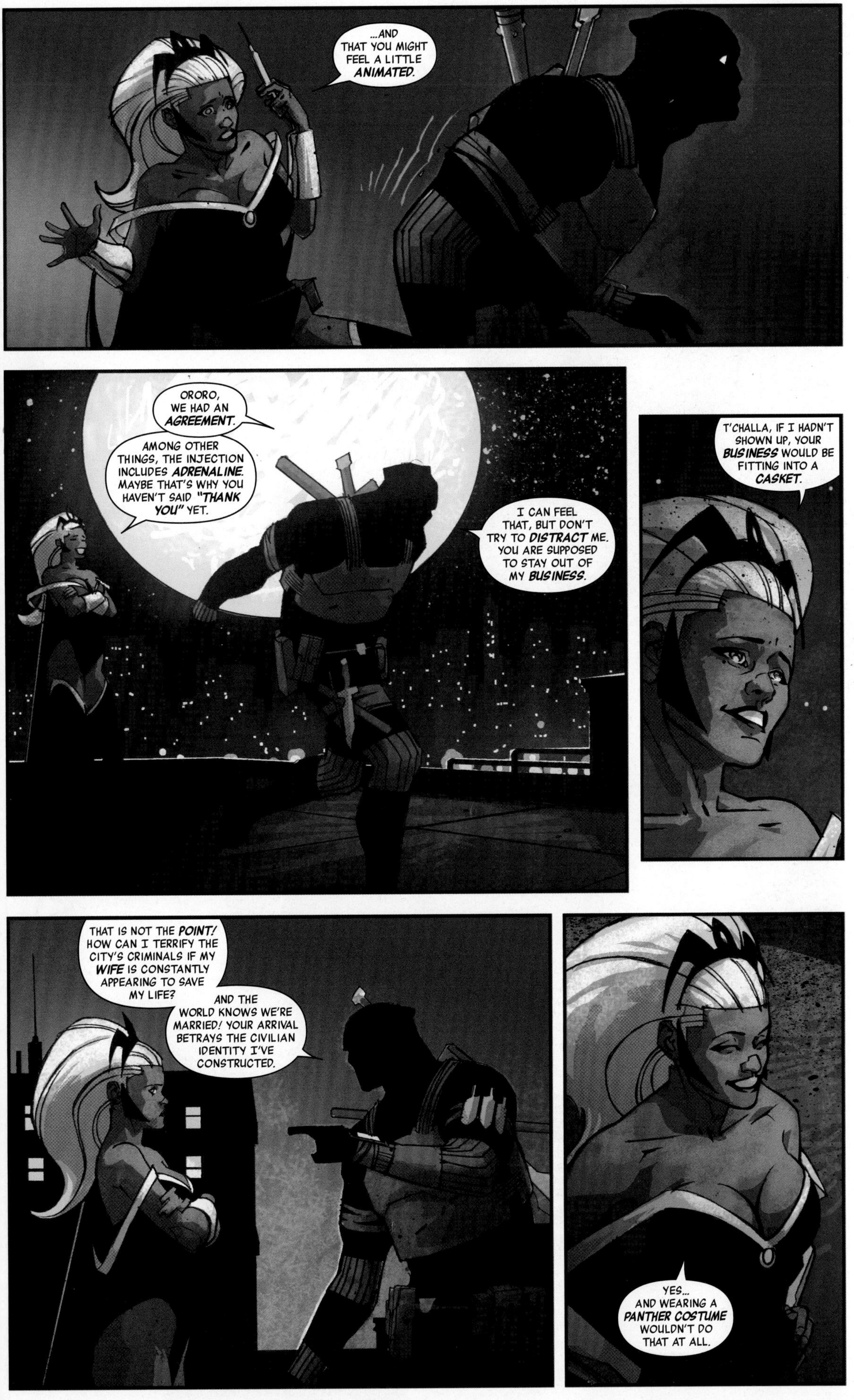

...AND THAT YOU MIGHT FEEL A LITTLE ANIMATED.
ORORO, WE HAD AN AGREEMENT.
AMONG OTHER THINGS, THE INJECTION INCLUDES ADRENALINE. MAYBE THAT'S WHY YOU HAVEN'T SAID "THANK YOU" YET.
I CAN FEEL THAT, BUT DON'T TRY TO DISTRACT ME. YOU ARE SUPPOSED TO STAY OUT OF MY BUSINESS.
T'CHALLA, IF I HADN'T SHOWN UP, YOUR BUSINESS WOULD BE FITTING INTO A CASKET.
THAT IS NOT THE POINT! HOW CAN I TERRIFY THE CITY'S CRIMINALS IF MY WIFE IS CONSTANTLY APPEARING TO SAVE MY LIFE?
AND THE WORLD KNOWS WE'RE MARRIED! YOUR ARRIVAL BETRAYS THE CIVILIAN IDENTITY I'VE CONSTRUCTED.
YES... AND WEARING A PANTHER COSTUME WOULDN'T DO THAT AT ALL.

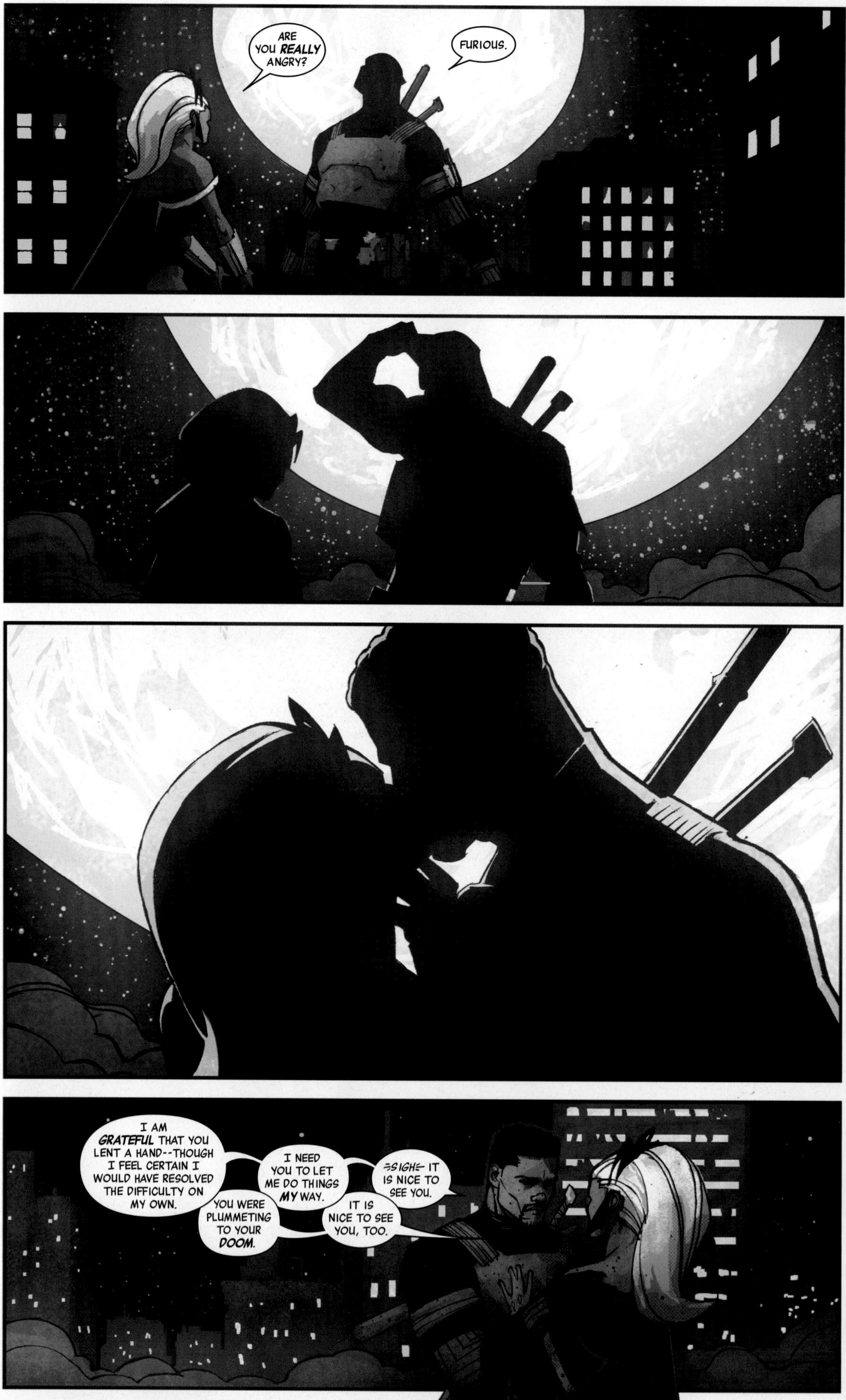
ARE YOU REALLY ANGRY?
FURIOUS.
I AM GRATEFUL THAT YOU LENT A HAND--THOUGH I FEEL CERTAIN I WOULD HAVE RESOLVED THE DIFFICULTY ON MY OWN.
YOU WERE PLUMMETING TO YOUR DOOM.
I NEED YOU TO LET ME DO THINGS MY WAY.
IT IS NICE TO SEE YOU, TOO.
=SIGH= IT IS NICE TO SEE YOU.

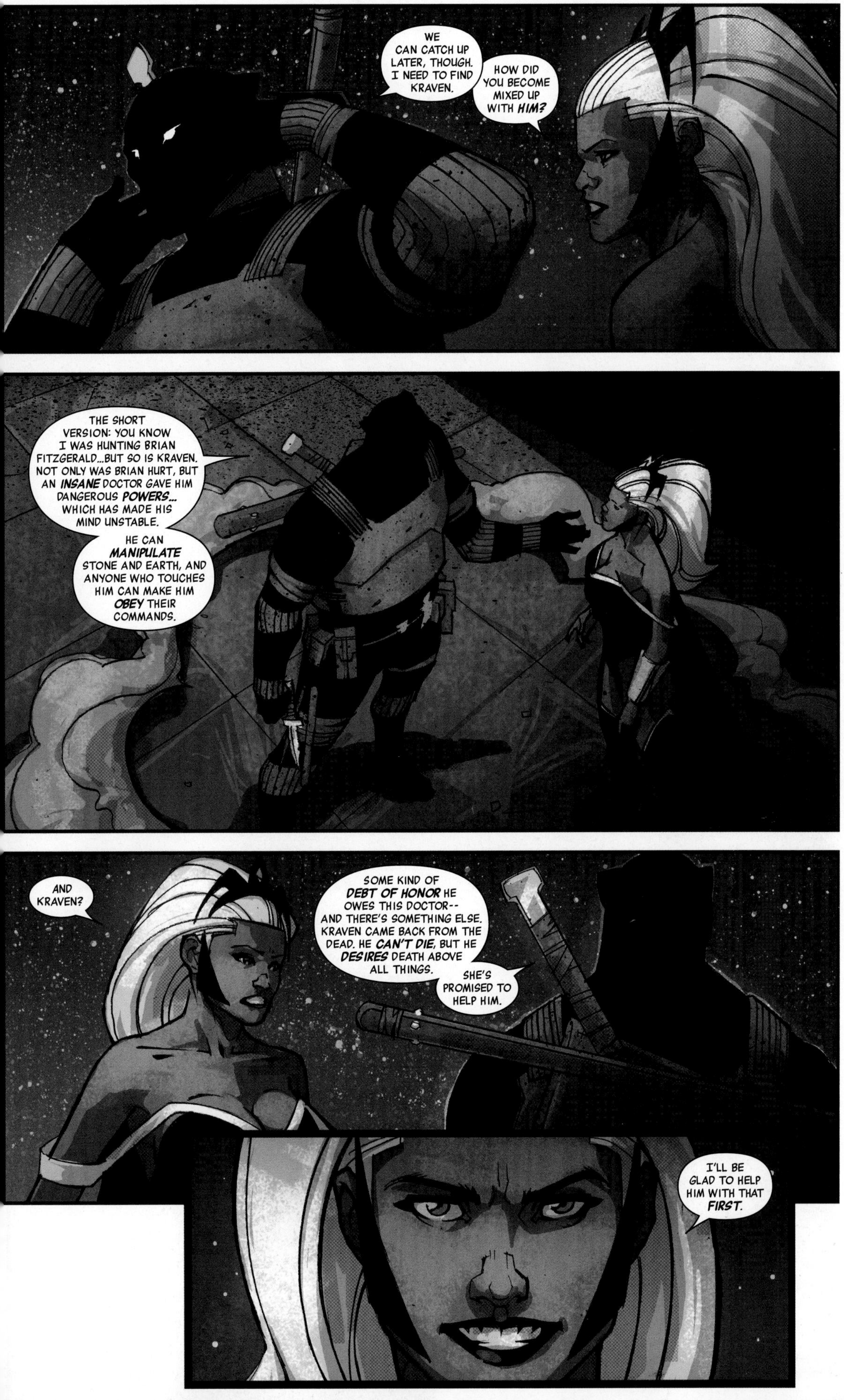
WE CAN CATCH UP LATER, THOUGH. I NEED TO FIND KRAVEN.
HOW DID YOU BECOME MIXED UP WITH HIM?
THE SHORT VERSION: YOU KNOW I WAS HUNTING BRIAN FITZGERALD...BUT SO IS KRAVEN. NOT ONLY WAS BRIAN HURT, BUT AN INSANE DOCTOR GAVE HIM DANGEROUS POWERS... WHICH HAS MADE HIS MIND UNSTABLE.
HE CAN MANIPULATE STONE AND EARTH, AND ANYONE WHO TOUCHES HIM CAN MAKE HIM OBEY THEIR COMMANDS.
AND KRAVEN?
SOME KIND OF DEBT OF HONOR HE OWES THIS DOCTOR-- AND THERE'S SOMETHING ELSE. KRAVEN CAME BACK FROM THE DEAD. HE CAN'T DIE, BUT HE DESIRES DEATH ABOVE ALL THINGS.
SHE'S PROMISED TO HELP HIM.
I'LL BE GLAD TO HELP HIM WITH THAT FIRST.

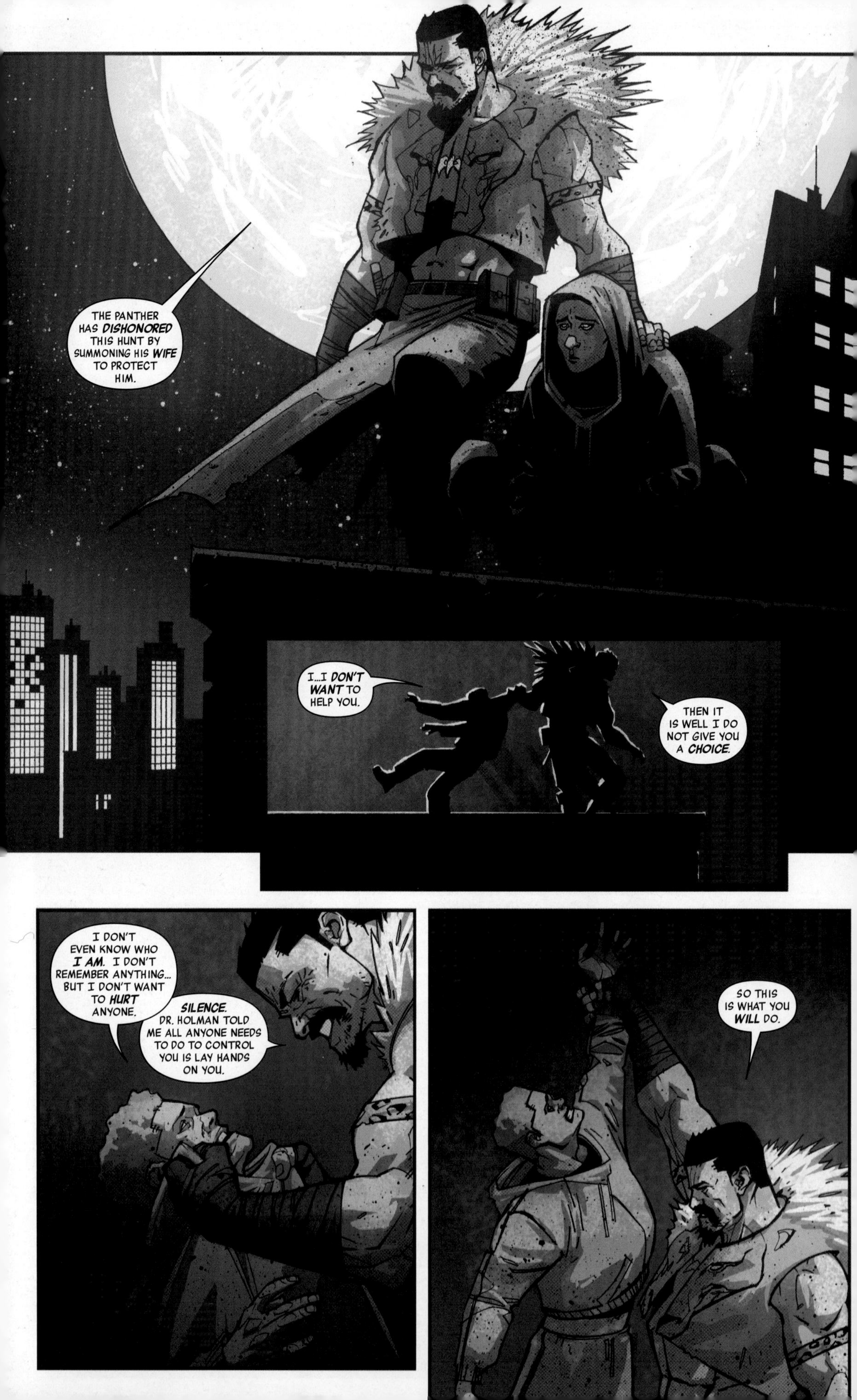
THE PANTHER HAS DISHONORED THIS HUNT BY SUMMONING HIS WIFE TO PROTECT HIM.
I...I DON'T WANT TO HELP YOU.
THEN IT IS WELL I DO NOT GIVE YOU A CHOICE.
I DON'T EVEN KNOW WHO I AM. I DON'T REMEMBER ANYTHING... BUT I DON'T WANT TO HURT ANYONE.
SILENCE. DR. HOLMAN TOLD ME ALL ANYONE NEEDS TO DO TO CONTROL YOU IS LAY HANDS ON YOU.
SO THIS IS WHAT YOU WILL DO.

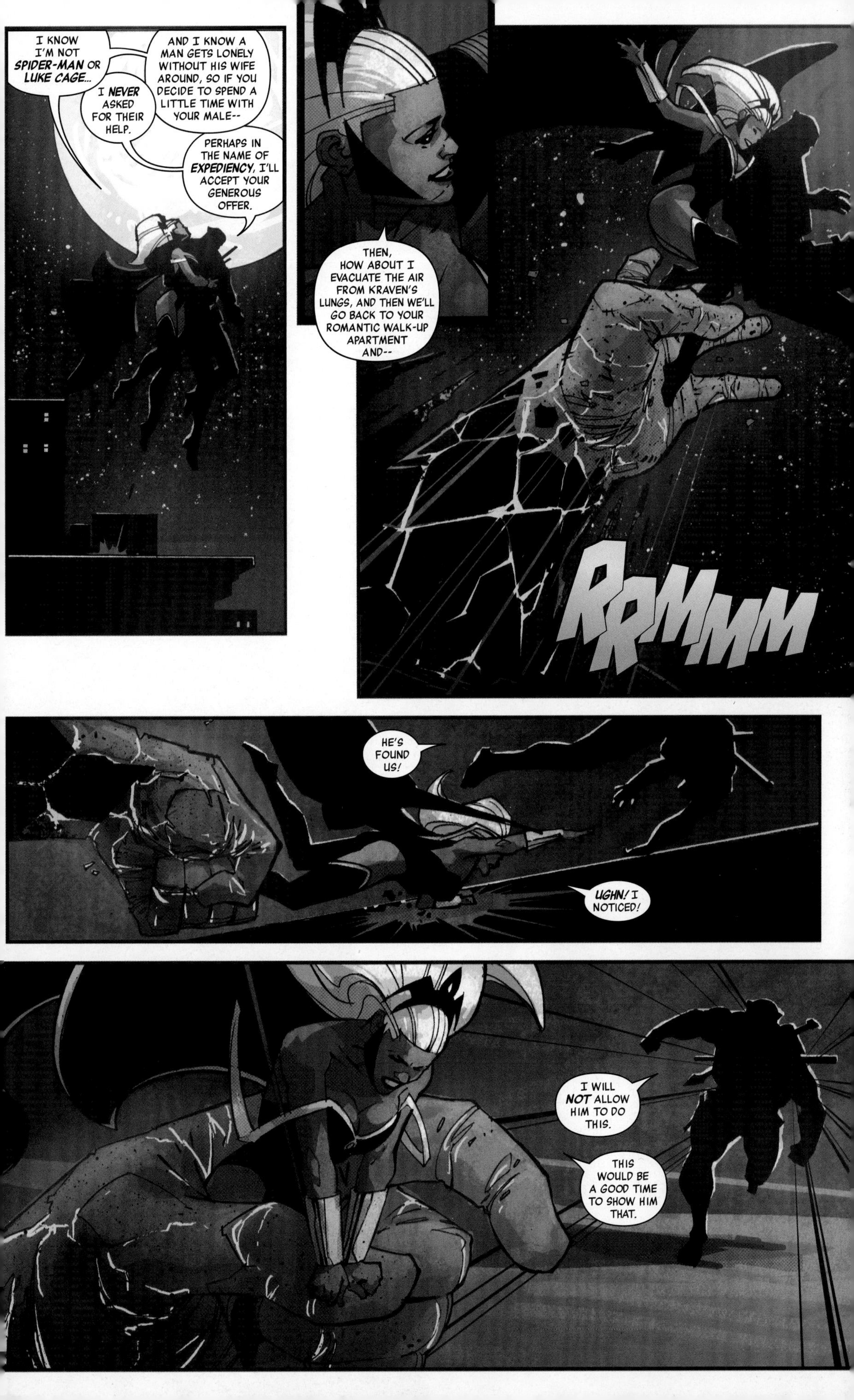

I KNOW I'M NOT SPIDER-MAN OR LUKE CAGE...
AND I KNOW A MAN GETS LONELY WITHOUT HIS WIFE AROUND, SO IF YOU DECIDE TO SPEND A LITTLE TIME WITH YOUR MALE--
I NEVER ASKED FOR THEIR HELP.
PERHAPS IN THE NAME OF EXPEDIENCY, I'LL ACCEPT YOUR GENEROUS OFFER.
THEN, HOW ABOUT I EVACUATE THE AIR FROM KRAVEN'S LUNGS, AND THEN WE'LL GO BACK TO YOUR ROMANTIC WALK-UP APARTMENT AND--
RRMMMM
HE'S FOUND US!
UGHN! I NOTICED!
I WILL NOT ALLOW HIM TO DO THIS.
THIS WOULD BE A GOOD TIME TO SHOW HIM THAT.

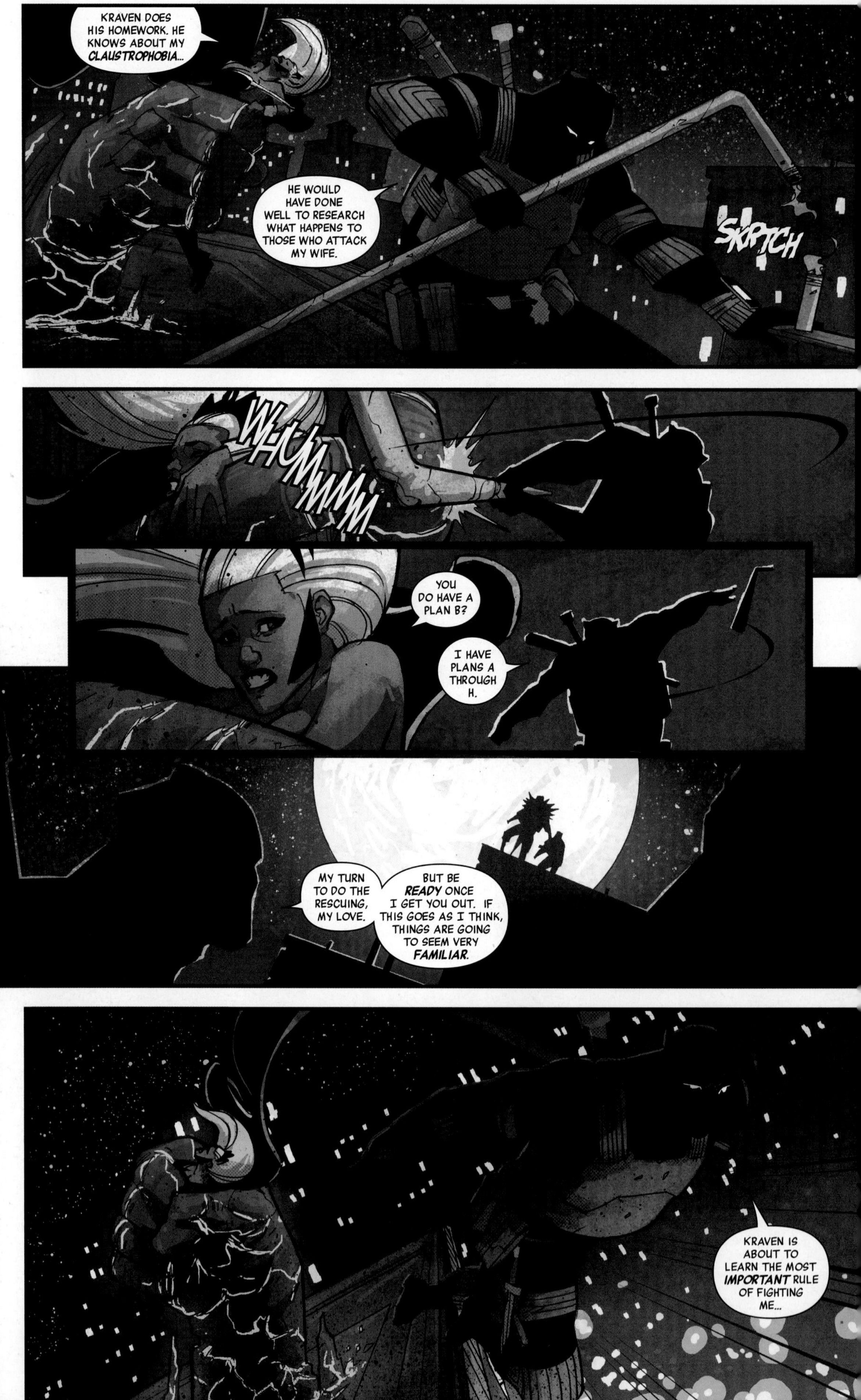
KRAVEN DOES HIS HOMEWORK. HE KNOWS ABOUT MY CLAUSTROPHOBIA...
HE WOULD HAVE DONE WELL TO RESEARCH WHAT HAPPENS TO THOSE WHO ATTACK MY WIFE.
SKRTCH
WHUMMMM
YOU DO HAVE A PLAN B?
I HAVE PLANS A THROUGH H.
MY TURN TO DO THE RESCUING, MY LOVE.
BUT BE READY ONCE I GET YOU OUT. IF THIS GOES AS I THINK, THINGS ARE GOING TO SEEM VERY FAMILIAR.
KRAVEN IS ABOUT TO LEARN THE MOST IMPORTANT RULE OF FIGHTING ME...

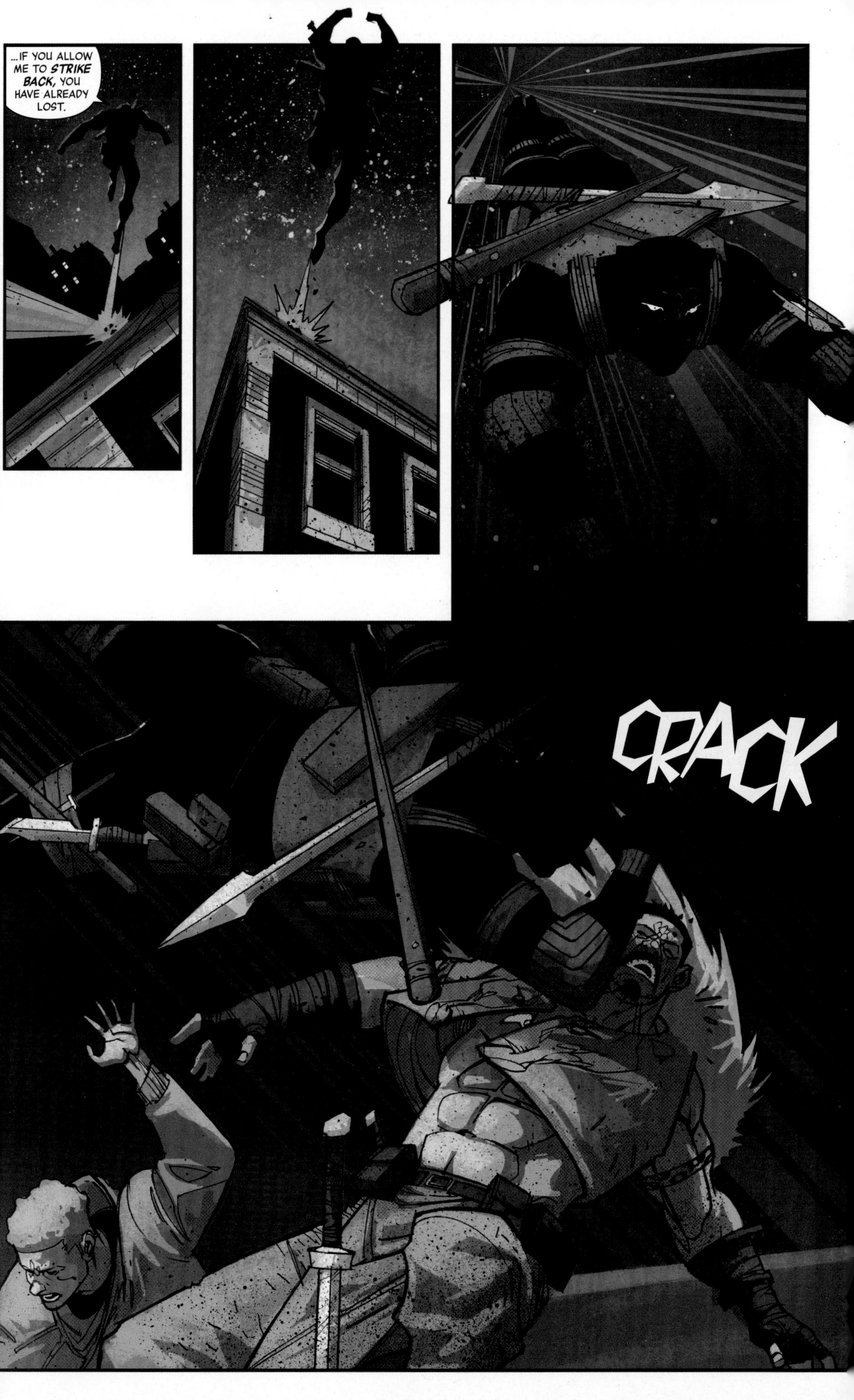
...IF YOU ALLOW ME TO STRIKE BACK, YOU HAVE ALREADY LOST.
CRACK

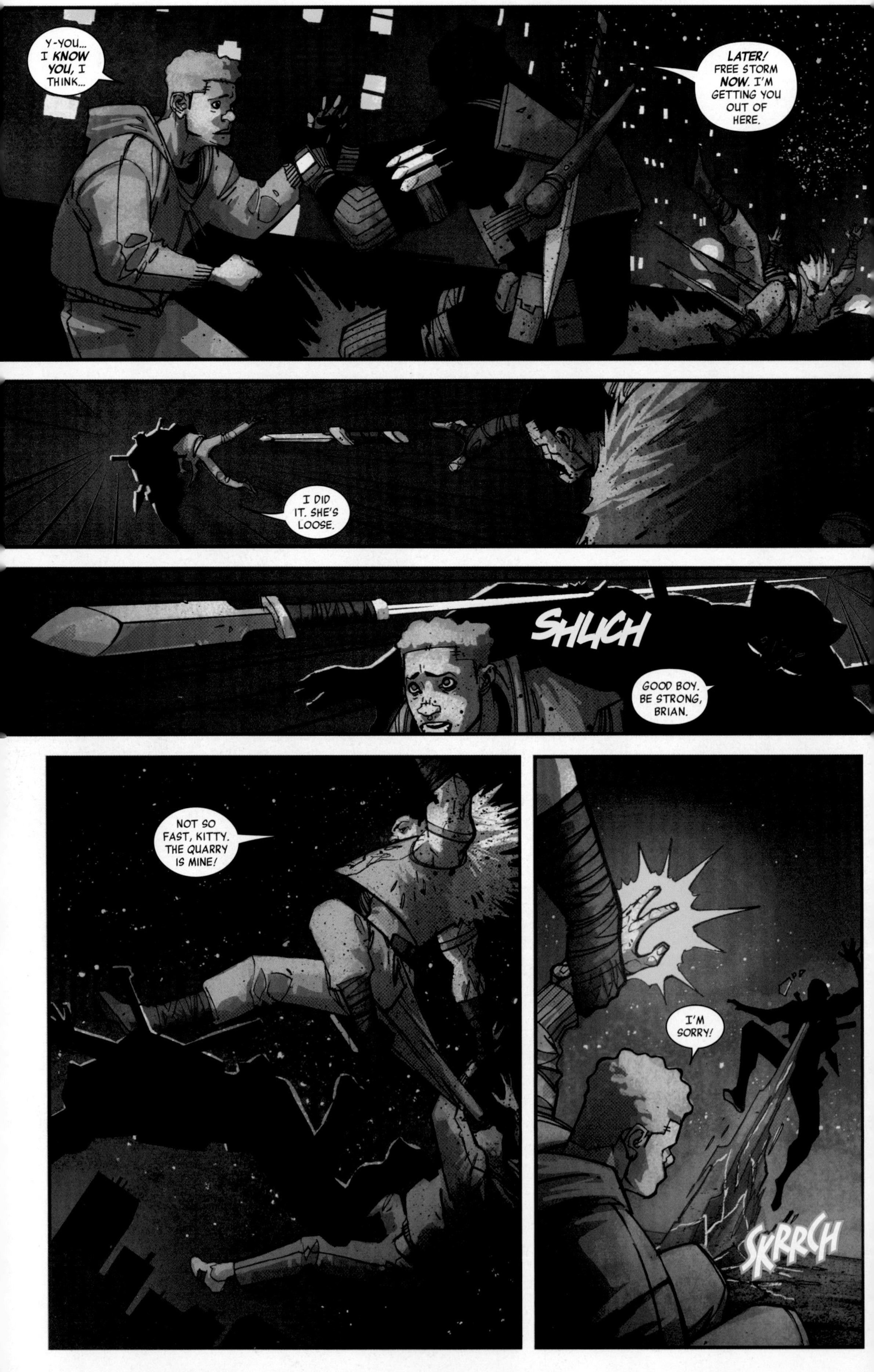
Y-YOU... I KNOW YOU, I THINK...
LATER! FREE STORM NOW. I'M GETTING YOU OUT OF HERE.
I DID IT. SHE'S LOOSE.
SHLICH
GOOD BOY. BE STRONG, BRIAN.
NOT SO FAST, KITTY. THE QUARRY IS MINE!
I'M SORRY!
SKRRCH

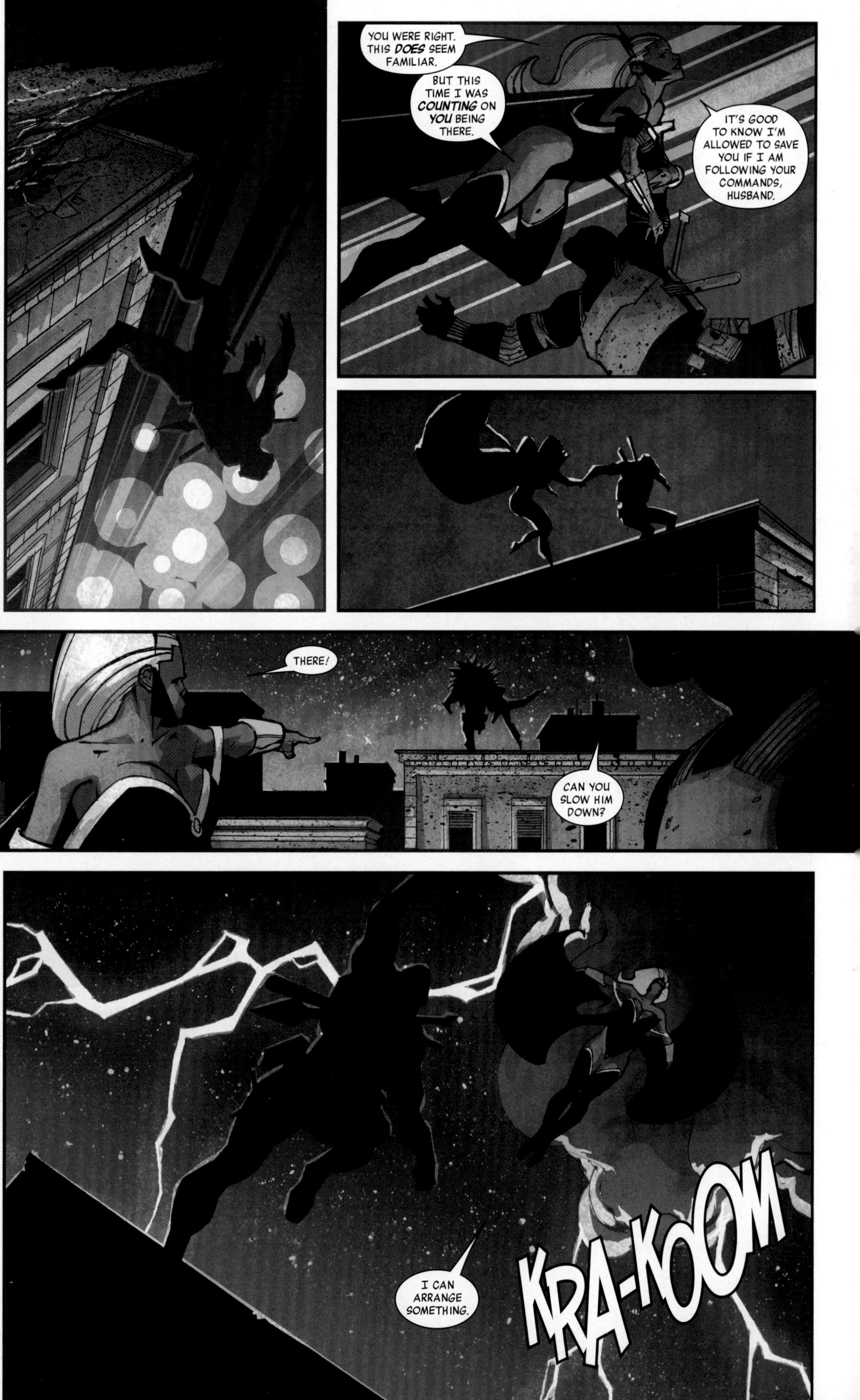
YOU WERE RIGHT. THIS DOES SEEM FAMILIAR.
BUT THIS TIME I WAS COUNTING ON YOU BEING THERE.
IT'S GOOD TO KNOW I'M ALLOWED TO SAVE YOU IF I AM FOLLOWING YOUR COMMANDS, HUSBAND.
THERE!
CAN YOU SLOW HIM DOWN?
I CAN ARRANGE SOMETHING.
KRA-KOOM

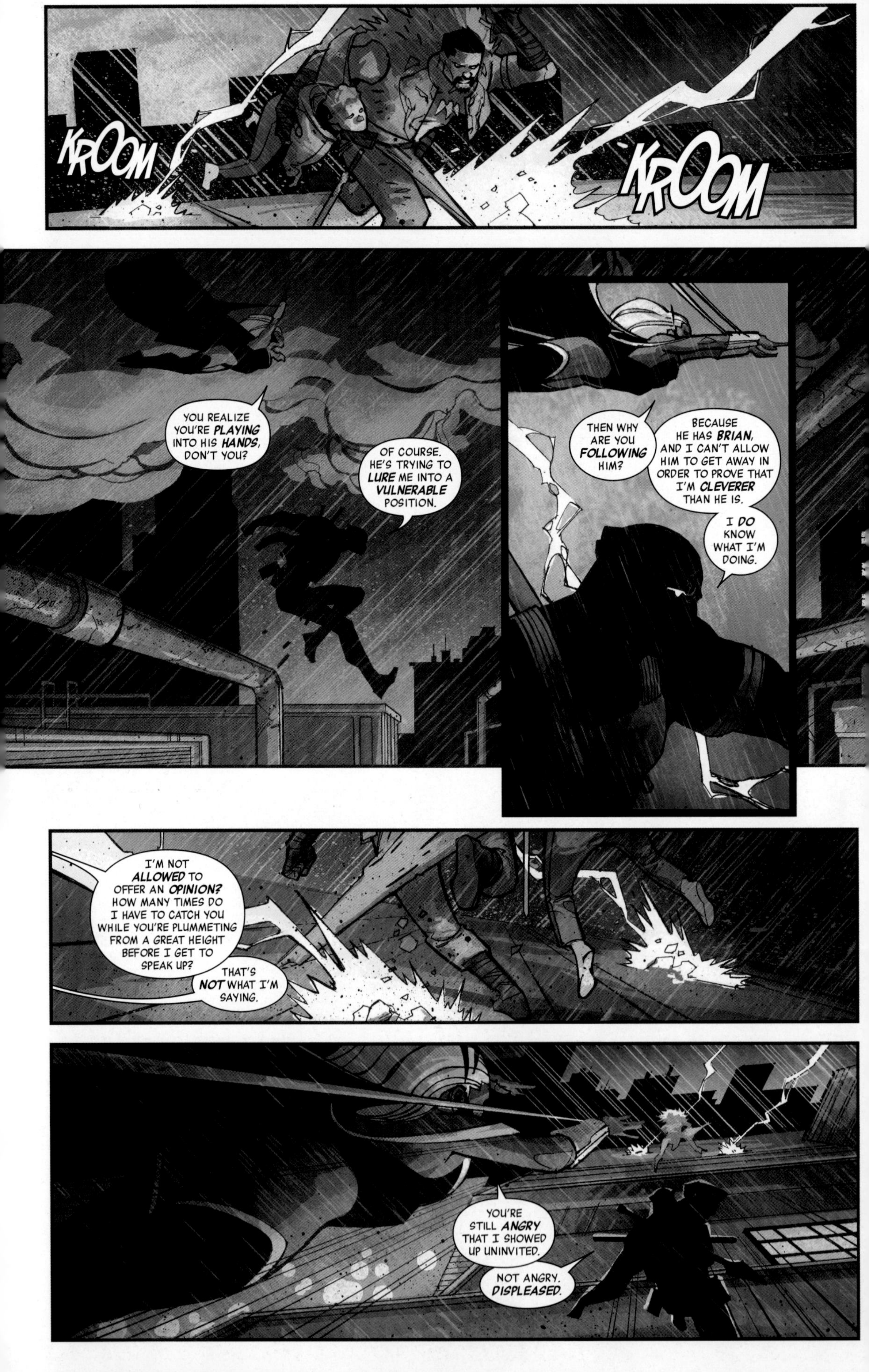
KROOM
KROOM
YOU REALIZE YOU'RE PLAYING INTO HIS HANDS, DON'T YOU?
OF COURSE. HE'S TRYING TO LURE ME INTO A VULNERABLE POSITION.
THEN WHY ARE YOU FOLLOWING HIM?
BECAUSE HE HAS BRIAN, AND I CAN'T ALLOW HIM TO GET AWAY IN ORDER TO PROVE THAT I'M CLEVERER THAN HE IS.
I DO KNOW WHAT I'M DOING.
I'M NOT ALLOWED TO OFFER AN OPINION? HOW MANY TIMES DO I HAVE TO CATCH YOU WHILE YOU'RE PLUMMETING FROM A GREAT HEIGHT BEFORE I GET TO SPEAK UP?
THAT'S NOT WHAT I'M SAYING.
YOU'RE STILL ANGRY THAT I SHOWED UP UNINVITED.
NOT ANGRY. DISPLEASED.

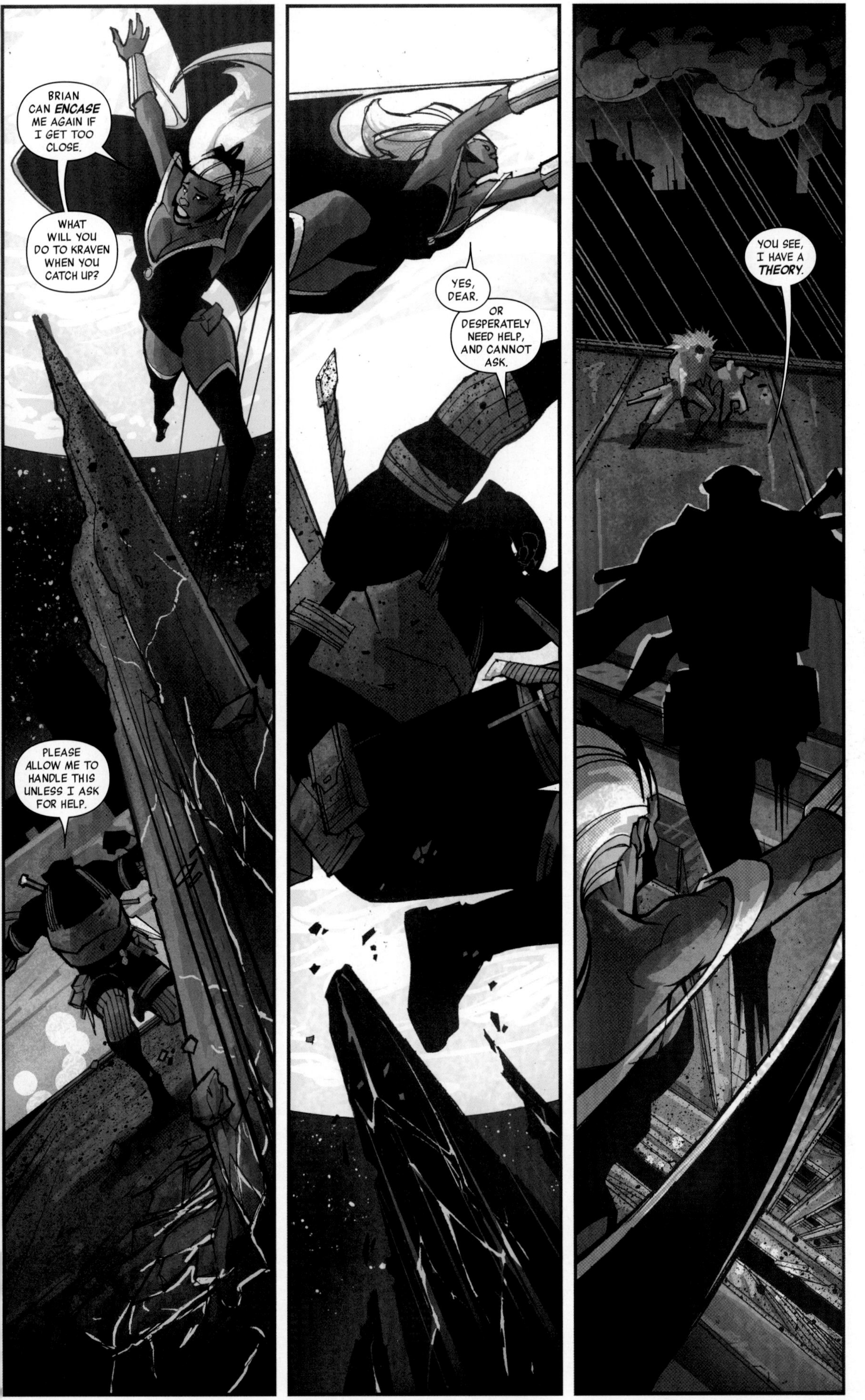
BRIAN CAN ENCASE ME AGAIN IF I GET TOO CLOSE.
WHAT WILL YOU DO TO KRAVEN WHEN YOU CATCH UP?
PLEASE ALLOW ME TO HANDLE THIS UNLESS I ASK FOR HELP.
YES, DEAR.
OR DESPERATELY NEED HELP, AND CANNOT ASK.
YOU SEE, I HAVE A THEORY.

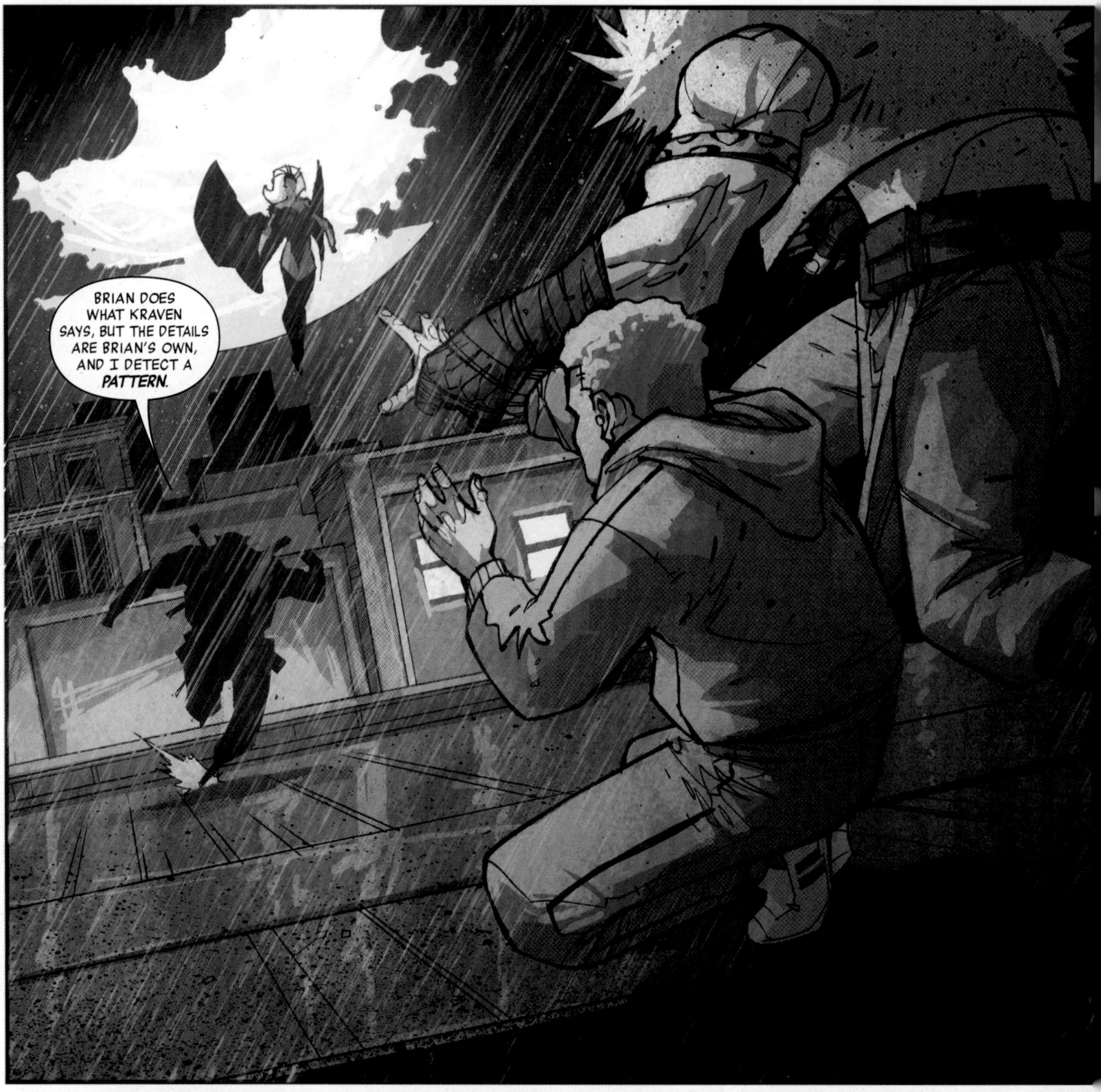
BRIAN DOES WHAT KRAVEN SAYS, BUT THE DETAILS ARE BRIAN'S OWN, AND I DETECT A *PATTERN*.

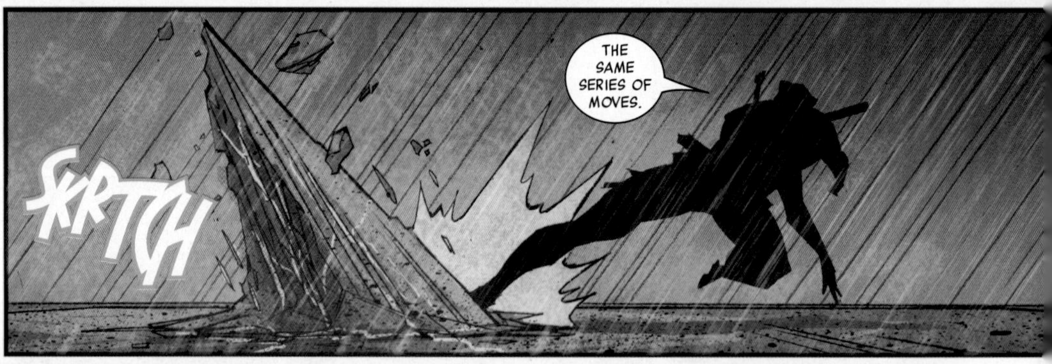
SKRTCH
THE SAME SERIES OF MOVES.

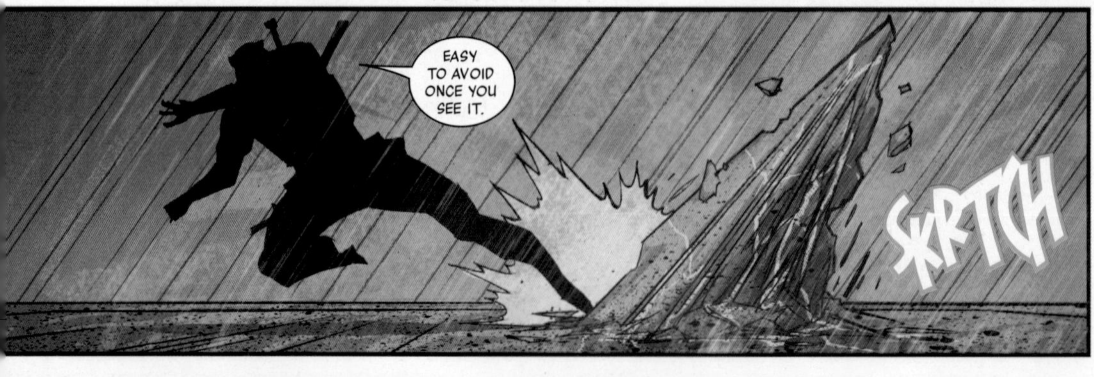
EASY TO AVOID ONCE YOU SEE IT.
SKRTCH

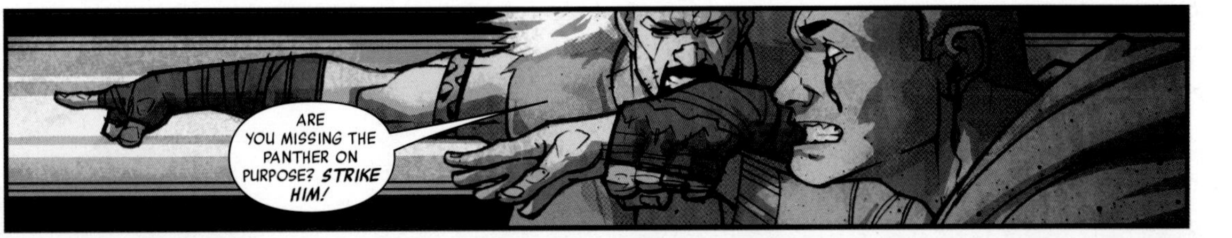
ARE YOU MISSING THE PANTHER ON PURPOSE? STRIKE HIM!

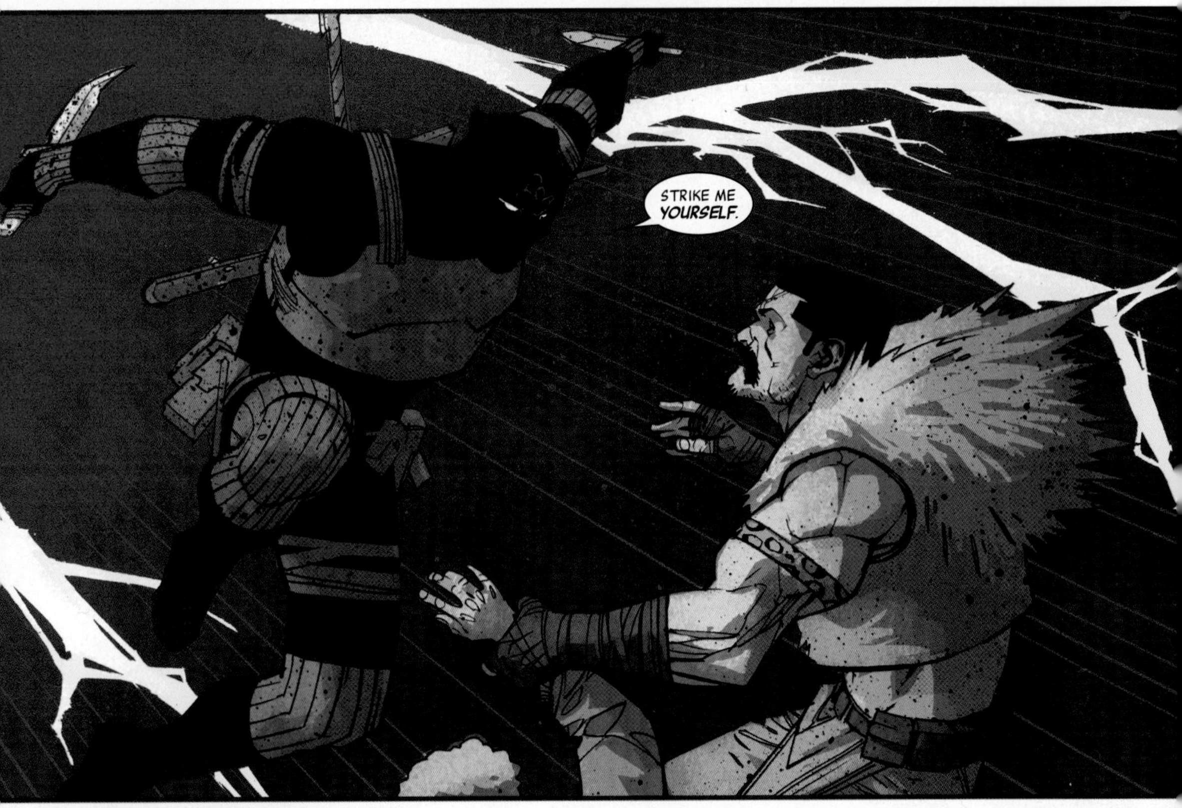
STRIKE ME YOURSELF.

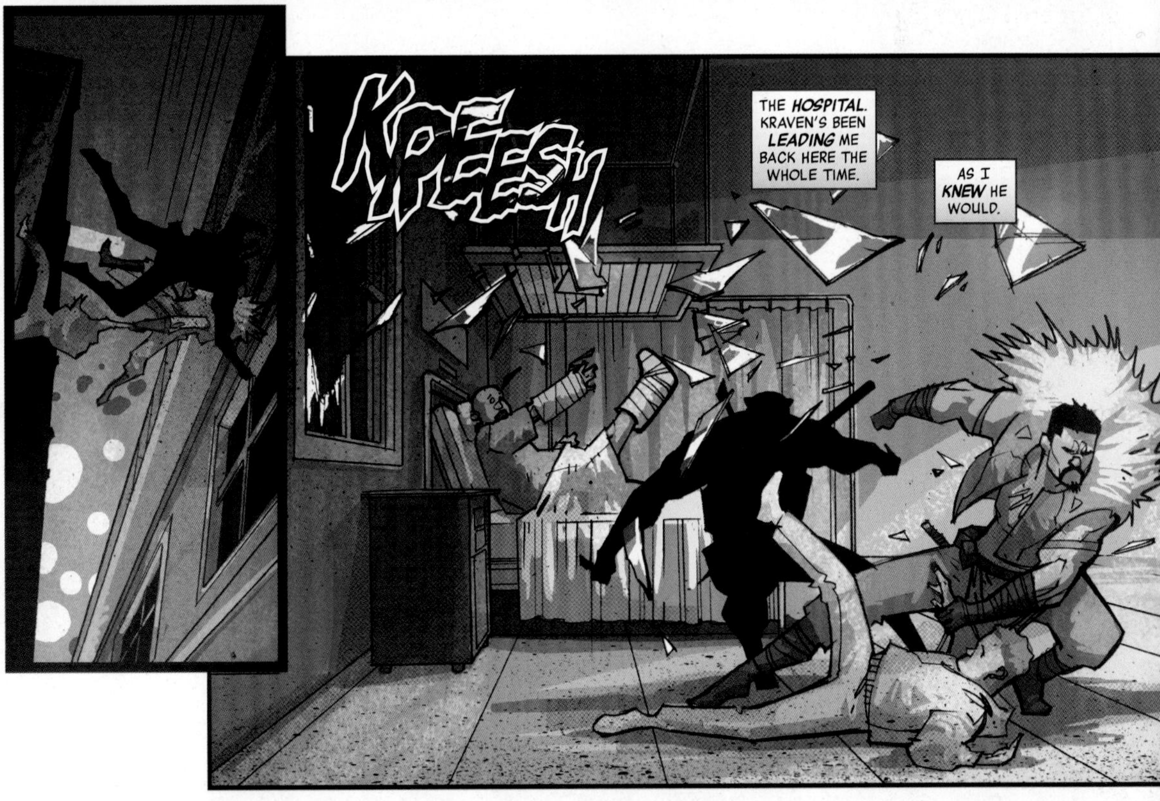
KREESH
THE HOSPITAL. KRAVEN'S BEEN LEADING ME BACK HERE THE WHOLE TIME.
AS I KNEW HE WOULD.

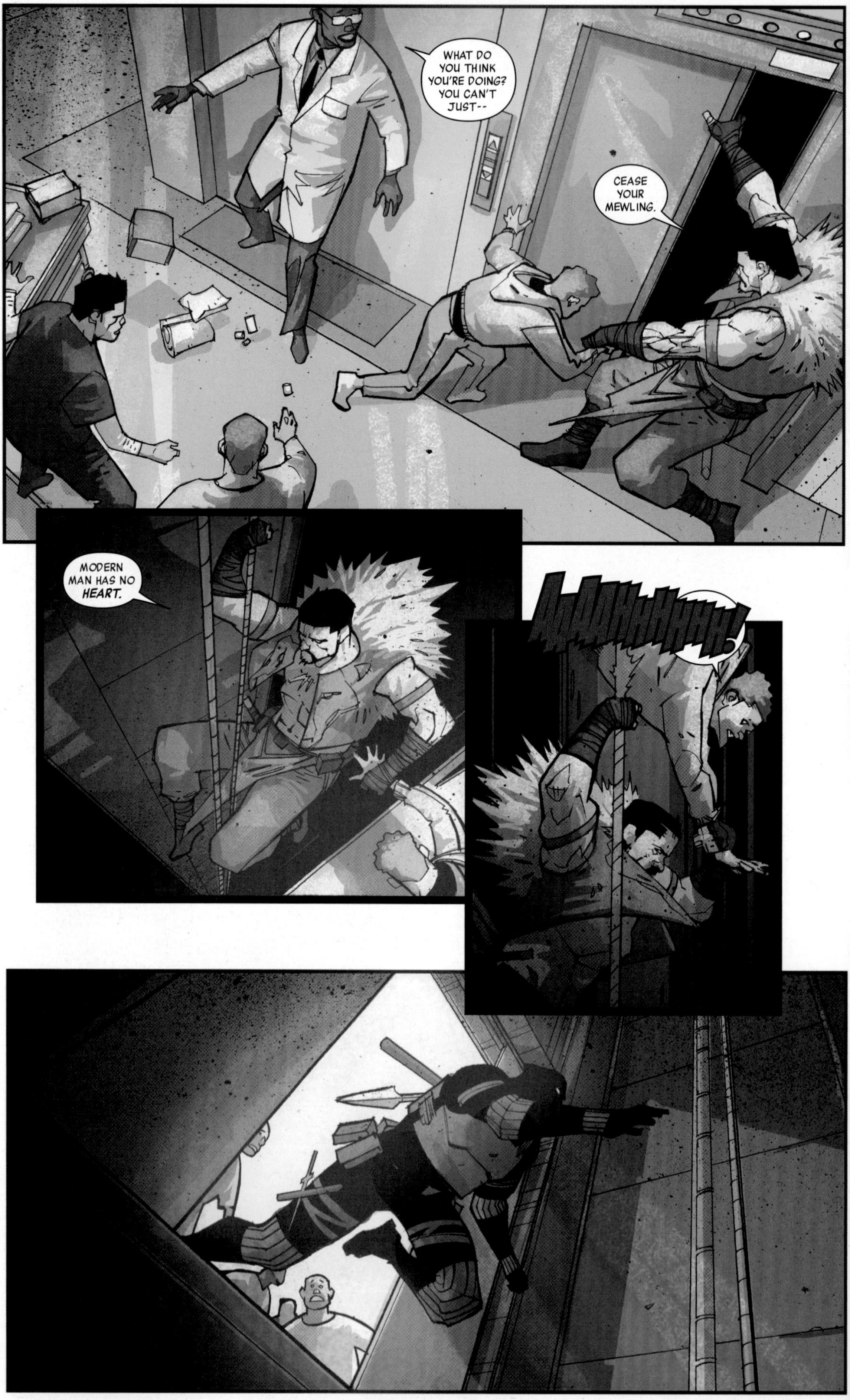
WHAT DO YOU THINK YOU'RE DOING? YOU CAN'T JUST--
CEASE YOUR MEWLING.
MODERN MAN HAS NO HEART.
AAAAHHHHHHH!

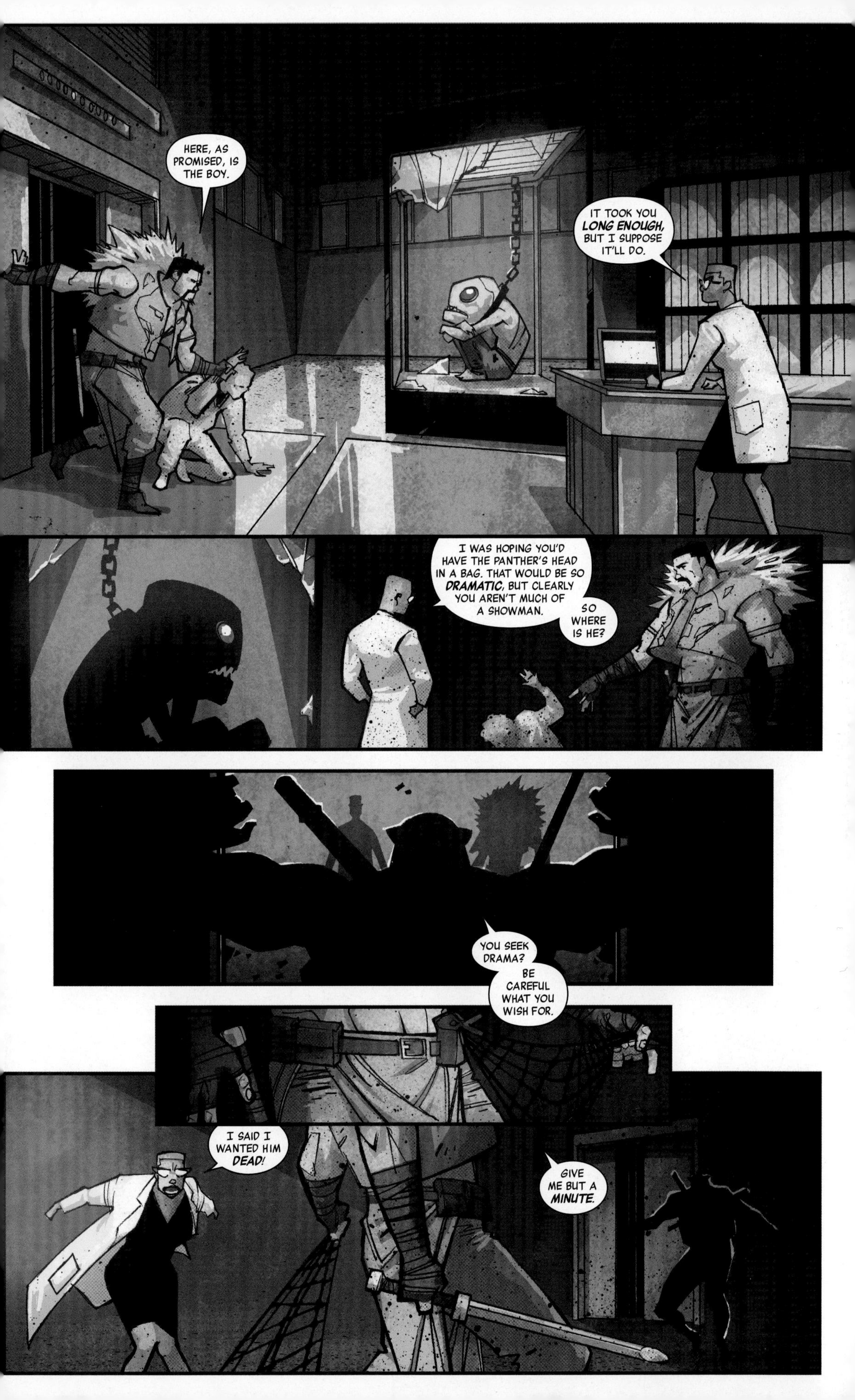
HERE, AS PROMISED, IS THE BOY.
IT TOOK YOU LONG ENOUGH, BUT I SUPPOSE IT'LL DO.
I WAS HOPING YOU'D HAVE THE PANTHER'S HEAD IN A BAG. THAT WOULD BE SO DRAMATIC, BUT CLEARLY YOU AREN'T MUCH OF A SHOWMAN.
SO WHERE IS HE?
YOU SEEK DRAMA?
BE CAREFUL WHAT YOU WISH FOR.
I SAID I WANTED HIM DEAD!
GIVE ME BUT A MINUTE.

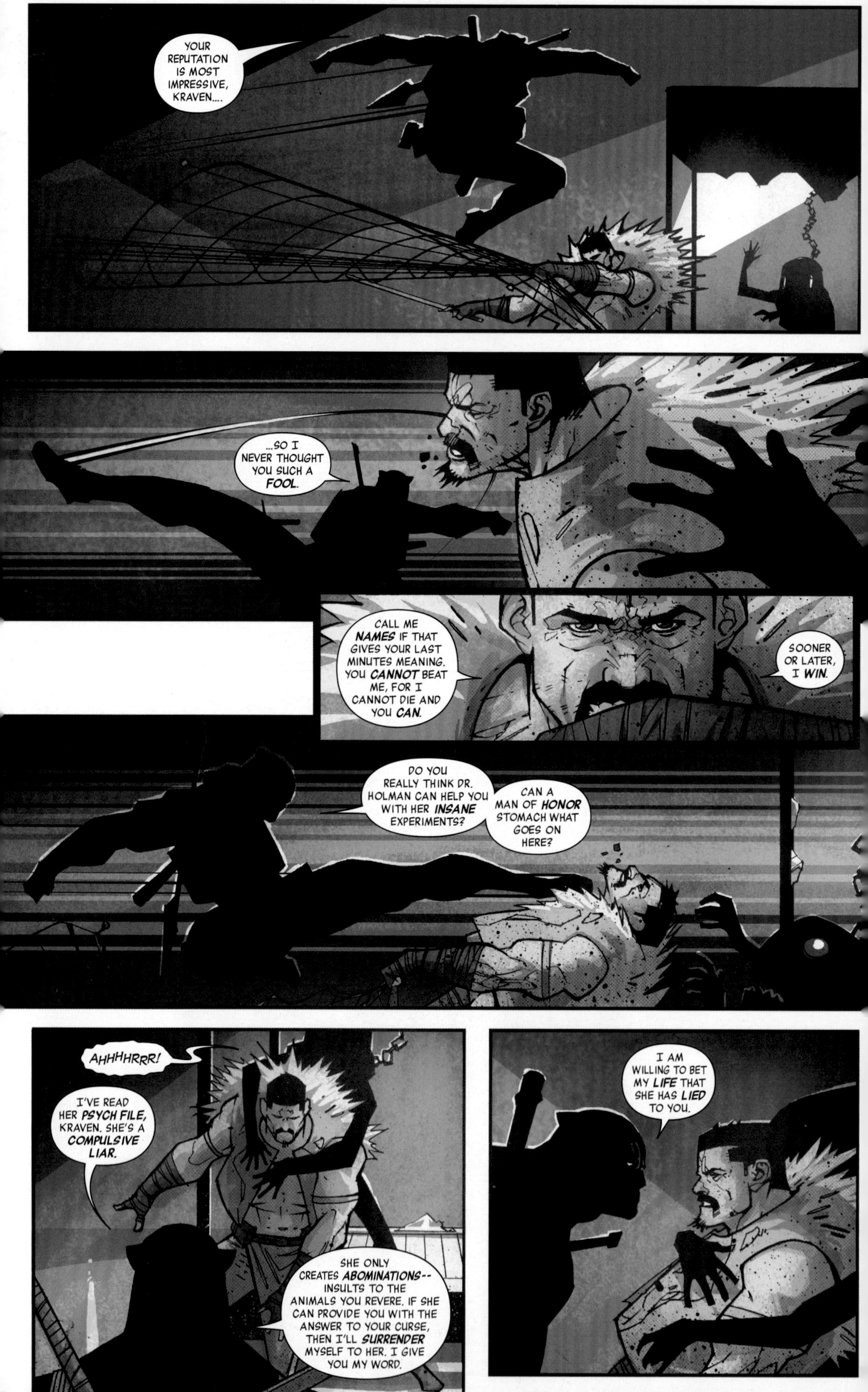

YOUR REPUTATION IS MOST IMPRESSIVE, KRAVEN....
...SO I NEVER THOUGHT YOU SUCH A FOOL.
CALL ME NAMES IF THAT GIVES YOUR LAST MINUTES MEANING. YOU CANNOT BEAT ME, FOR I CANNOT DIE AND YOU CAN.
SOONER OR LATER, I WIN.
DO YOU REALLY THINK DR. HOLMAN CAN HELP YOU WITH HER INSANE EXPERIMENTS?
CAN A MAN OF HONOR STOMACH WHAT GOES ON HERE?
AHHHHRRR!
I'VE READ HER PSYCH FILE, KRAVEN. SHE'S A COMPULSIVE LIAR.
SHE ONLY CREATES ABOMINATIONS-- INSULTS TO THE ANIMALS YOU REVERE. IF SHE CAN PROVIDE YOU WITH THE ANSWER TO YOUR CURSE, THEN I'LL SURRENDER MYSELF TO HER. I GIVE YOU MY WORD.
I AM WILLING TO BET MY LIFE THAT SHE HAS LIED TO YOU.

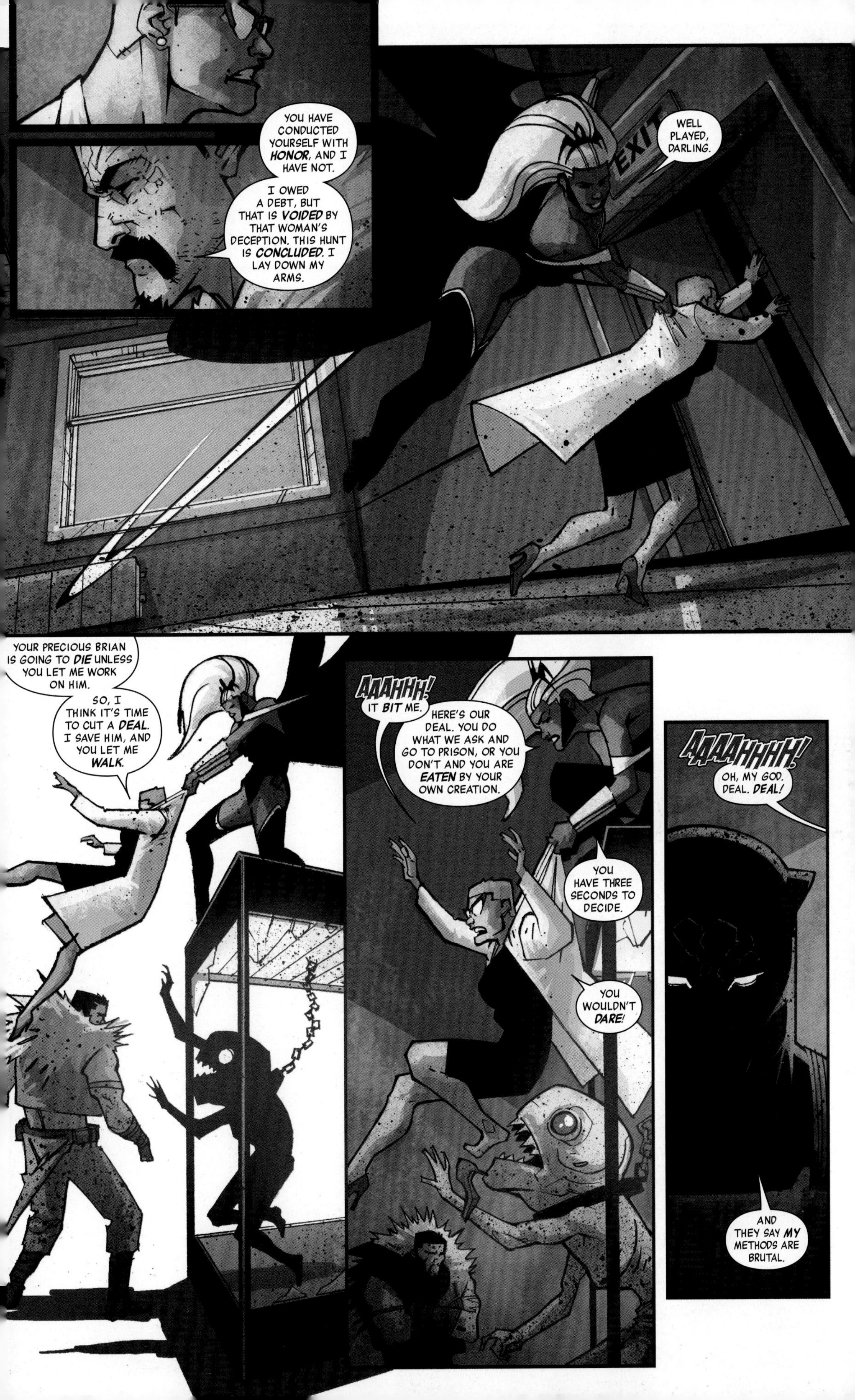
YOU HAVE CONDUCTED YOURSELF WITH HONOR, AND I HAVE NOT.
I OWED A DEBT, BUT THAT IS VOIDED BY THAT WOMAN'S DECEPTION. THIS HUNT IS CONCLUDED. I LAY DOWN MY ARMS.
EXIT
WELL PLAYED, DARLING.
YOUR PRECIOUS BRIAN IS GOING TO DIE UNLESS YOU LET ME WORK ON HIM.
SO, I THINK IT'S TIME TO CUT A DEAL. I SAVE HIM, AND YOU LET ME WALK.
AAAHHH!
IT BIT ME.
HERE'S OUR DEAL. YOU DO WHAT WE ASK AND GO TO PRISON, OR YOU DON'T AND YOU ARE EATEN BY YOUR OWN CREATION.
YOU HAVE THREE SECONDS TO DECIDE.
YOU WOULDN'T DARE!
AAAAHHHH!
OH, MY GOD. DEAL. DEAL!
AND THEY SAY MY METHODS ARE BRUTAL.

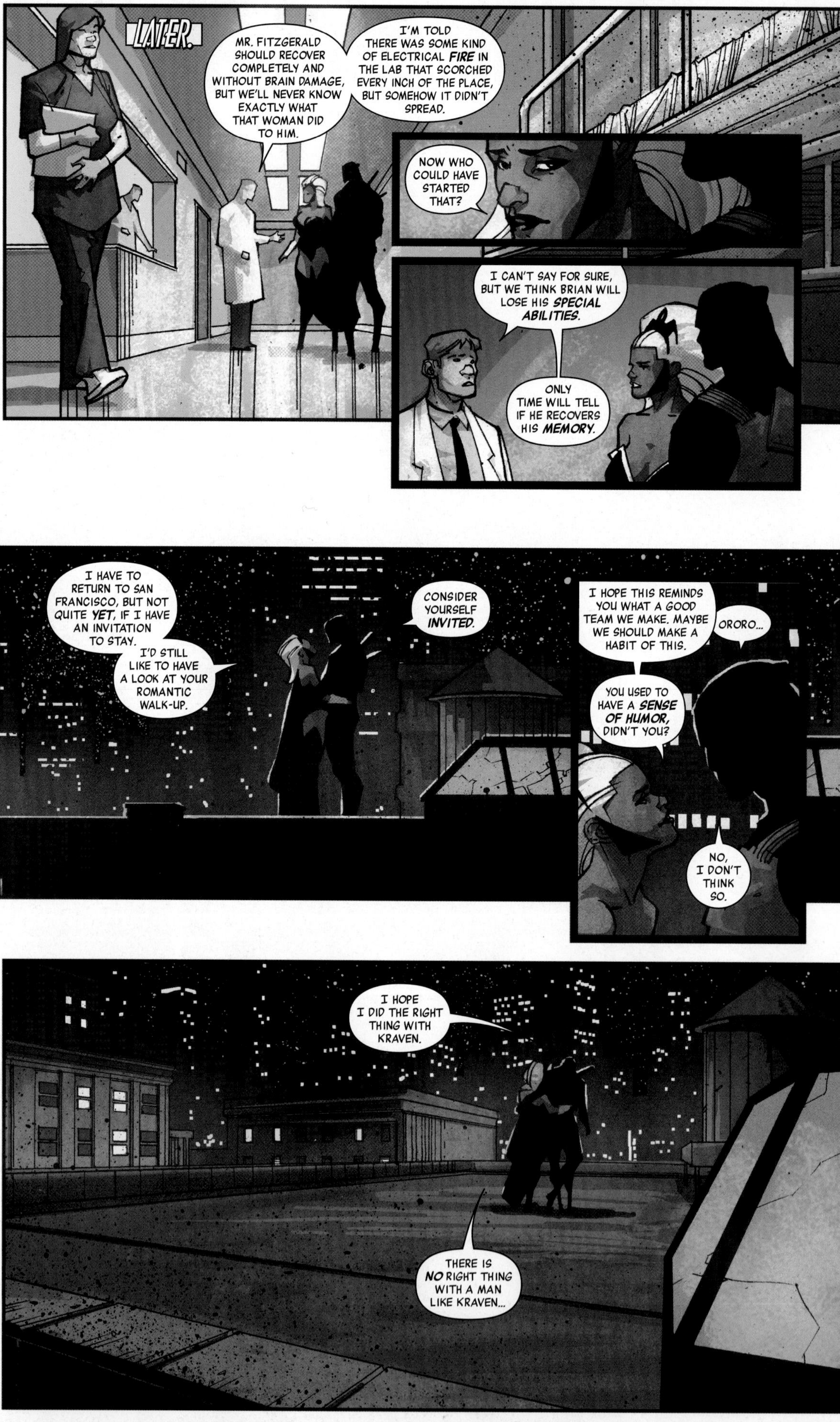
LATER.
MR. FITZGERALD SHOULD RECOVER COMPLETELY AND WITHOUT BRAIN DAMAGE, BUT WE'LL NEVER KNOW EXACTLY WHAT THAT WOMAN DID TO HIM.
I'M TOLD THERE WAS SOME KIND OF ELECTRICAL FIRE IN THE LAB THAT SCORCHED EVERY INCH OF THE PLACE, BUT SOMEHOW IT DIDN'T SPREAD.
NOW WHO COULD HAVE STARTED THAT?
I CAN'T SAY FOR SURE, BUT WE THINK BRIAN WILL LOSE HIS SPECIAL ABILITIES.
ONLY TIME WILL TELL IF HE RECOVERS HIS MEMORY.
I HAVE TO RETURN TO SAN FRANCISCO, BUT NOT QUITE YET, IF I HAVE AN INVITATION TO STAY.
I'D STILL LIKE TO HAVE A LOOK AT YOUR ROMANTIC WALK-UP.
CONSIDER YOURSELF INVITED.
I HOPE THIS REMINDS YOU WHAT A GOOD TEAM WE MAKE. MAYBE WE SHOULD MAKE A HABIT OF THIS.
ORORO...
YOU USED TO HAVE A SENSE OF HUMOR, DIDN'T YOU?
NO, I DON'T THINK SO.
I HOPE I DID THE RIGHT THING WITH KRAVEN.
THERE IS NO RIGHT THING WITH A MAN LIKE KRAVEN...

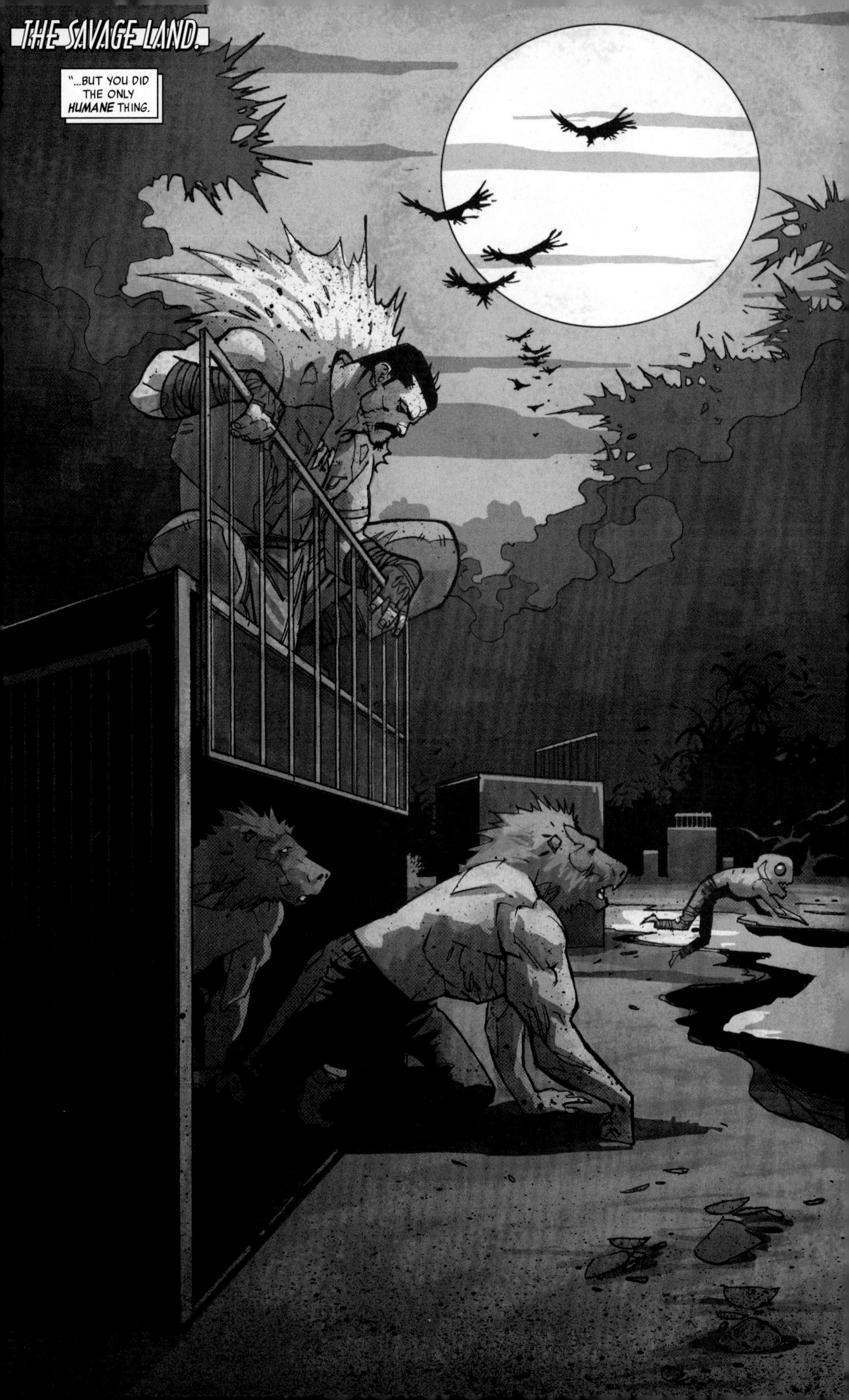
THE SAVAGE LAND.
"...BUT YOU DID THE ONLY HUMANE THING.

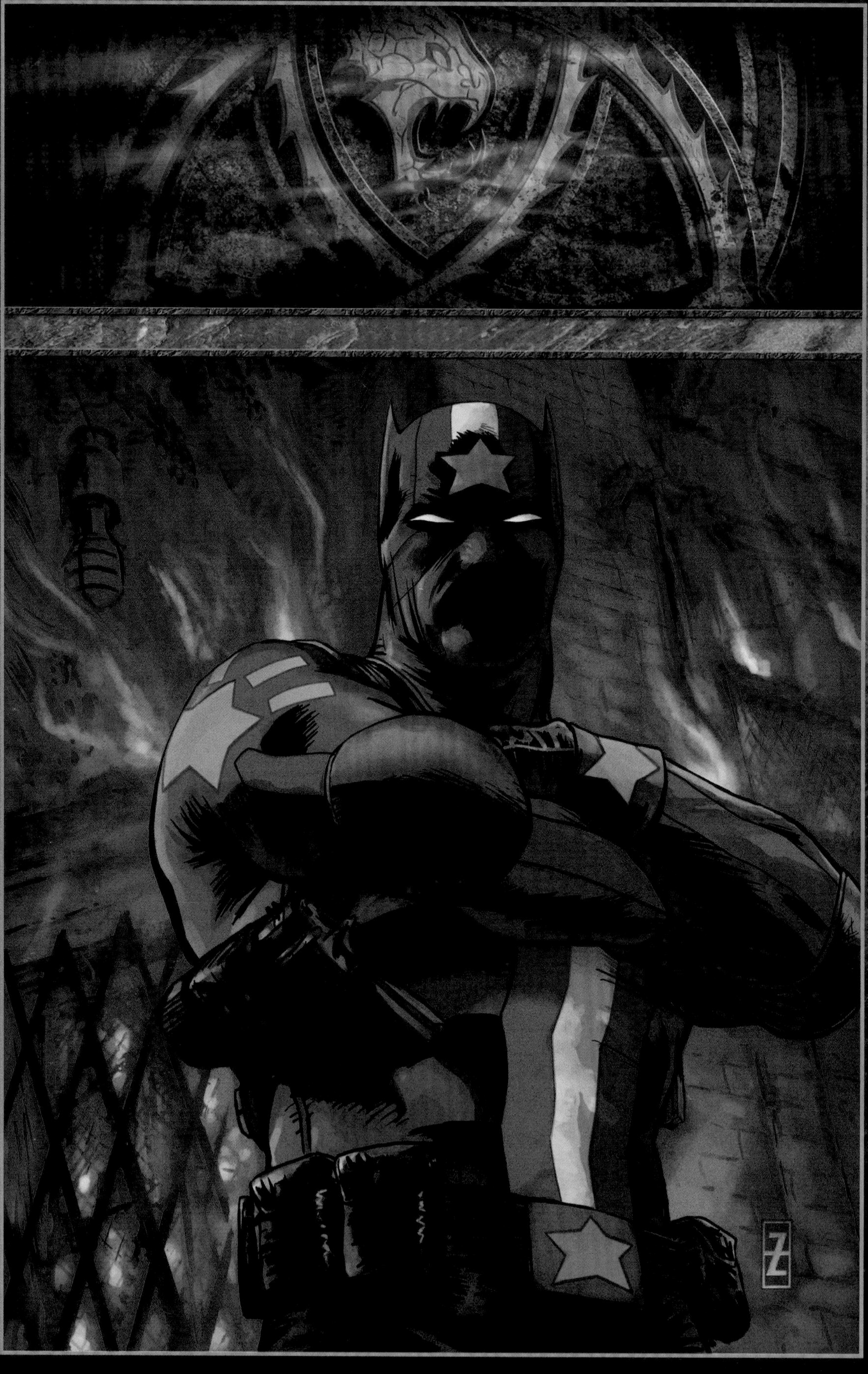

BLACK PANTHER:
THE MAN WITHOUT FEAR #521

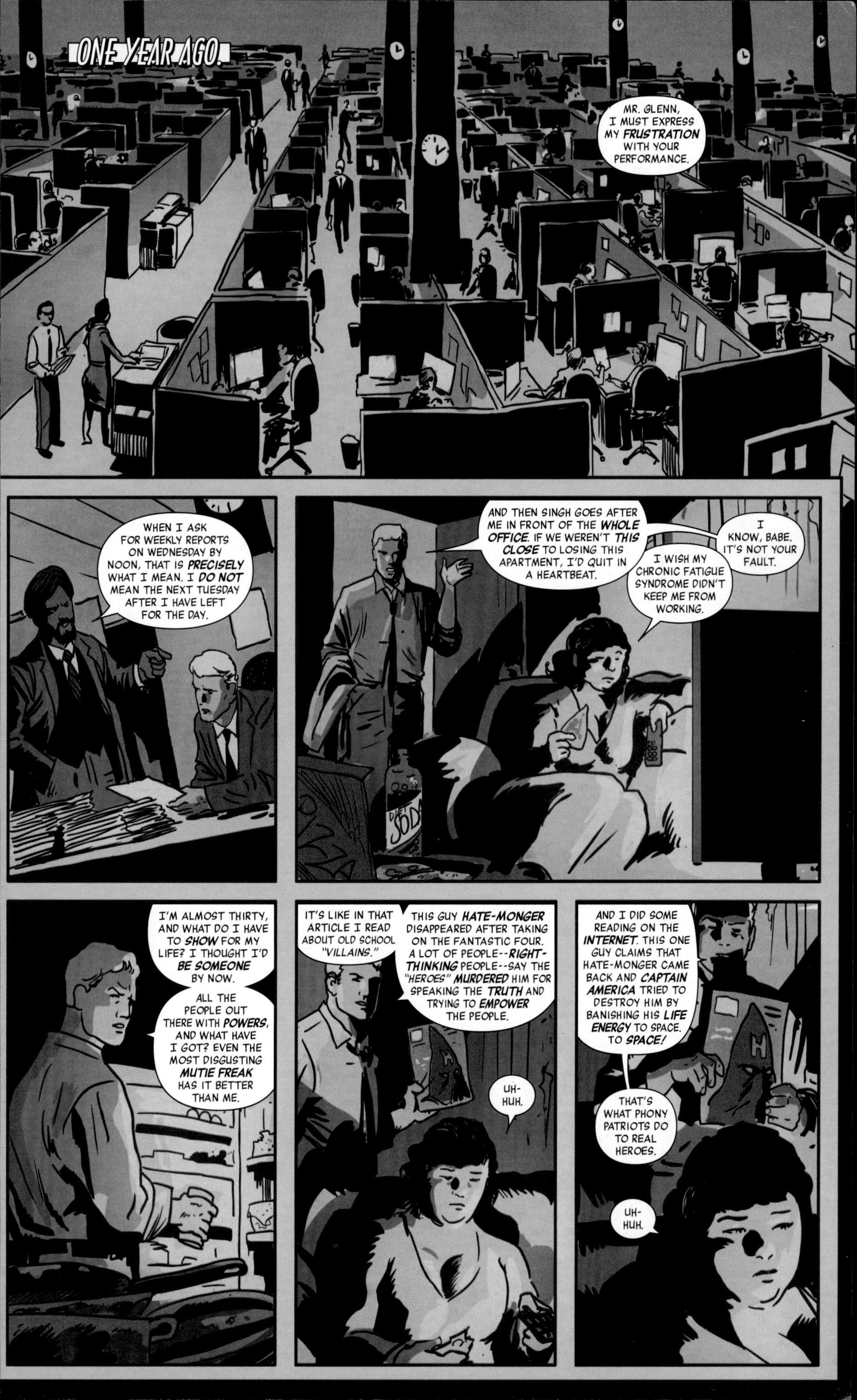
ONE YEAR AGO.
MR. GLENN, I MUST EXPRESS MY FRUSTRATION WITH YOUR PERFORMANCE.
WHEN I ASK FOR WEEKLY REPORTS ON WEDNESDAY BY NOON, THAT IS PRECISELY WHAT I MEAN. I DO NOT MEAN THE NEXT TUESDAY AFTER I HAVE LEFT FOR THE DAY.
AND THEN SINGH GOES AFTER ME IN FRONT OF THE WHOLE OFFICE. IF WE WEREN'T THIS CLOSE TO LOSING THIS APARTMENT, I'D QUIT IN A HEARTBEAT.
I KNOW, BABE. IT'S NOT YOUR FAULT.
I WISH MY CHRONIC FATIGUE SYNDROME DIDN'T KEEP ME FROM WORKING.
DIET SODA
I'M ALMOST THIRTY, AND WHAT DO I HAVE TO SHOW FOR MY LIFE? I THOUGHT I'D BE SOMEONE BY NOW.
ALL THE PEOPLE OUT THERE WITH POWERS, AND WHAT HAVE I GOT? EVEN THE MOST DISGUSTING MUTIE FREAK HAS IT BETTER THAN ME.
IT'S LIKE IN THAT ARTICLE I READ ABOUT OLD SCHOOL "VILLAINS."
THIS GUY HATE-MONGER DISAPPEARED AFTER TAKING ON THE FANTASTIC FOUR. A LOT OF PEOPLE--RIGHT-THINKING PEOPLE--SAY THE "HEROES" MURDERED HIM FOR SPEAKING THE TRUTH AND TRYING TO EMPOWER THE PEOPLE.
UH-HUH.
AND I DID SOME READING ON THE INTERNET. THIS ONE GUY CLAIMS THAT HATE-MONGER CAME BACK AND CAPTAIN AMERICA TRIED TO DESTROY HIM BY BANISHING HIS LIFE ENERGY TO SPACE. TO SPACE!
THAT'S WHAT PHONY PATRIOTS DO TO REAL HEROES.
UH-HUH.

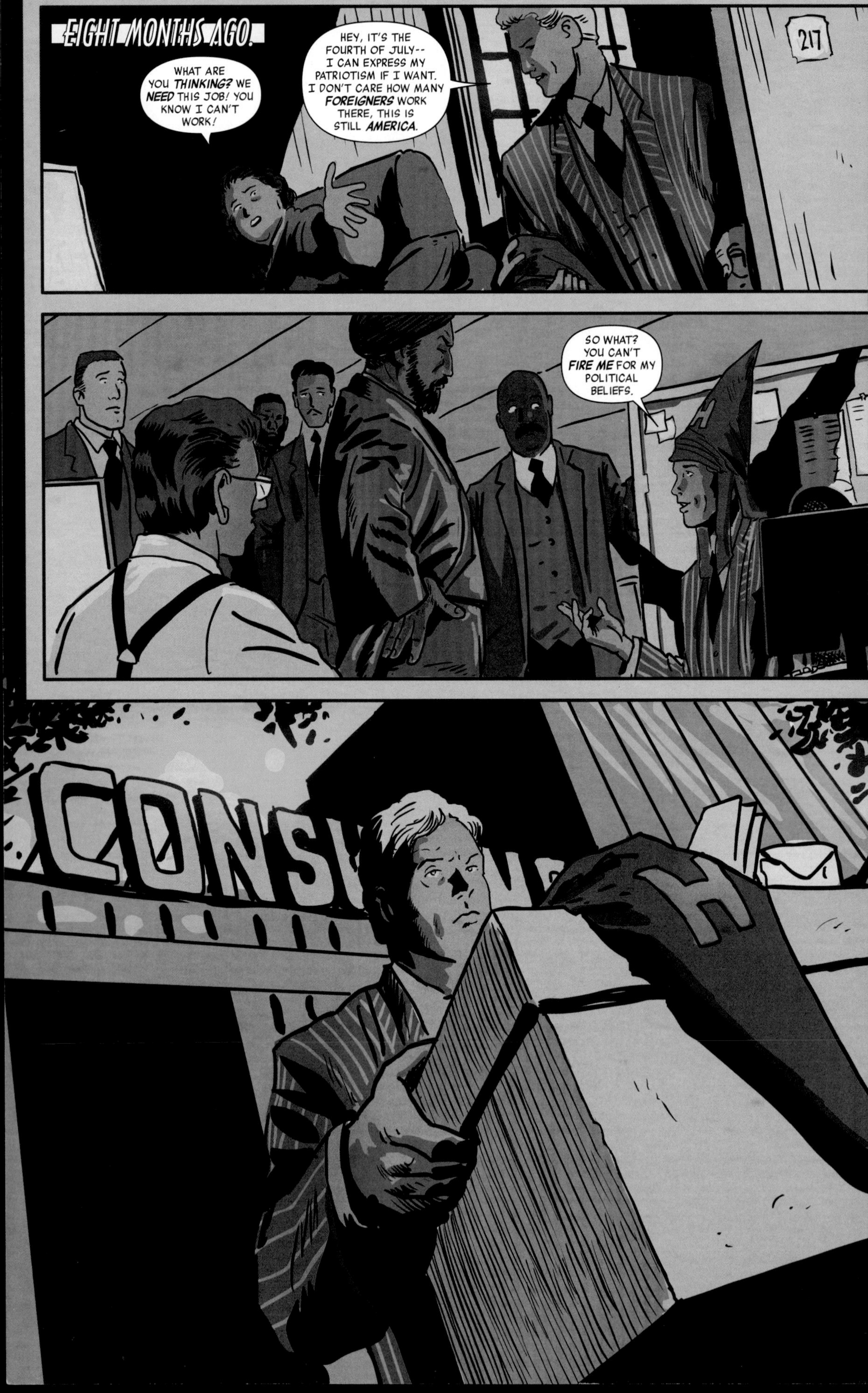
EIGHT MONTHS AGO.
217
WHAT ARE YOU THINKING? WE NEED THIS JOB! YOU KNOW I CAN'T WORK!
HEY, IT'S THE FOURTH OF JULY-- I CAN EXPRESS MY PATRIOTISM IF I WANT. I DON'T CARE HOW MANY FOREIGNERS WORK THERE, THIS IS STILL AMERICA.
SO WHAT? YOU CAN'T FIRE ME FOR MY POLITICAL BELIEFS.
CONSU

FIVE MONTHS AGO.

SO, DON'T TELL ME AMERICA IS A COUNTRY OF *IMMIGRANTS*. AMERICA IS A COUNTRY OF *AMERICANS!*

IMMIGRANTS CAN WORK THEIR WAY UP, BUT WHEN THEY GET *EVERYTHING* HANDED TO THEM, SOMETHING IS *WRONG!*

JOSH?

NOT *NOW*. I'M RECORDING MY BLOG!

I *KNOW*, BUT YOU *PROMISED* YOU WOULD LOOK FOR WORK TODAY. THE RENT IS ALMOST DUE--

LET YOUR PARENTS PAY IT AGAIN. IT'S THE LEAST A COUPLE OF *ILLEGALS* LIKE THEM CAN DO FOR A *REAL* AMERICAN.

JOSH, THEY'RE *CANADIAN*.

SOMETHING HAS TO *CHANGE*. WE CAN'T LIVE LIKE THIS.

COME ON. YOU *KNOW* WHAT A *RESTRAINING ORDER* MEANS.

I SUPPORTED THAT *FAT COW* FOR YEARS...AND SHE KICKS ME *OUT?*

THREE MONTHS AGO.

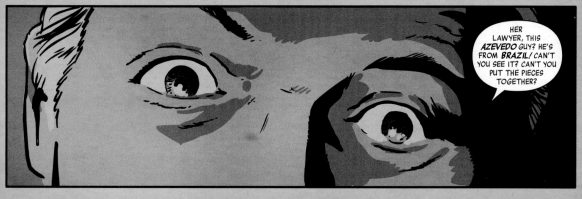

HER LAWYER, THIS *AZEVEDO* GUY? HE'S FROM *BRAZIL!* CAN'T YOU SEE IT? CAN'T YOU PUT THE PIECES TOGETHER?

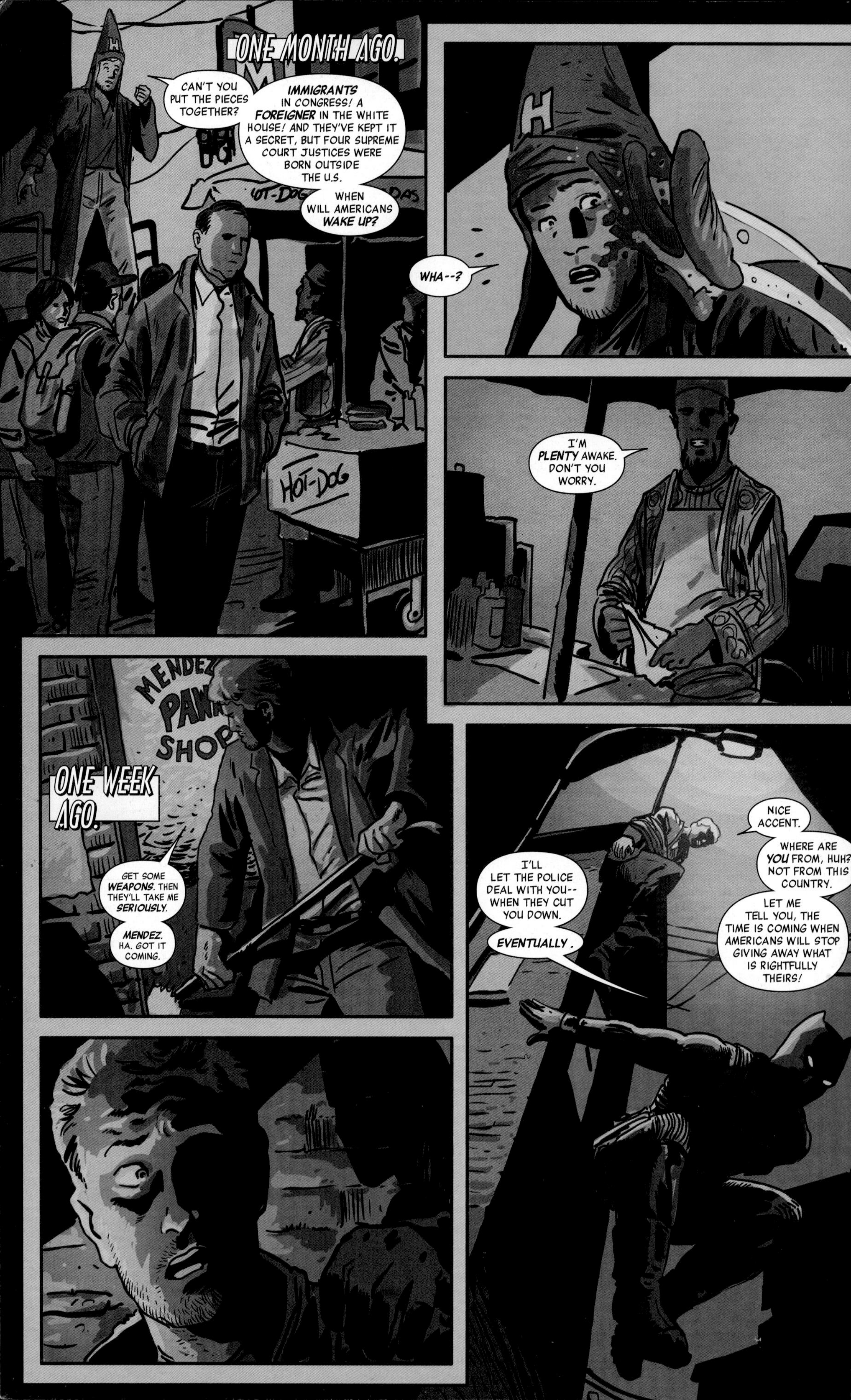
ONE MONTH AGO.
CAN'T YOU PUT THE PIECES TOGETHER?
IMMIGRANTS IN CONGRESS! A FOREIGNER IN THE WHITE HOUSE! AND THEY'VE KEPT IT A SECRET, BUT FOUR SUPREME COURT JUSTICES WERE BORN OUTSIDE THE U.S.
WHEN WILL AMERICANS WAKE UP?
HOT-DOG
WHA--?
I'M PLENTY AWAKE. DON'T YOU WORRY.
MENDEZ PAWN SHOP
ONE WEEK AGO.
GET SOME WEAPONS. THEN THEY'LL TAKE ME SERIOUSLY.
MENDEZ. HA. GOT IT COMING.
NICE ACCENT.
WHERE ARE YOU FROM, HUH? NOT FROM THIS COUNTRY.
LET ME TELL YOU, THE TIME IS COMING WHEN AMERICANS WILL STOP GIVING AWAY WHAT IS RIGHTFULLY THEIRS!
I'LL LET THE POLICE DEAL WITH YOU-- WHEN THEY CUT YOU DOWN.
EVENTUALLY.

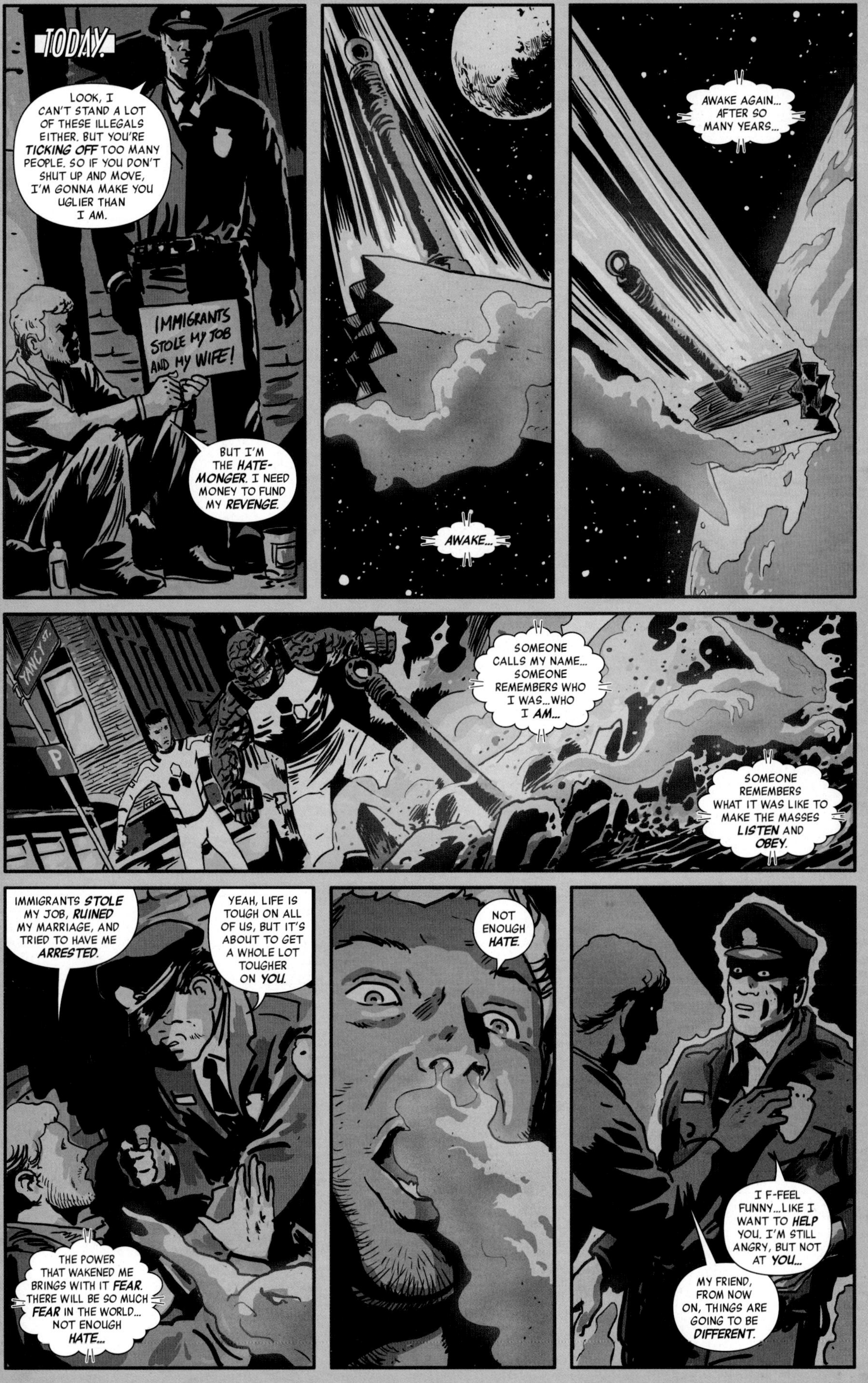
TODAY.
LOOK, I CAN'T STAND A LOT OF THESE ILLEGALS EITHER. BUT YOU'RE TICKING OFF TOO MANY PEOPLE. SO IF YOU DON'T SHUT UP AND MOVE, I'M GONNA MAKE YOU UGLIER THAN I AM.
IMMIGRANTS STOLE MY JOB AND MY WIFE!
BUT I'M THE HATE-MONGER. I NEED MONEY TO FUND MY REVENGE.
AWAKE...
AWAKE AGAIN... AFTER SO MANY YEARS...
YANCY ST.
P
SOMEONE CALLS MY NAME... SOMEONE REMEMBERS WHO I WAS...WHO I AM...
SOMEONE REMEMBERS WHAT IT WAS LIKE TO MAKE THE MASSES LISTEN AND OBEY.
IMMIGRANTS STOLE MY JOB, RUINED MY MARRIAGE, AND TRIED TO HAVE ME ARRESTED.
YEAH, LIFE IS TOUGH ON ALL OF US, BUT IT'S ABOUT TO GET A WHOLE LOT TOUGHER ON YOU.
THE POWER THAT WAKENED ME BRINGS WITH IT FEAR. THERE WILL BE SO MUCH FEAR IN THE WORLD... NOT ENOUGH HATE...
NOT ENOUGH HATE.
I F-FEEL FUNNY...LIKE I WANT TO HELP YOU. I'M STILL ANGRY, BUT NOT AT YOU...
MY FRIEND, FROM NOW ON, THINGS ARE GOING TO BE DIFFERENT.

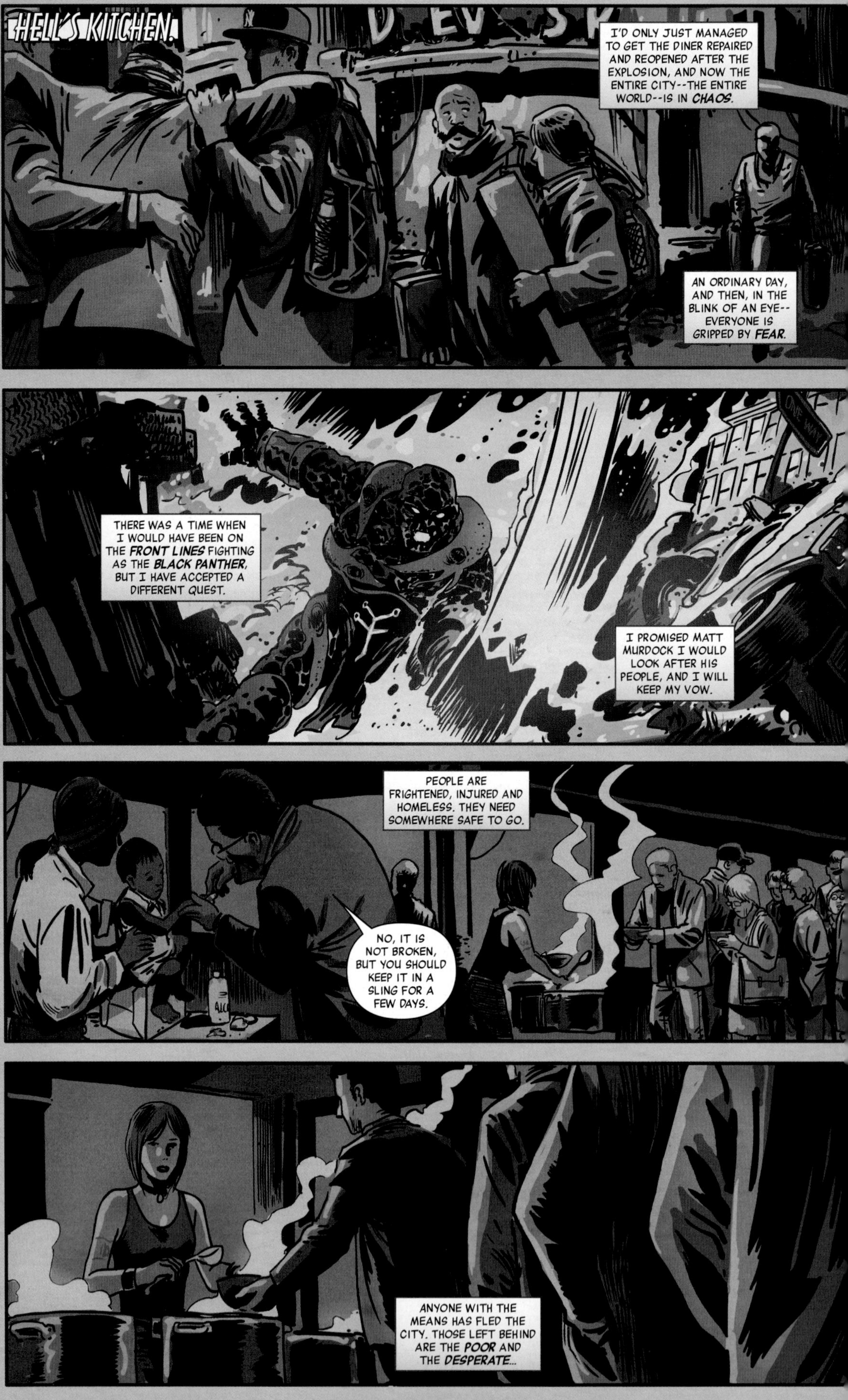
HELL'S KITCHEN.
I'D ONLY JUST MANAGED TO GET THE DINER REPAIRED AND REOPENED AFTER THE EXPLOSION, AND NOW THE ENTIRE CITY--THE ENTIRE WORLD--IS IN CHAOS.
AN ORDINARY DAY, AND THEN, IN THE BLINK OF AN EYE--EVERYONE IS GRIPPED BY FEAR.
THERE WAS A TIME WHEN I WOULD HAVE BEEN ON THE FRONT LINES FIGHTING AS THE BLACK PANTHER, BUT I HAVE ACCEPTED A DIFFERENT QUEST.
I PROMISED MATT MURDOCK I WOULD LOOK AFTER HIS PEOPLE, AND I WILL KEEP MY VOW.
PEOPLE ARE FRIGHTENED, INJURED AND HOMELESS. THEY NEED SOMEWHERE SAFE TO GO.
NO, IT IS NOT BROKEN, BUT YOU SHOULD KEEP IT IN A SLING FOR A FEW DAYS.
ANYONE WITH THE MEANS HAS FLED THE CITY. THOSE LEFT BEHIND ARE THE POOR AND THE DESPERATE...

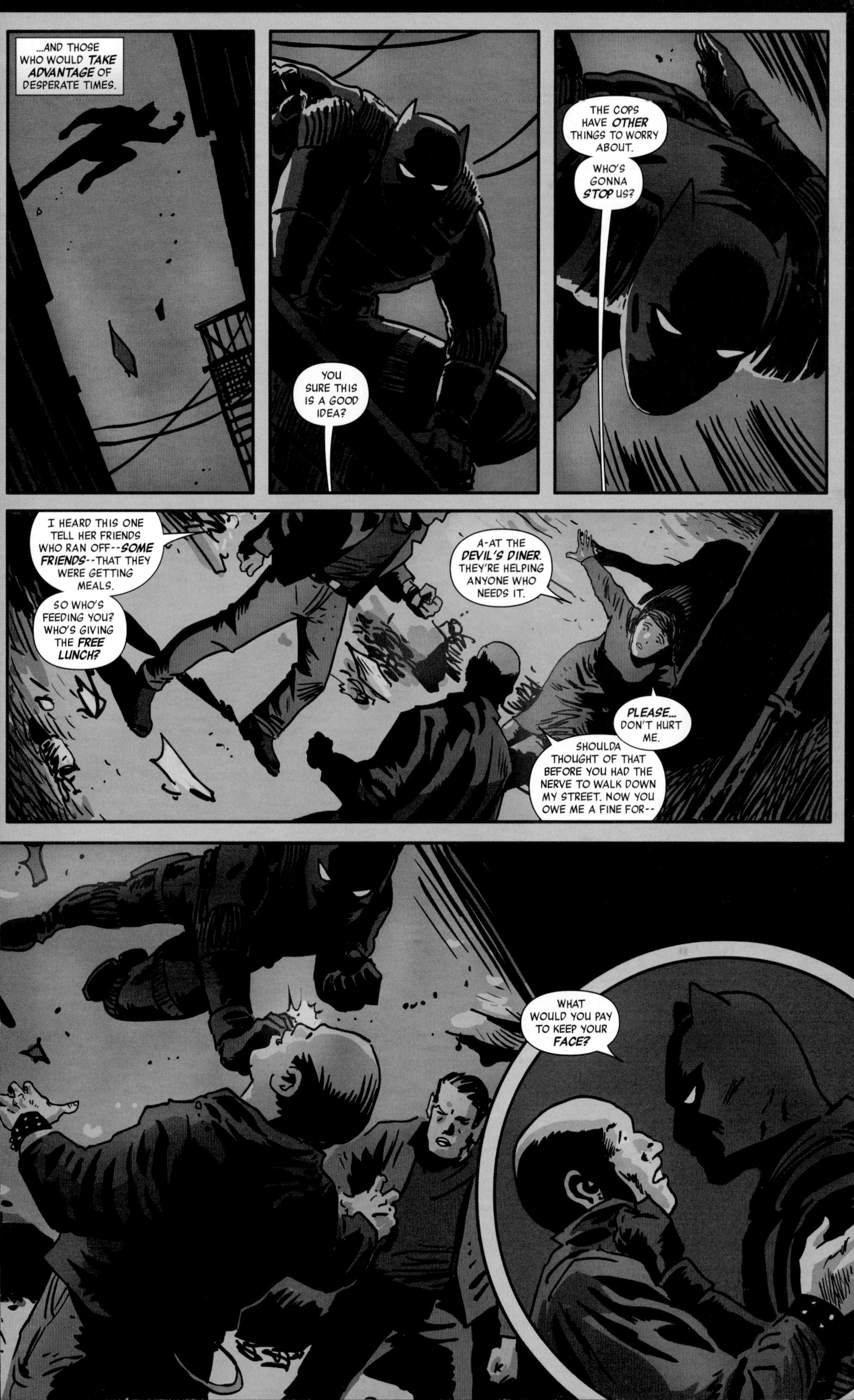
...AND THOSE WHO WOULD TAKE ADVANTAGE OF DESPERATE TIMES.
YOU SURE THIS IS A GOOD IDEA?
THE COPS HAVE OTHER THINGS TO WORRY ABOUT.
WHO'S GONNA STOP US?
I HEARD THIS ONE TELL HER FRIENDS WHO RAN OFF--SOME FRIENDS--THAT THEY WERE GETTING MEALS.
SO WHO'S FEEDING YOU? WHO'S GIVING THE FREE LUNCH?
A-AT THE DEVIL'S DINER. THEY'RE HELPING ANYONE WHO NEEDS IT.
PLEASE... DON'T HURT ME.
SHOULDA THOUGHT OF THAT BEFORE YOU HAD THE NERVE TO WALK DOWN MY STREET. NOW YOU OWE ME A FINE FOR--
WHAT WOULD YOU PAY TO KEEP YOUR FACE?

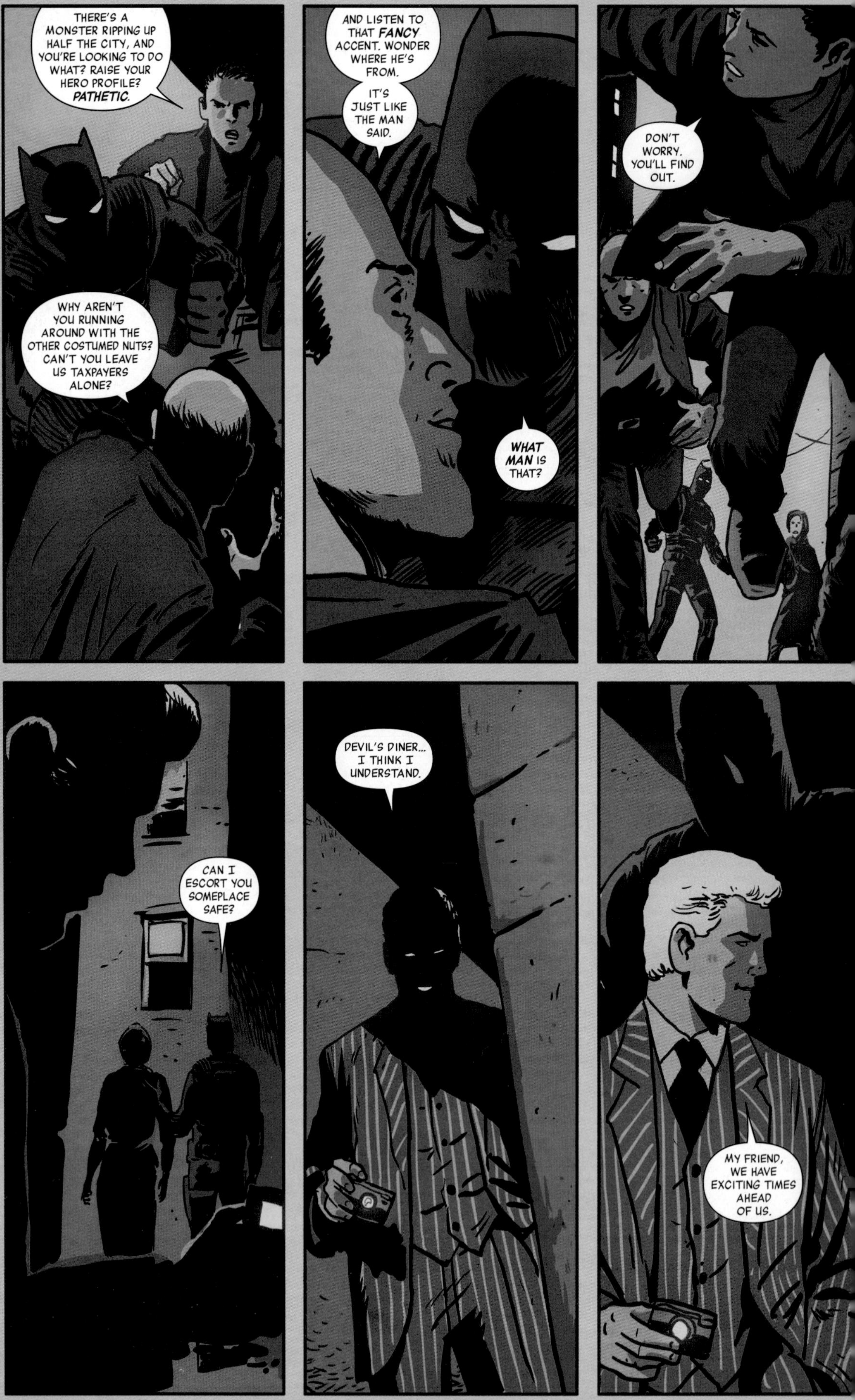
THERE'S A MONSTER RIPPING UP HALF THE CITY, AND YOU'RE LOOKING TO DO WHAT? RAISE YOUR HERO PROFILE? PATHETIC.
WHY AREN'T YOU RUNNING AROUND WITH THE OTHER COSTUMED NUTS? CAN'T YOU LEAVE US TAXPAYERS ALONE?
AND LISTEN TO THAT FANCY ACCENT. WONDER WHERE HE'S FROM.
IT'S JUST LIKE THE MAN SAID.
WHAT MAN IS THAT?
DON'T WORRY. YOU'LL FIND OUT.
CAN I ESCORT YOU SOMEPLACE SAFE?
DEVIL'S DINER... I THINK I UNDERSTAND.
MY FRIEND, WE HAVE EXCITING TIMES AHEAD OF US.

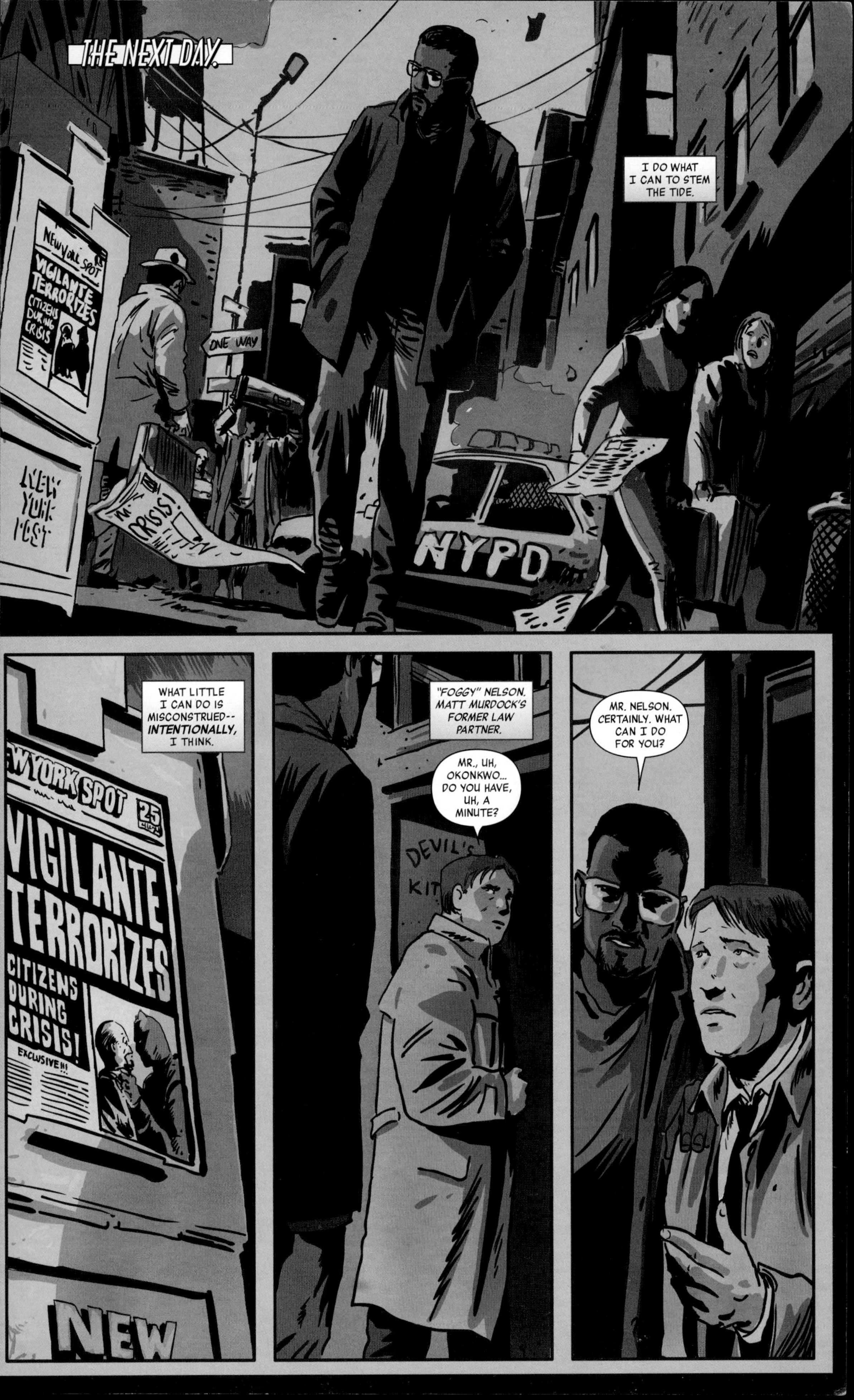

THE NEXT DAY.
NEW YORK SPOT
VIGILANTE TERRORIZES CITIZENS DURING CRISIS
ONE WAY
CRISIS!
NYPD
I DO WHAT I CAN TO STEM THE TIDE.
WHAT LITTLE I CAN DO IS MISCONSTRUED-- INTENTIONALLY, I THINK.
NEW YORK SPOT
25
VIGILANTE TERRORIZES CITIZENS DURING CRISIS!
EXCLUSIVE!!!
NEW
"FOGGY" NELSON. MATT MURDOCK'S FORMER LAW PARTNER.
MR., UH, OKONKWO... DO YOU HAVE, UH, A MINUTE?
DEVIL'S KIT
MR. NELSON. CERTAINLY. WHAT CAN I DO FOR YOU?

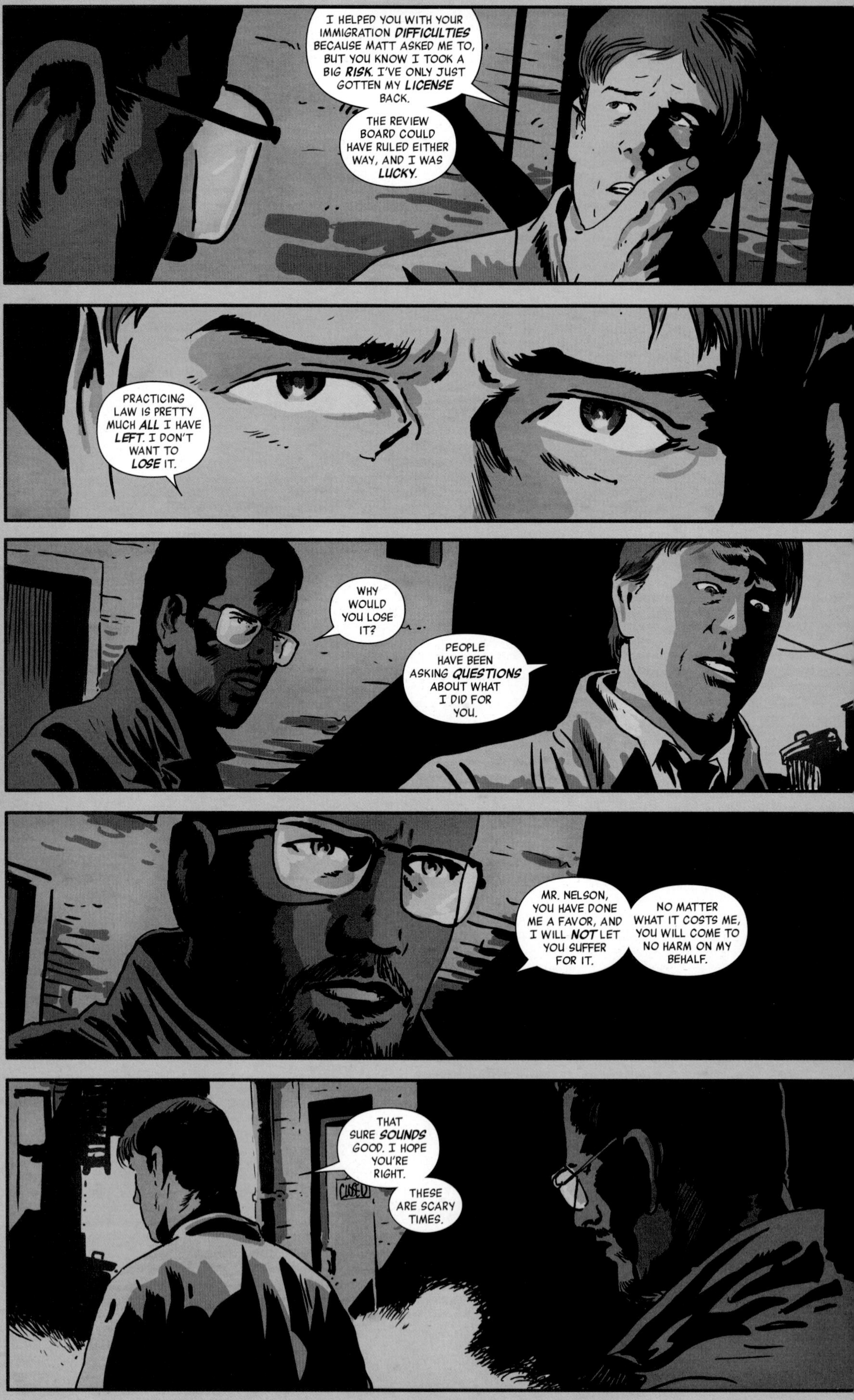
I HELPED YOU WITH YOUR IMMIGRATION DIFFICULTIES BECAUSE MATT ASKED ME TO, BUT YOU KNOW I TOOK A BIG RISK. I'VE ONLY JUST GOTTEN MY LICENSE BACK.
THE REVIEW BOARD COULD HAVE RULED EITHER WAY, AND I WAS LUCKY.
PRACTICING LAW IS PRETTY MUCH ALL I HAVE LEFT. I DON'T WANT TO LOSE IT.
WHY WOULD YOU LOSE IT?
PEOPLE HAVE BEEN ASKING QUESTIONS ABOUT WHAT I DID FOR YOU.
MR. NELSON, YOU HAVE DONE ME A FAVOR, AND I WILL NOT LET YOU SUFFER FOR IT.
NO MATTER WHAT IT COSTS ME, YOU WILL COME TO NO HARM ON MY BEHALF.
THAT SURE SOUNDS GOOD. I HOPE YOU'RE RIGHT.
CLOSED
THESE ARE SCARY TIMES.

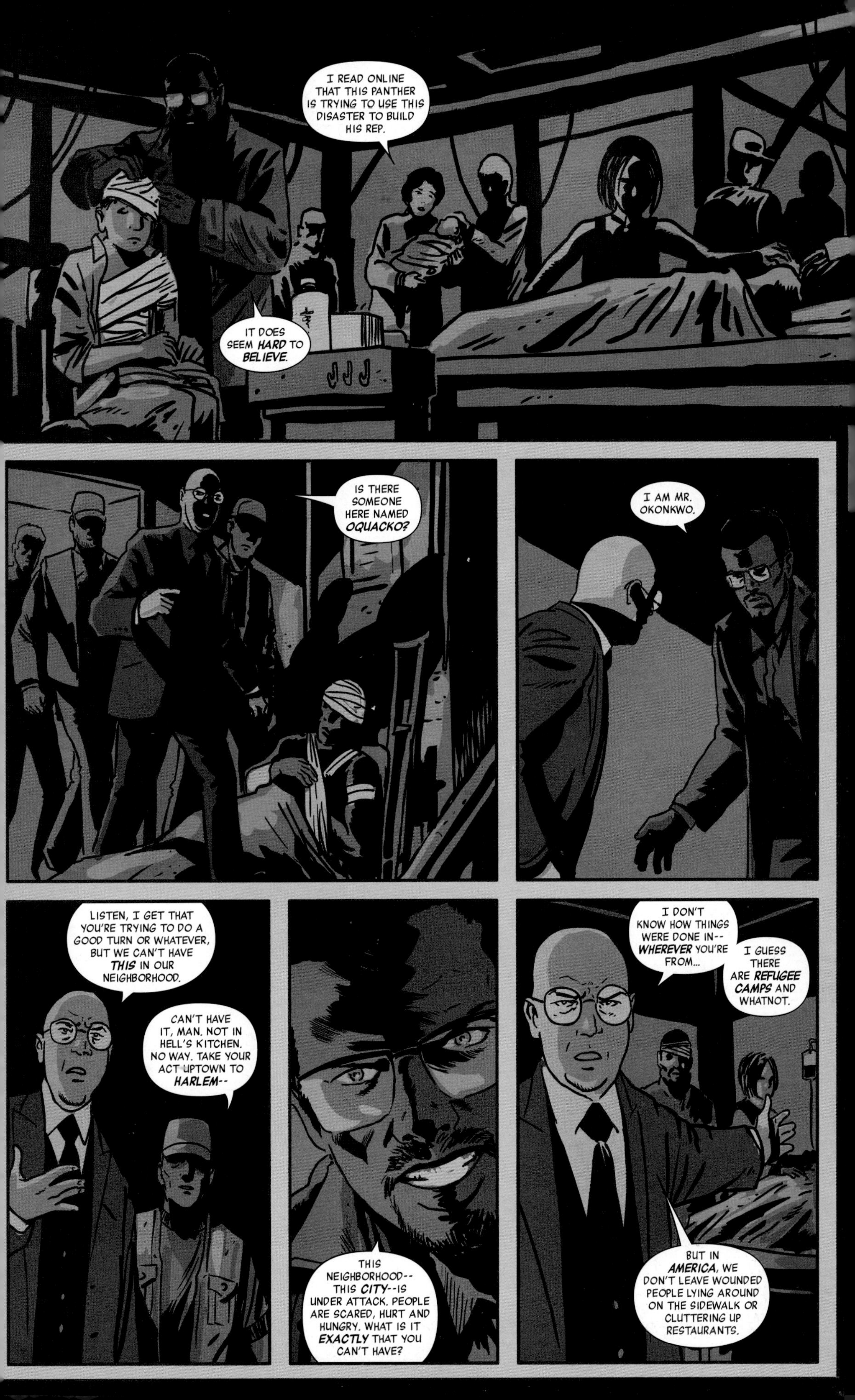
I READ ONLINE THAT THIS PANTHER IS TRYING TO USE THIS DISASTER TO BUILD HIS REP.
IT DOES SEEM HARD TO BELIEVE.
IS THERE SOMEONE HERE NAMED OQUACKO?
I AM MR. OKONKWO.
LISTEN, I GET THAT YOU'RE TRYING TO DO A GOOD TURN OR WHATEVER, BUT WE CAN'T HAVE THIS IN OUR NEIGHBORHOOD.
CAN'T HAVE IT, MAN. NOT IN HELL'S KITCHEN. NO WAY. TAKE YOUR ACT UPTOWN TO HARLEM--
THIS NEIGHBORHOOD-- THIS CITY--IS UNDER ATTACK. PEOPLE ARE SCARED, HURT AND HUNGRY. WHAT IS IT EXACTLY THAT YOU CAN'T HAVE?
I DON'T KNOW HOW THINGS WERE DONE IN-- WHEREVER YOU'RE FROM...
I GUESS THERE ARE REFUGEE CAMPS AND WHATNOT.
BUT IN AMERICA, WE DON'T LEAVE WOUNDED PEOPLE LYING AROUND ON THE SIDEWALK OR CLUTTERING UP RESTAURANTS.

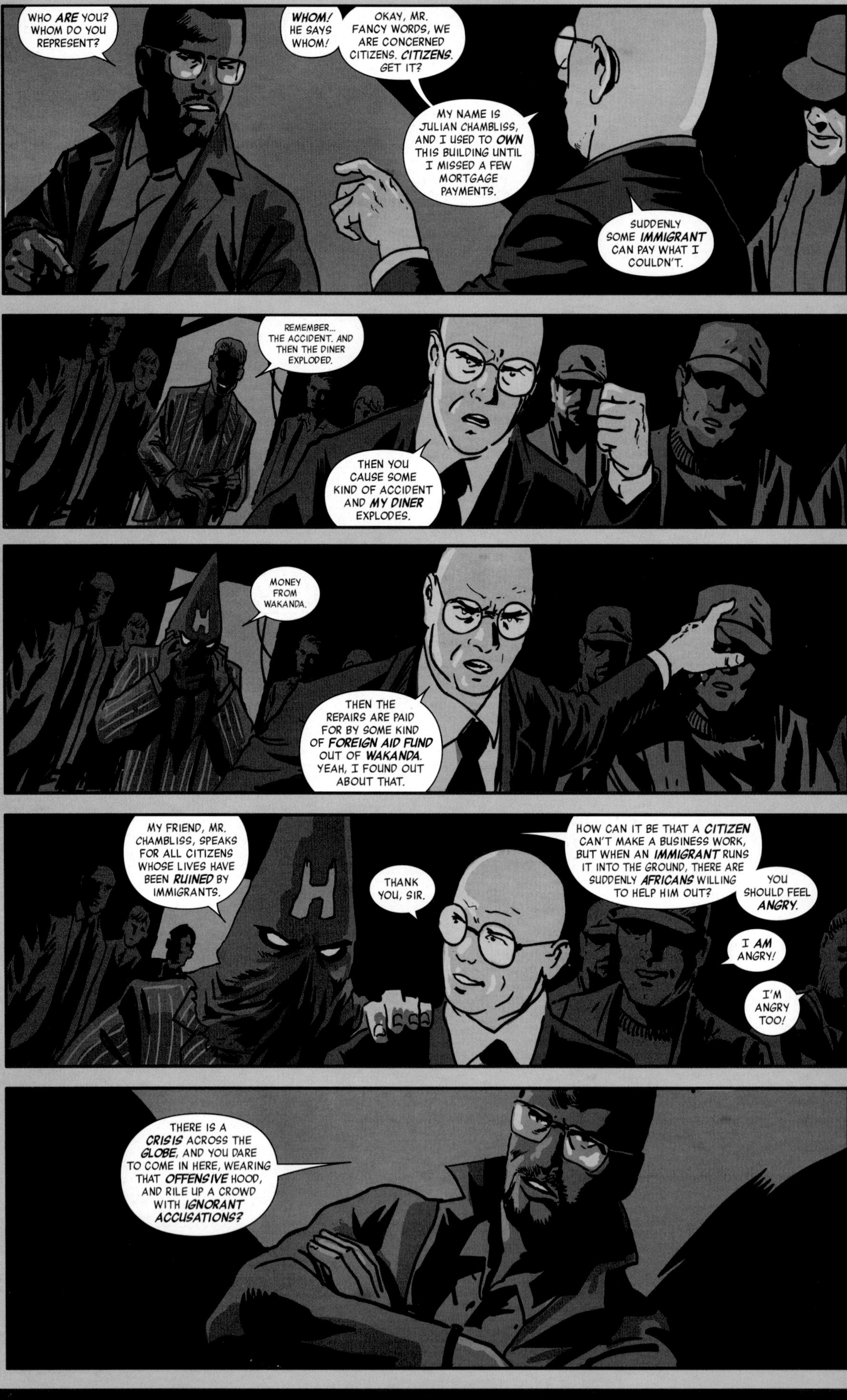
WHO ARE YOU? WHOM DO YOU REPRESENT?
WHOM! HE SAYS WHOM!
OKAY, MR. FANCY WORDS, WE ARE CONCERNED CITIZENS. CITIZENS. GET IT?
MY NAME IS JULIAN CHAMBLISS, AND I USED TO OWN THIS BUILDING UNTIL I MISSED A FEW MORTGAGE PAYMENTS.
SUDDENLY SOME IMMIGRANT CAN PAY WHAT I COULDN'T.
REMEMBER... THE ACCIDENT. AND THEN THE DINER EXPLODED.
THEN YOU CAUSE SOME KIND OF ACCIDENT AND MY DINER EXPLODES.
MONEY FROM WAKANDA.
THEN THE REPAIRS ARE PAID FOR BY SOME KIND OF FOREIGN AID FUND OUT OF WAKANDA. YEAH, I FOUND OUT ABOUT THAT.
MY FRIEND, MR. CHAMBLISS, SPEAKS FOR ALL CITIZENS WHOSE LIVES HAVE BEEN RUINED BY IMMIGRANTS.
THANK YOU, SIR.
HOW CAN IT BE THAT A CITIZEN CAN'T MAKE A BUSINESS WORK, BUT WHEN AN IMMIGRANT RUNS IT INTO THE GROUND, THERE ARE SUDDENLY AFRICANS WILLING TO HELP HIM OUT?
YOU SHOULD FEEL ANGRY.
I AM ANGRY!
I'M ANGRY TOO!
THERE IS A CRISIS ACROSS THE GLOBE, AND YOU DARE TO COME IN HERE, WEARING THAT OFFENSIVE HOOD, AND RILE UP A CROWD WITH IGNORANT ACCUSATIONS?

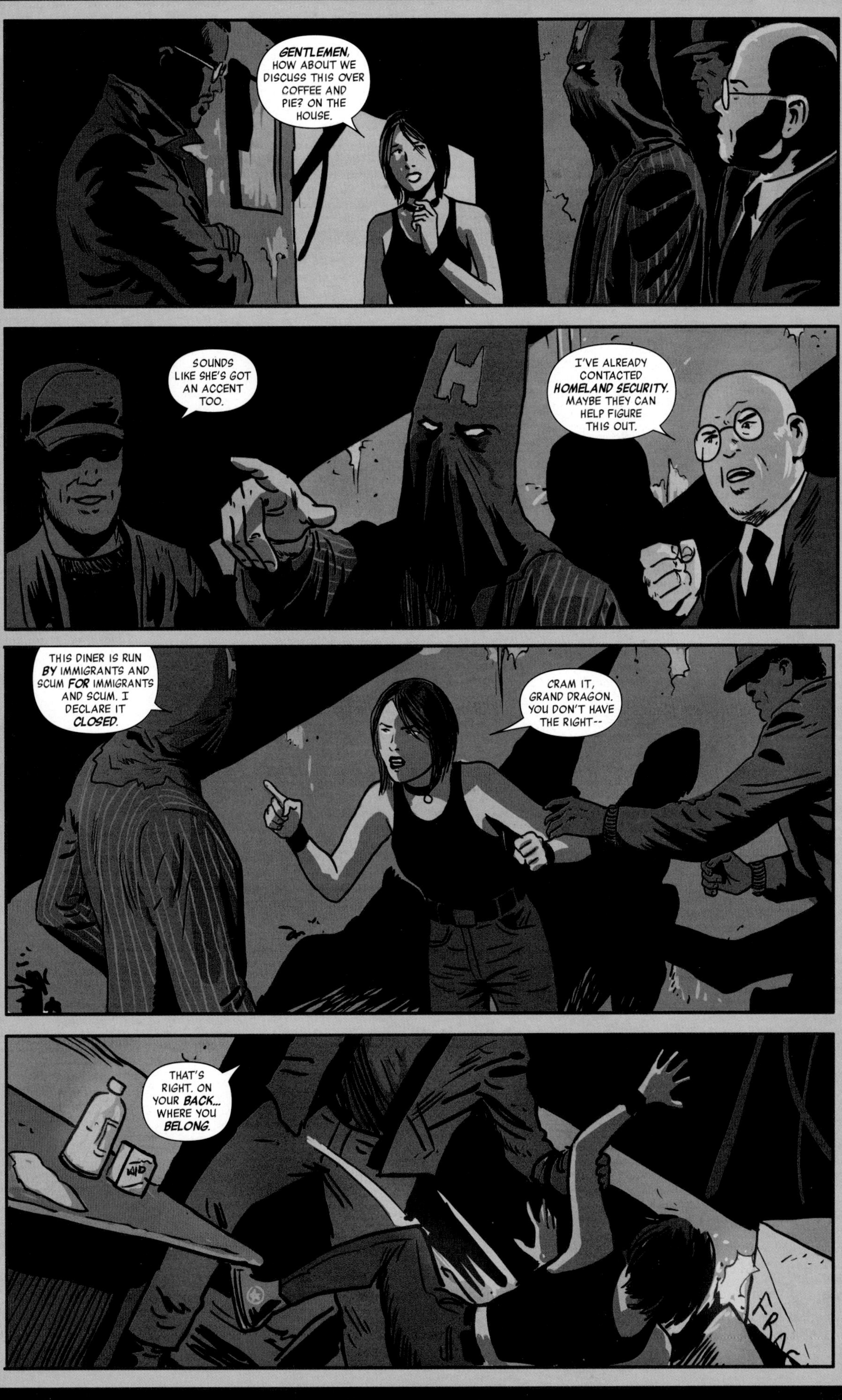
GENTLEMEN, HOW ABOUT WE DISCUSS THIS OVER COFFEE AND PIE? ON THE HOUSE.
SOUNDS LIKE SHE'S GOT AN ACCENT TOO.
I'VE ALREADY CONTACTED HOMELAND SECURITY. MAYBE THEY CAN HELP FIGURE THIS OUT.
THIS DINER IS RUN BY IMMIGRANTS AND SCUM FOR IMMIGRANTS AND SCUM. I DECLARE IT CLOSED.
CRAM IT, GRAND DRAGON. YOU DON'T HAVE THE RIGHT--
THAT'S RIGHT. ON YOUR BACK... WHERE YOU BELONG.

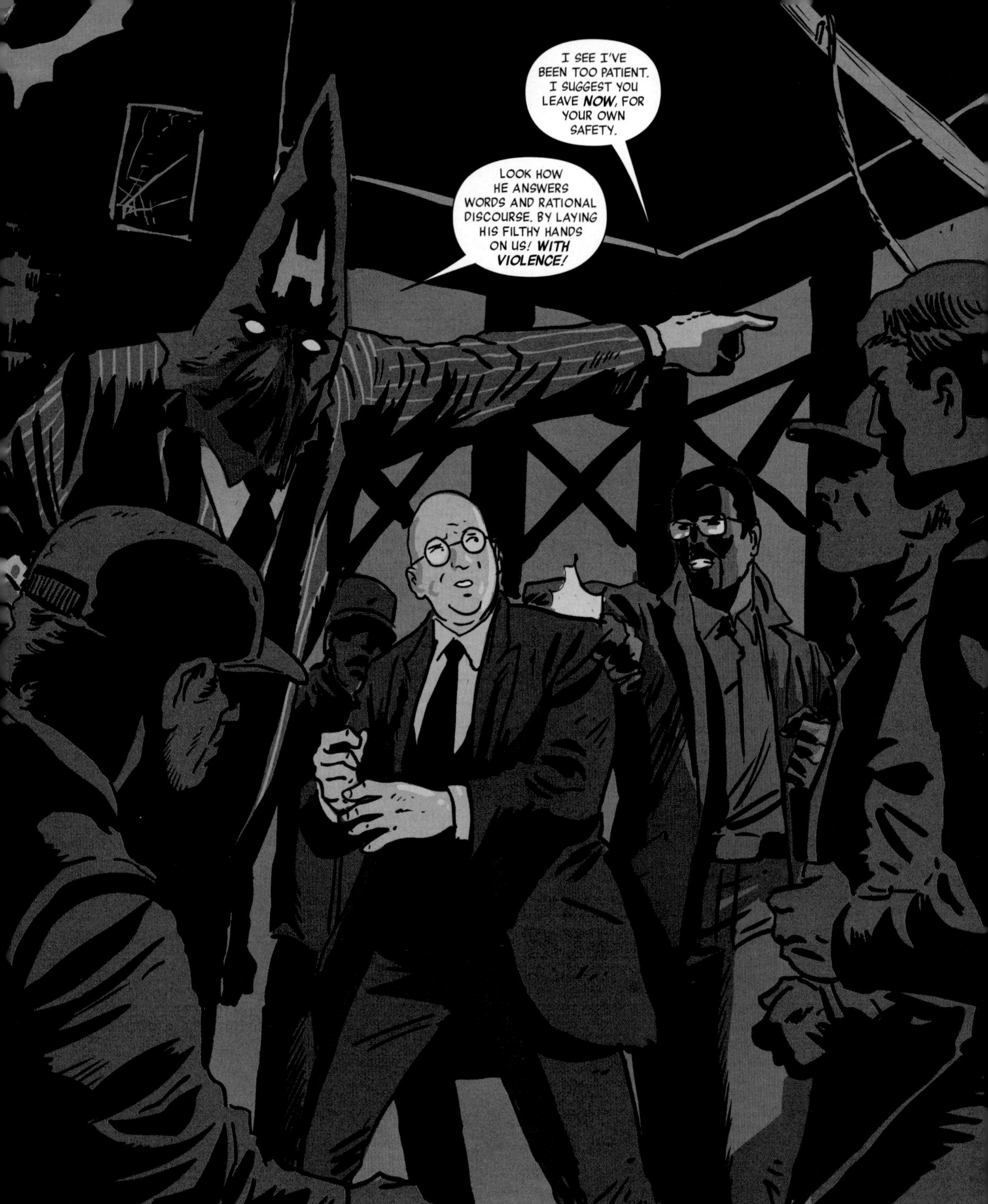
I SEE I'VE BEEN TOO PATIENT. I SUGGEST YOU LEAVE NOW, FOR YOUR OWN SAFETY.
LOOK HOW HE ANSWERS WORDS AND RATIONAL DISCOURSE. BY LAYING HIS FILTHY HANDS ON US! WITH VIOLENCE!

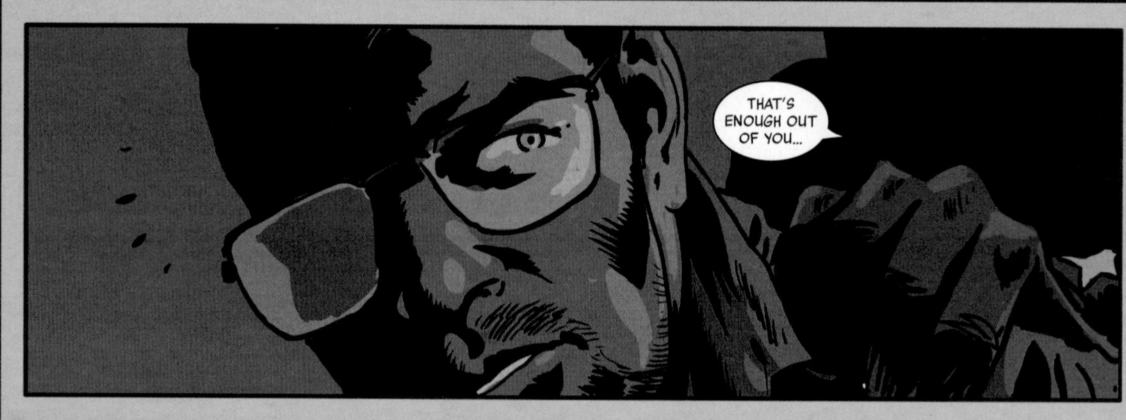
THAT'S ENOUGH OUT OF YOU...

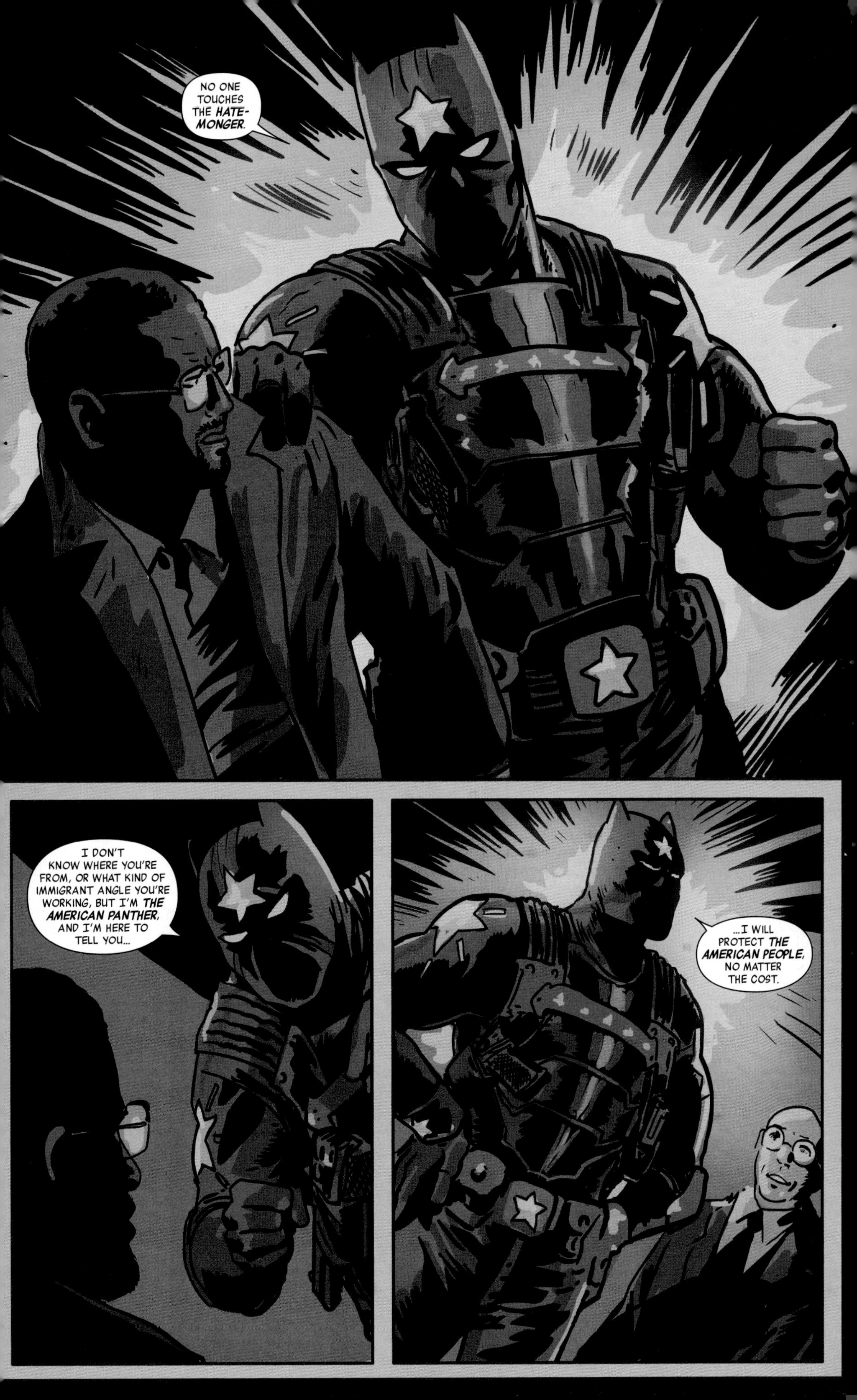

NO ONE TOUCHES THE **HATE-MONGER**.
I DON'T KNOW WHERE YOU'RE FROM, OR WHAT KIND OF IMMIGRANT ANGLE YOU'RE WORKING, BUT I'M **THE AMERICAN PANTHER**, AND I'M HERE TO TELL YOU...
...I WILL PROTECT **THE AMERICAN PEOPLE**, NO MATTER THE COST.

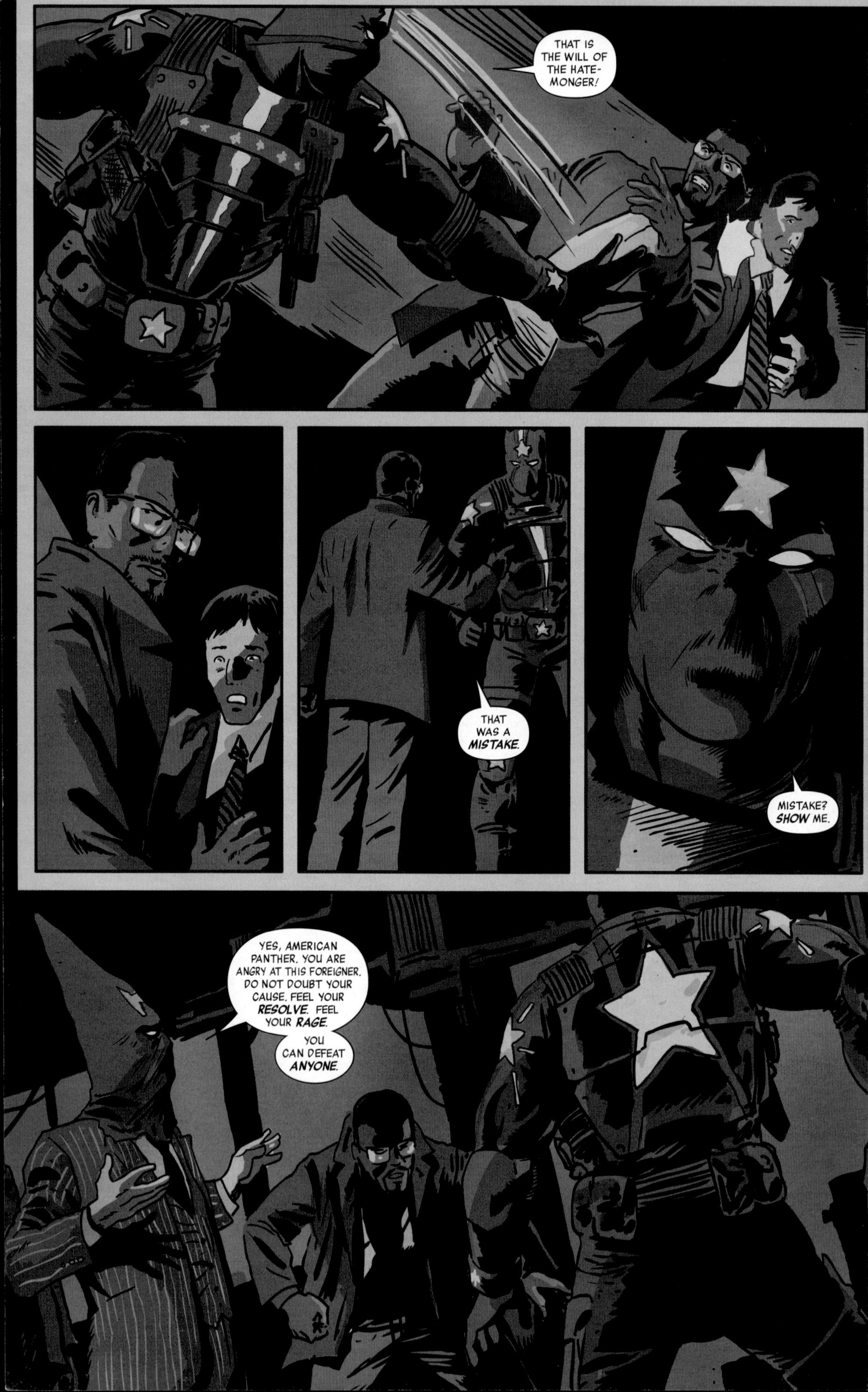
THAT IS THE WILL OF THE HATE-MONGER!
THAT WAS A MISTAKE.
MISTAKE? SHOW ME.
YES, AMERICAN PANTHER. YOU ARE ANGRY AT THIS FOREIGNER. DO NOT DOUBT YOUR CAUSE. FEEL YOUR RESOLVE. FEEL YOUR RAGE.
YOU CAN DEFEAT ANYONE.

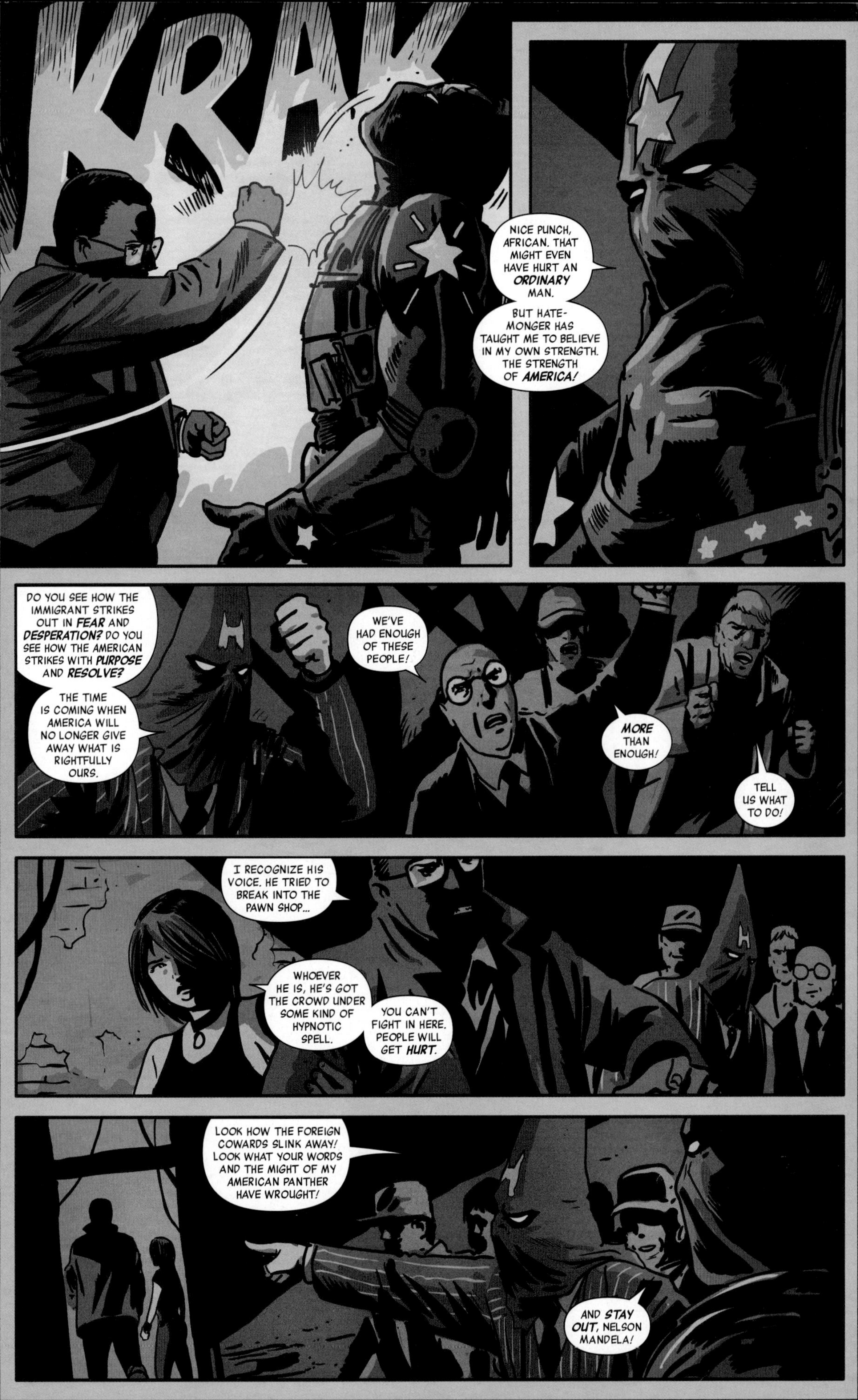
KRAK
NICE PUNCH, AFRICAN. THAT MIGHT EVEN HAVE HURT AN ORDINARY MAN.
BUT HATE-MONGER HAS TAUGHT ME TO BELIEVE IN MY OWN STRENGTH. THE STRENGTH OF AMERICA!
DO YOU SEE HOW THE IMMIGRANT STRIKES OUT IN FEAR AND DESPERATION? DO YOU SEE HOW THE AMERICAN STRIKES WITH PURPOSE AND RESOLVE?
THE TIME IS COMING WHEN AMERICA WILL NO LONGER GIVE AWAY WHAT IS RIGHTFULLY OURS.
WE'VE HAD ENOUGH OF THESE PEOPLE!
MORE THAN ENOUGH!
TELL US WHAT TO DO!
I RECOGNIZE HIS VOICE. HE TRIED TO BREAK INTO THE PAWN SHOP...
WHOEVER HE IS, HE'S GOT THE CROWD UNDER SOME KIND OF HYPNOTIC SPELL.
YOU CAN'T FIGHT IN HERE. PEOPLE WILL GET HURT.
LOOK HOW THE FOREIGN COWARDS SLINK AWAY! LOOK WHAT YOUR WORDS AND THE MIGHT OF MY AMERICAN PANTHER HAVE WROUGHT!
AND STAY OUT, NELSON MANDELA!

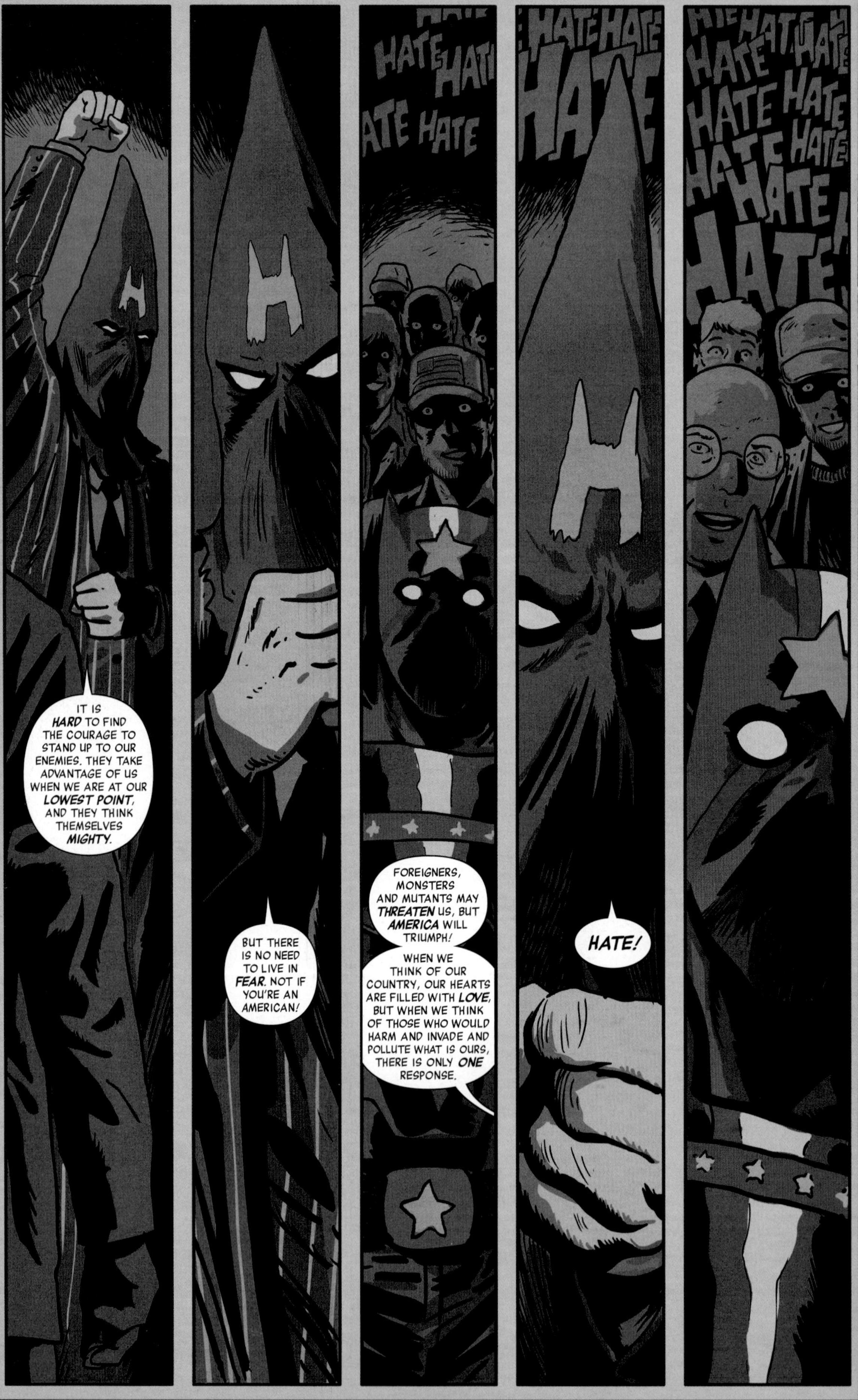
IT IS HARD TO FIND THE COURAGE TO STAND UP TO OUR ENEMIES. THEY TAKE ADVANTAGE OF US WHEN WE ARE AT OUR LOWEST POINT, AND THEY THINK THEMSELVES MIGHTY.
BUT THERE IS NO NEED TO LIVE IN FEAR. NOT IF YOU'RE AN AMERICAN!
HATE HATE HATE HATE
FOREIGNERS, MONSTERS AND MUTANTS MAY THREATEN US, BUT AMERICA WILL TRIUMPH!
WHEN WE THINK OF OUR COUNTRY, OUR HEARTS ARE FILLED WITH LOVE, BUT WHEN WE THINK OF THOSE WHO WOULD HARM AND INVADE AND POLLUTE WHAT IS OURS, THERE IS ONLY ONE RESPONSE.
HATE!

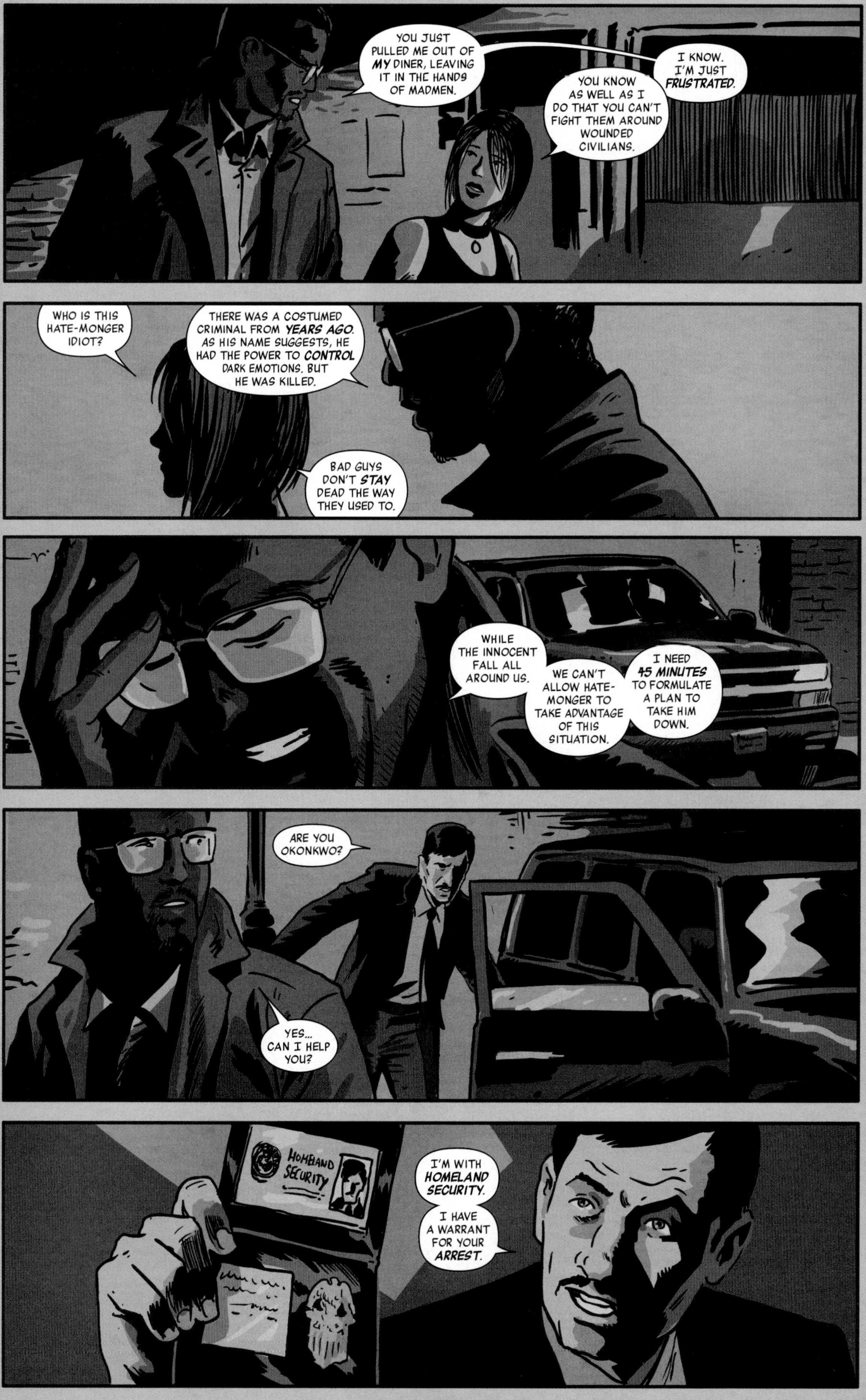
YOU JUST PULLED ME OUT OF MY DINER, LEAVING IT IN THE HANDS OF MADMEN.
YOU KNOW AS WELL AS I DO THAT YOU CAN'T FIGHT THEM AROUND WOUNDED CIVILIANS.
I KNOW. I'M JUST FRUSTRATED.
WHO IS THIS HATE-MONGER IDIOT?
THERE WAS A COSTUMED CRIMINAL FROM YEARS AGO. AS HIS NAME SUGGESTS, HE HAD THE POWER TO CONTROL DARK EMOTIONS. BUT HE WAS KILLED.
BAD GUYS DON'T STAY DEAD THE WAY THEY USED TO.
WHILE THE INNOCENT FALL ALL AROUND US.
WE CAN'T ALLOW HATE-MONGER TO TAKE ADVANTAGE OF THIS SITUATION.
I NEED 45 MINUTES TO FORMULATE A PLAN TO TAKE HIM DOWN.
ARE YOU OKONKWO?
YES... CAN I HELP YOU?
HOMELAND SECURITY
I'M WITH HOMELAND SECURITY.
I HAVE A WARRANT FOR YOUR ARREST.

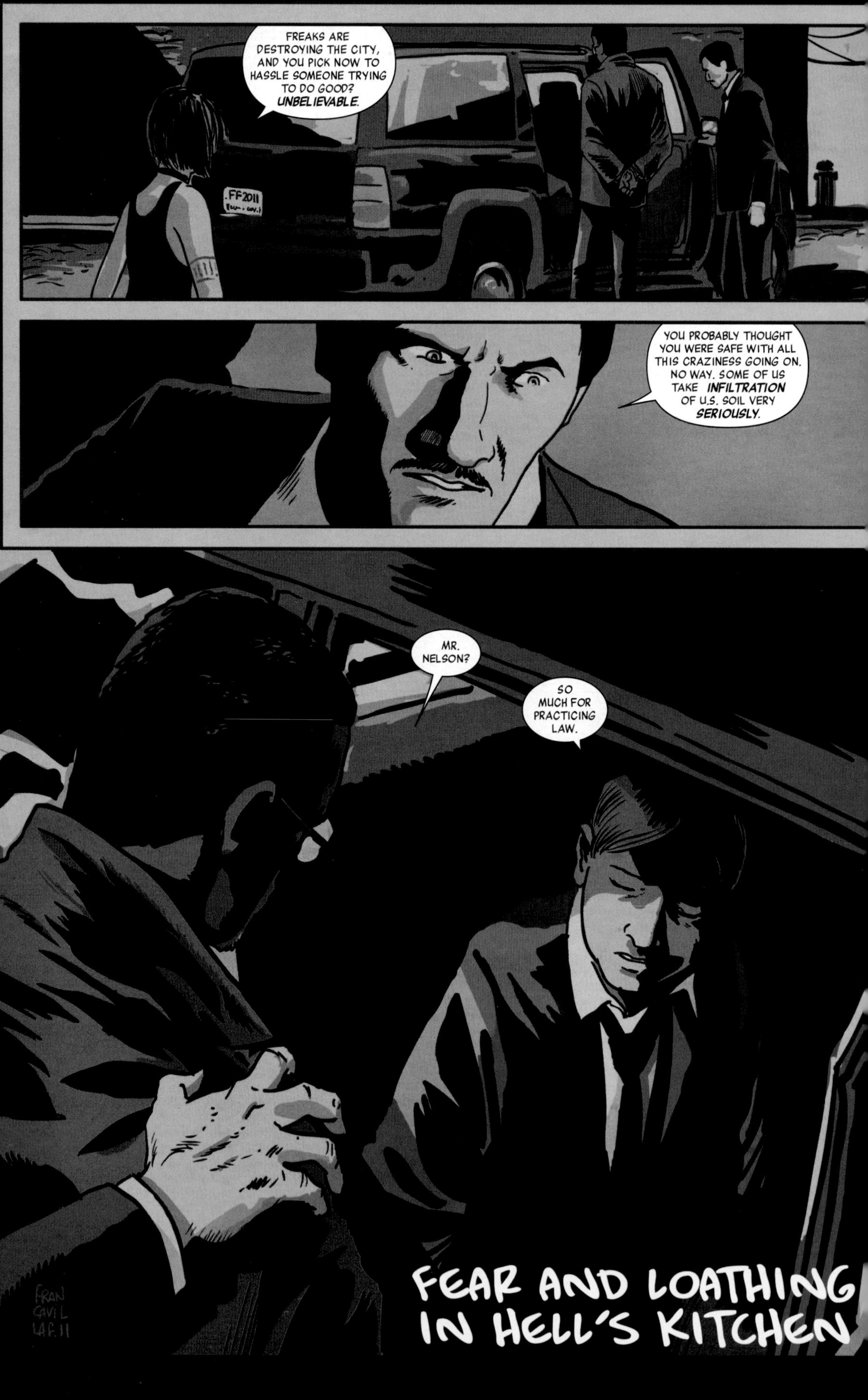
FREAKS ARE DESTROYING THE CITY, AND YOU PICK NOW TO HASSLE SOMEONE TRYING TO DO GOOD? UNBELIEVABLE.
FF2011
YOU PROBABLY THOUGHT YOU WERE SAFE WITH ALL THIS CRAZINESS GOING ON. NO WAY. SOME OF US TAKE INFILTRATION OF U.S. SOIL VERY SERIOUSLY.
MR. NELSON?
SO MUCH FOR PRACTICING LAW.
FEAR AND LOATHING IN HELL'S KITCHEN

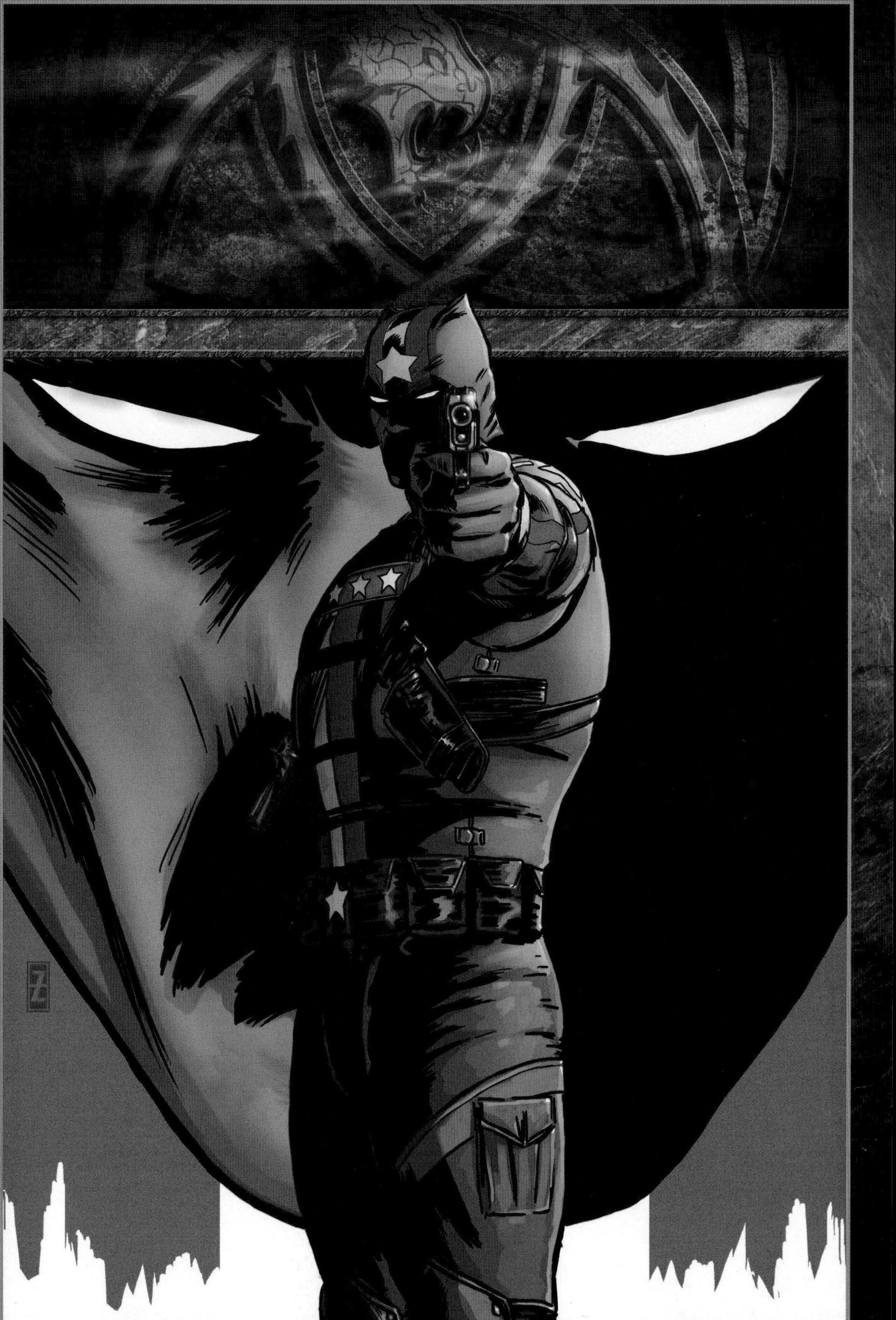

BLACK PANTHER:
THE MAN WITHOUT FEAR #522

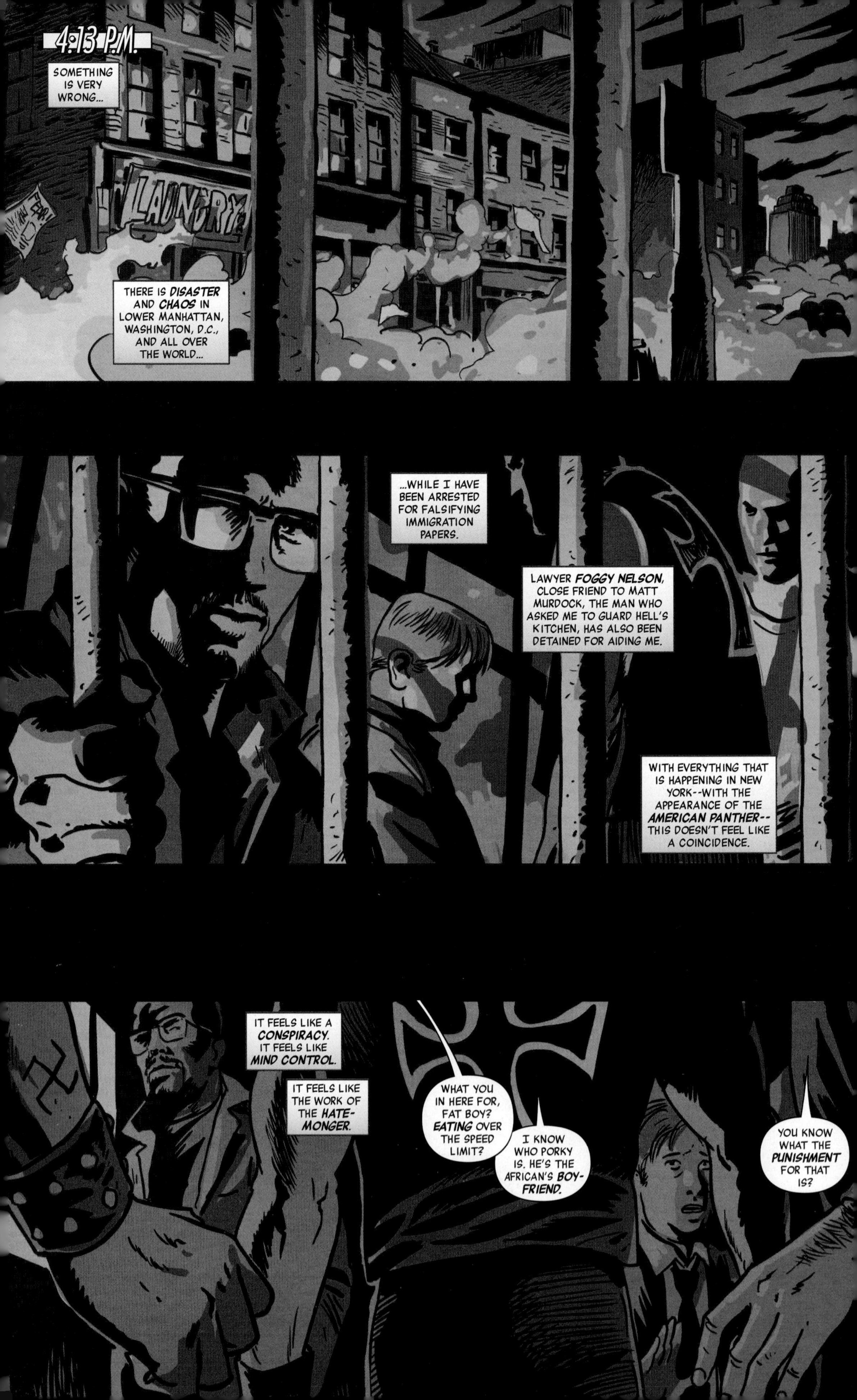
4:13 P.M.
SOMETHING IS VERY WRONG...
LAUNDRY
THERE IS DISASTER AND CHAOS IN LOWER MANHATTAN, WASHINGTON, D.C., AND ALL OVER THE WORLD...
...WHILE I HAVE BEEN ARRESTED FOR FALSIFYING IMMIGRATION PAPERS.
LAWYER FOGGY NELSON, CLOSE FRIEND TO MATT MURDOCK, THE MAN WHO ASKED ME TO GUARD HELL'S KITCHEN, HAS ALSO BEEN DETAINED FOR AIDING ME.
WITH EVERYTHING THAT IS HAPPENING IN NEW YORK--WITH THE APPEARANCE OF THE AMERICAN PANTHER--THIS DOESN'T FEEL LIKE A COINCIDENCE.
IT FEELS LIKE A CONSPIRACY. IT FEELS LIKE MIND CONTROL.
IT FEELS LIKE THE WORK OF THE HATE-MONGER.
WHAT YOU IN HERE FOR, FAT BOY? EATING OVER THE SPEED LIMIT?
I KNOW WHO PORKY IS. HE'S THE AFRICAN'S BOY-FRIEND.
YOU KNOW WHAT THE PUNISHMENT FOR THAT IS?

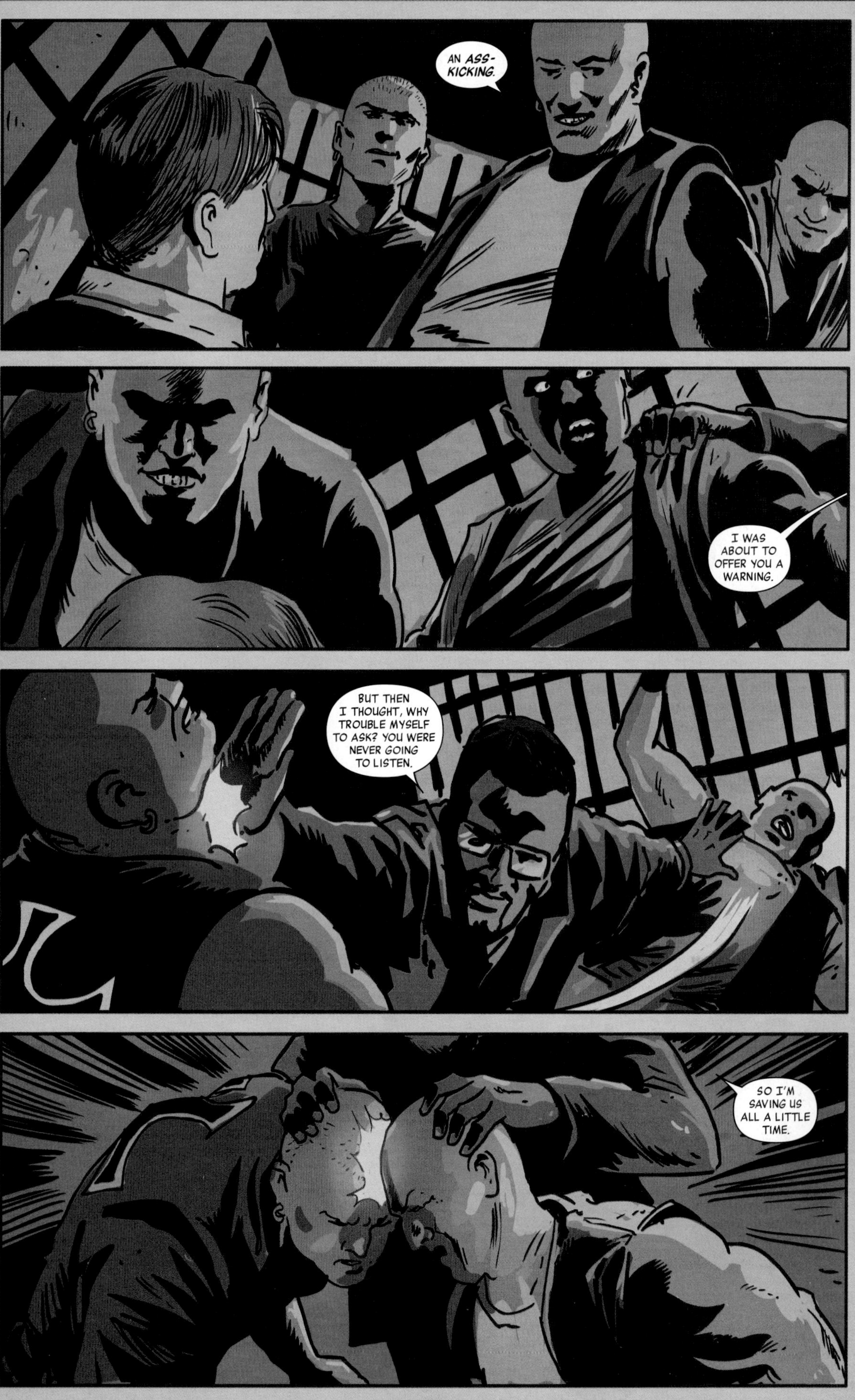
AN ASS-KICKING.
I WAS ABOUT TO OFFER YOU A WARNING.
BUT THEN I THOUGHT, WHY TROUBLE MYSELF TO ASK? YOU WERE NEVER GOING TO LISTEN.
SO I'M SAVING US ALL A LITTLE TIME.

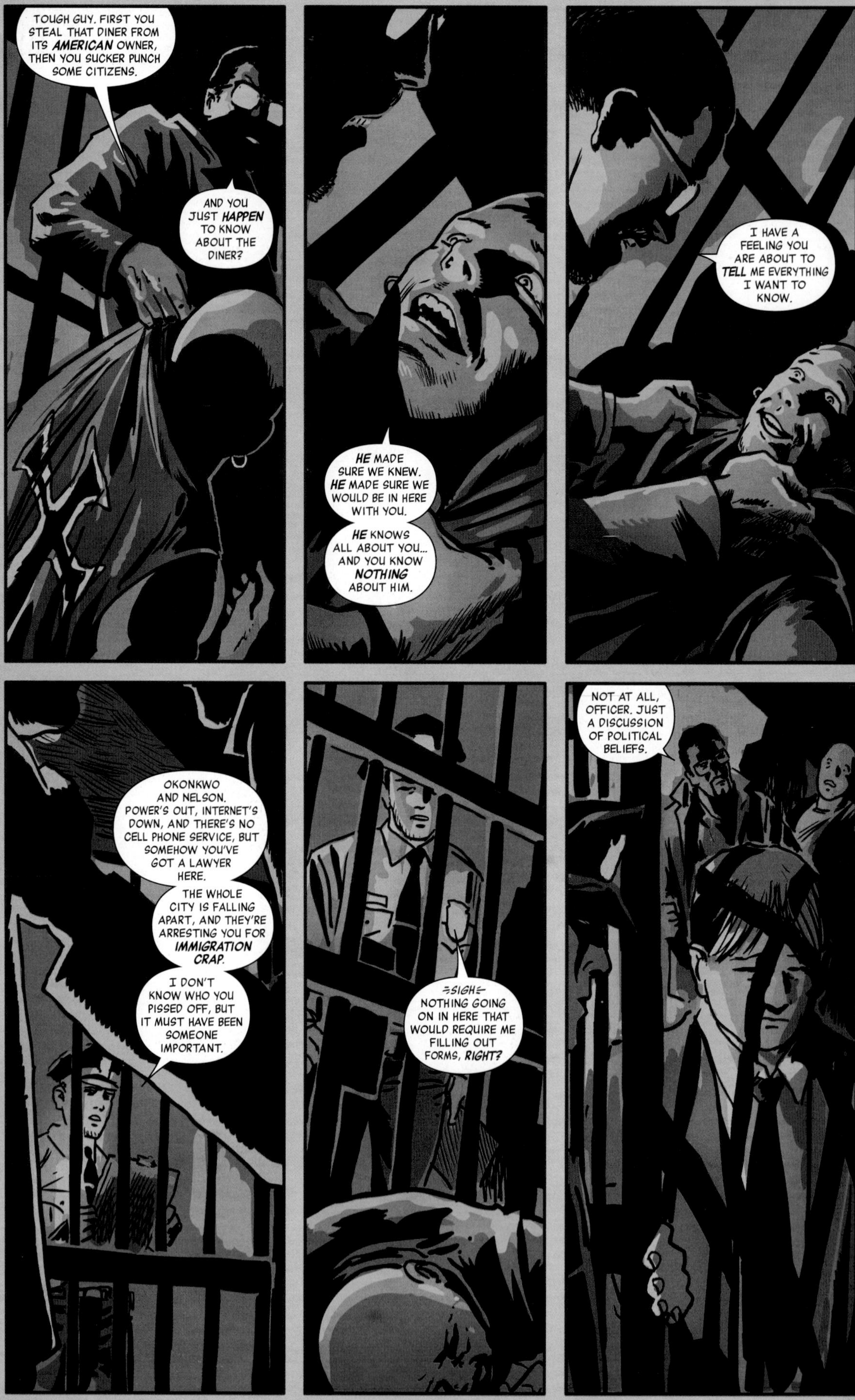
TOUGH GUY. FIRST YOU STEAL THAT DINER FROM ITS AMERICAN OWNER, THEN YOU SUCKER PUNCH SOME CITIZENS.
AND YOU JUST HAPPEN TO KNOW ABOUT THE DINER?
HE MADE SURE WE KNEW. HE MADE SURE WE WOULD BE IN HERE WITH YOU.
HE KNOWS ALL ABOUT YOU... AND YOU KNOW NOTHING ABOUT HIM.
I HAVE A FEELING YOU ARE ABOUT TO TELL ME EVERYTHING I WANT TO KNOW.
OKONKWO AND NELSON. POWER'S OUT, INTERNET'S DOWN, AND THERE'S NO CELL PHONE SERVICE, BUT SOMEHOW YOU'VE GOT A LAWYER HERE.
THE WHOLE CITY IS FALLING APART, AND THEY'RE ARRESTING YOU FOR IMMIGRATION CRAP.
I DON'T KNOW WHO YOU PISSED OFF, BUT IT MUST HAVE BEEN SOMEONE IMPORTANT.
=SIGH= NOTHING GOING ON IN HERE THAT WOULD REQUIRE ME FILLING OUT FORMS, RIGHT?
NOT AT ALL, OFFICER. JUST A DISCUSSION OF POLITICAL BELIEFS.

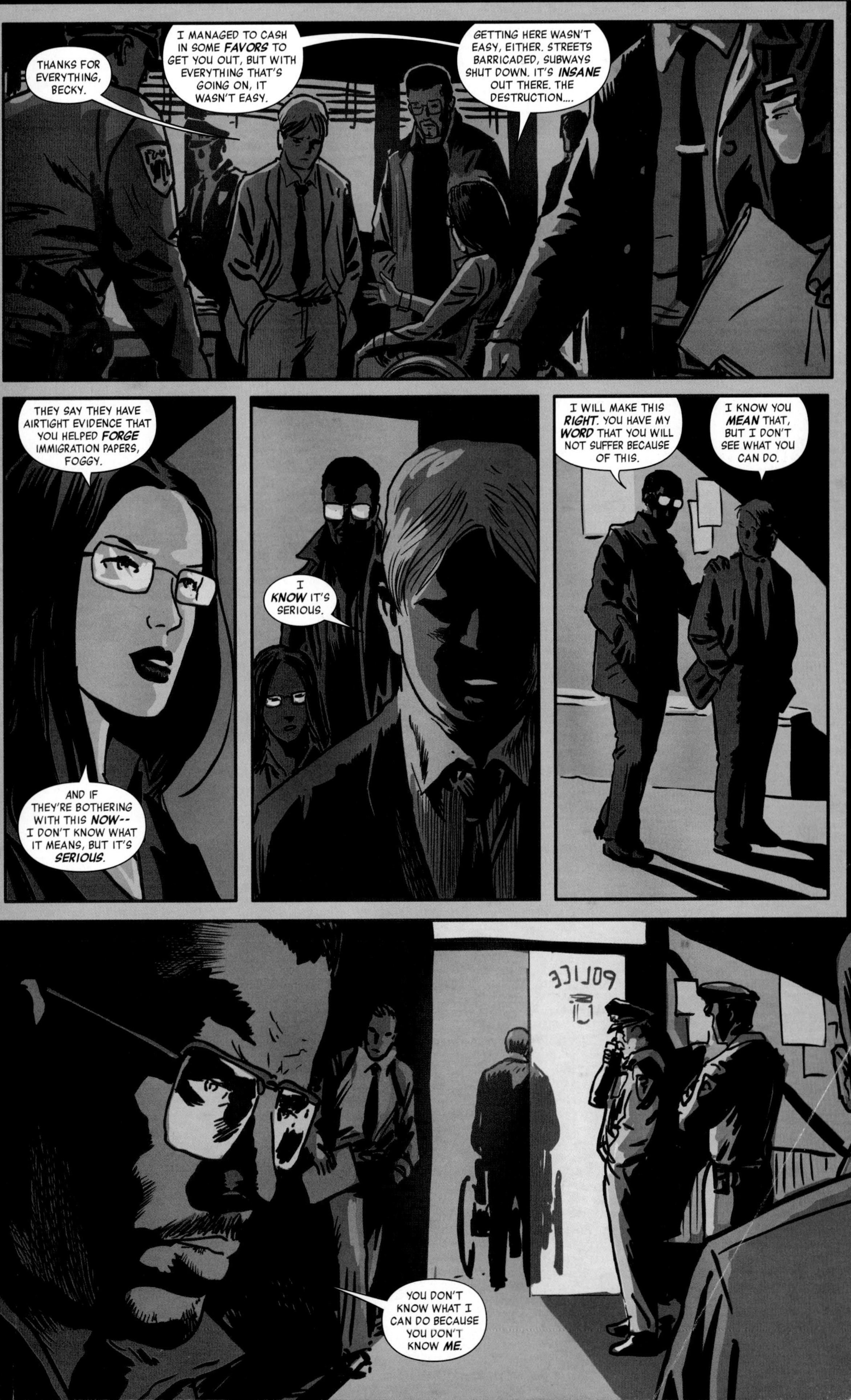
THANKS FOR EVERYTHING, BECKY.
I MANAGED TO CASH IN SOME FAVORS TO GET YOU OUT, BUT WITH EVERYTHING THAT'S GOING ON, IT WASN'T EASY.
GETTING HERE WASN'T EASY, EITHER. STREETS BARRICADED, SUBWAYS SHUT DOWN. IT'S INSANE OUT THERE. THE DESTRUCTION....
THEY SAY THEY HAVE AIRTIGHT EVIDENCE THAT YOU HELPED FORGE IMMIGRATION PAPERS, FOGGY.
AND IF THEY'RE BOTHERING WITH THIS NOW-- I DON'T KNOW WHAT IT MEANS, BUT IT'S SERIOUS.
I KNOW IT'S SERIOUS.
I WILL MAKE THIS RIGHT. YOU HAVE MY WORD THAT YOU WILL NOT SUFFER BECAUSE OF THIS.
I KNOW YOU MEAN THAT, BUT I DON'T SEE WHAT YOU CAN DO.
YOU DON'T KNOW WHAT I CAN DO BECAUSE YOU DON'T KNOW ME.

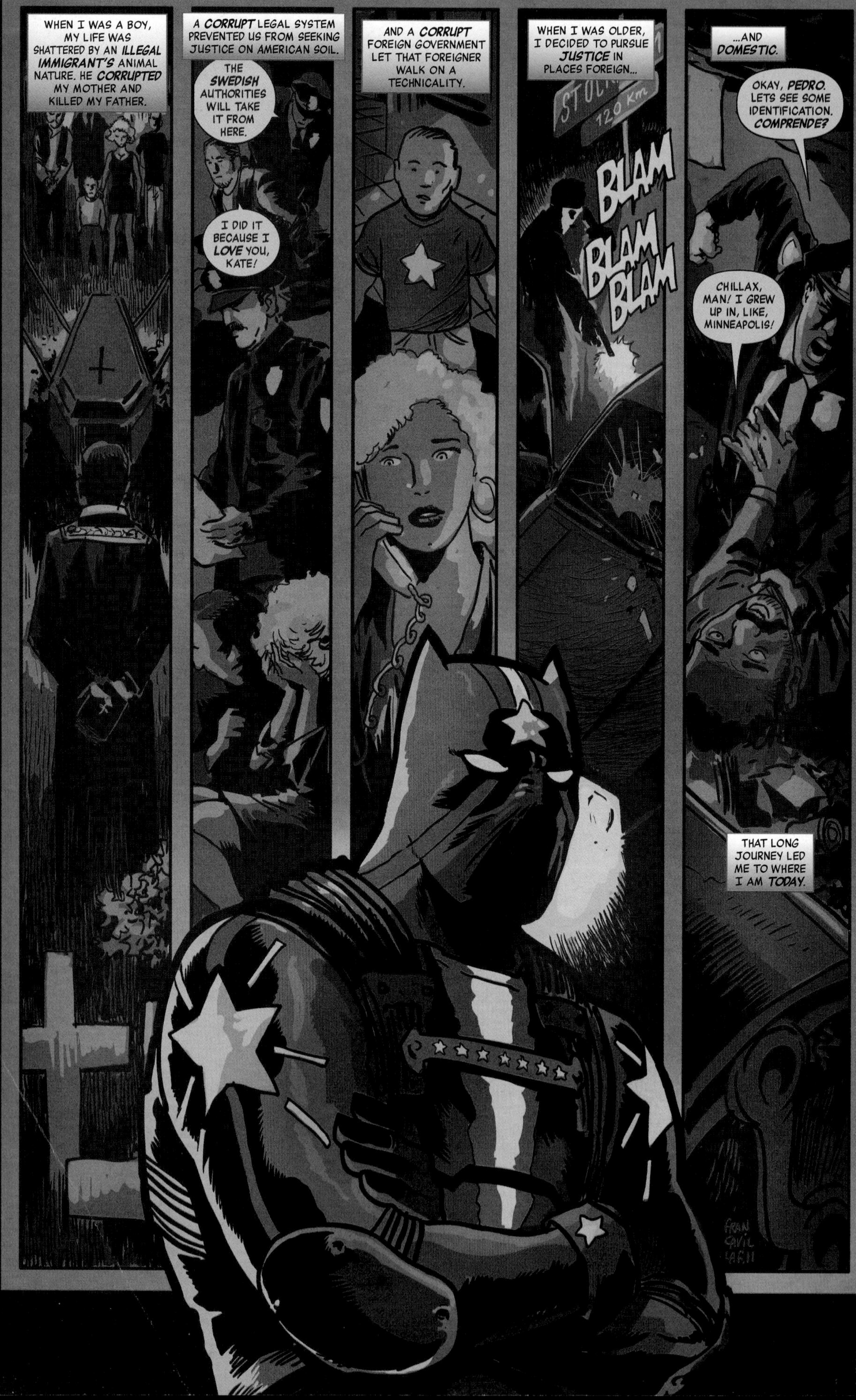
WHEN I WAS A BOY, MY LIFE WAS SHATTERED BY AN ILLEGAL IMMIGRANT'S ANIMAL NATURE. HE CORRUPTED MY MOTHER AND KILLED MY FATHER.
A CORRUPT LEGAL SYSTEM PREVENTED US FROM SEEKING JUSTICE ON AMERICAN SOIL.
THE SWEDISH AUTHORITIES WILL TAKE IT FROM HERE.
I DID IT BECAUSE I LOVE YOU, KATE!
AND A CORRUPT FOREIGN GOVERNMENT LET THAT FOREIGNER WALK ON A TECHNICALITY.
WHEN I WAS OLDER, I DECIDED TO PURSUE JUSTICE IN PLACES FOREIGN...
120 Km
BLAM
BLAM BLAM
...AND DOMESTIC.
OKAY, PEDRO. LETS SEE SOME IDENTIFICATION. COMPRENDE?
CHILLAX, MAN! I GREW UP IN, LIKE, MINNEAPOLIS!
THAT LONG JOURNEY LED ME TO WHERE I AM TODAY.

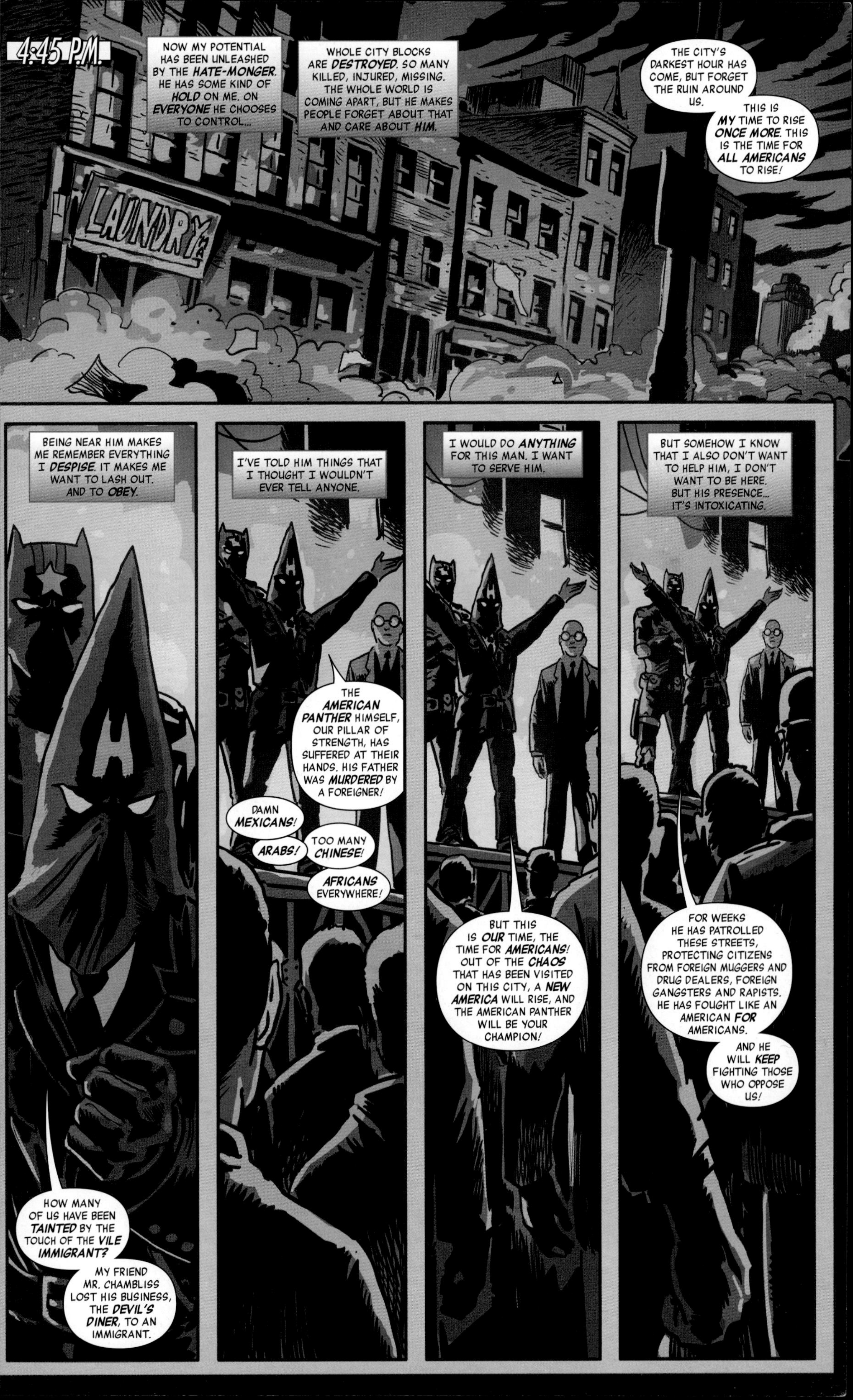
4:45 P.M.
NOW MY POTENTIAL HAS BEEN UNLEASHED BY THE HATE-MONGER. HE HAS SOME KIND OF HOLD ON ME. ON EVERYONE HE CHOOSES TO CONTROL...
WHOLE CITY BLOCKS ARE DESTROYED. SO MANY KILLED, INJURED, MISSING. THE WHOLE WORLD IS COMING APART, BUT HE MAKES PEOPLE FORGET ABOUT THAT AND CARE ABOUT HIM.
THE CITY'S DARKEST HOUR HAS COME, BUT FORGET THE RUIN AROUND US.
THIS IS MY TIME TO RISE ONCE MORE. THIS IS THE TIME FOR ALL AMERICANS TO RISE!
LAUNDRY
BEING NEAR HIM MAKES ME REMEMBER EVERYTHING I DESPISE. IT MAKES ME WANT TO LASH OUT. AND TO OBEY.
HOW MANY OF US HAVE BEEN TAINTED BY THE TOUCH OF THE VILE IMMIGRANT?
MY FRIEND MR. CHAMBLISS LOST HIS BUSINESS, THE DEVIL'S DINER, TO AN IMMIGRANT.
I'VE TOLD HIM THINGS THAT I THOUGHT I WOULDN'T EVER TELL ANYONE.
THE AMERICAN PANTHER HIMSELF, OUR PILLAR OF STRENGTH, HAS SUFFERED AT THEIR HANDS. HIS FATHER WAS MURDERED BY A FOREIGNER!
DAMN MEXICANS!
ARABS!
TOO MANY CHINESE!
AFRICANS EVERYWHERE!
I WOULD DO ANYTHING FOR THIS MAN. I WANT TO SERVE HIM.
BUT THIS IS OUR TIME, THE TIME FOR AMERICANS! OUT OF THE CHAOS THAT HAS BEEN VISITED ON THIS CITY, A NEW AMERICA WILL RISE, AND THE AMERICAN PANTHER WILL BE YOUR CHAMPION!
BUT SOMEHOW I KNOW THAT I ALSO DON'T WANT TO HELP HIM, I DON'T WANT TO BE HERE. BUT HIS PRESENCE... IT'S INTOXICATING.
FOR WEEKS HE HAS PATROLLED THESE STREETS, PROTECTING CITIZENS FROM FOREIGN MUGGERS AND DRUG DEALERS, FOREIGN GANGSTERS AND RAPISTS. HE HAS FOUGHT LIKE AN AMERICAN FOR AMERICANS.
AND HE WILL KEEP FIGHTING THOSE WHO OPPOSE US!

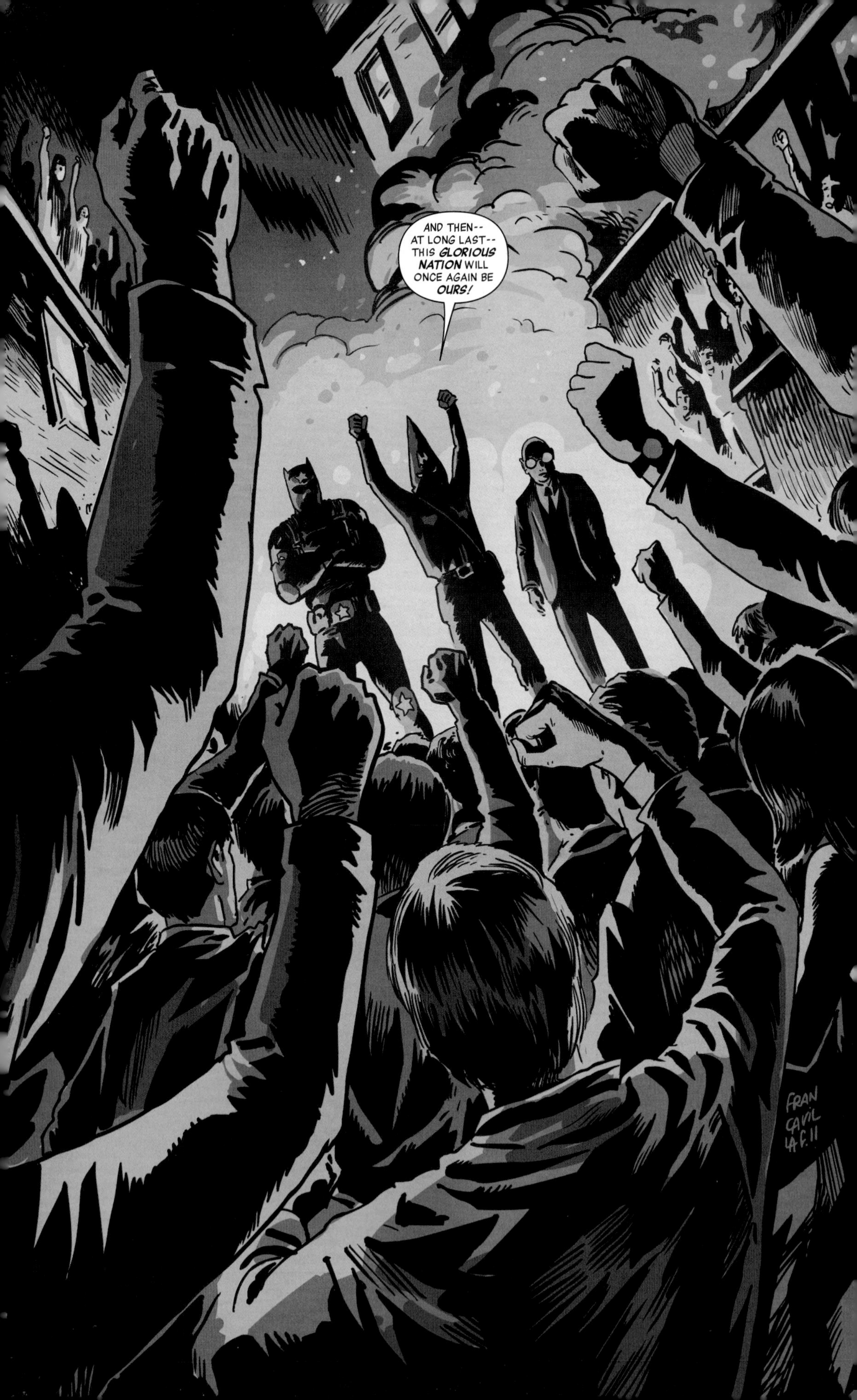
AND THEN-- AT LONG LAST-- THIS GLORIOUS NATION WILL ONCE AGAIN BE OURS!
FRAN CAVIL LA F.11

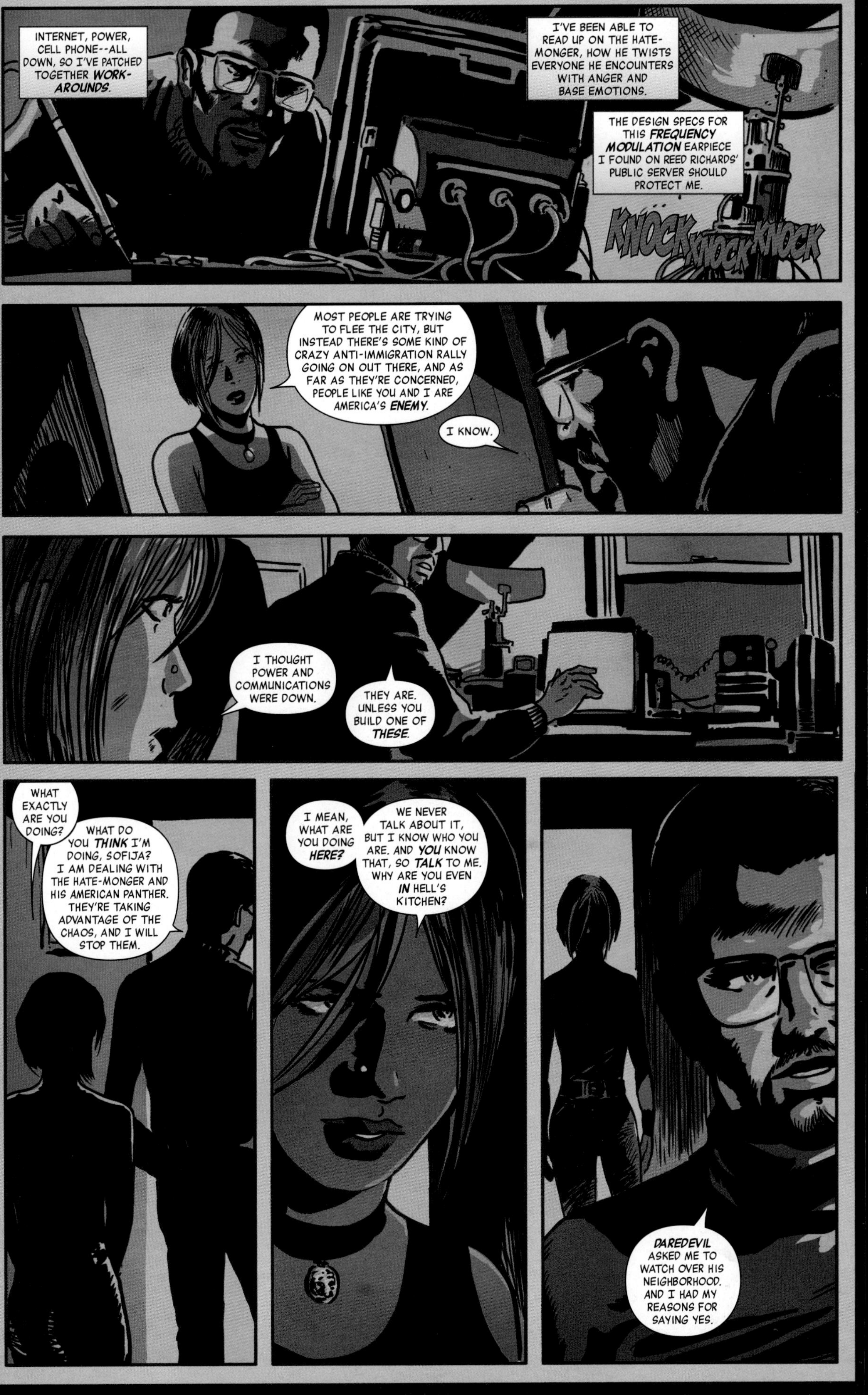
INTERNET, POWER, CELL PHONE--ALL DOWN, SO I'VE PATCHED TOGETHER WORK-AROUNDS.
I'VE BEEN ABLE TO READ UP ON THE HATE-MONGER, HOW HE TWISTS EVERYONE HE ENCOUNTERS WITH ANGER AND BASE EMOTIONS.
THE DESIGN SPECS FOR THIS FREQUENCY MODULATION EARPIECE I FOUND ON REED RICHARDS' PUBLIC SERVER SHOULD PROTECT ME.
KNOCK KNOCK KNOCK
MOST PEOPLE ARE TRYING TO FLEE THE CITY, BUT INSTEAD THERE'S SOME KIND OF CRAZY ANTI-IMMIGRATION RALLY GOING ON OUT THERE, AND AS FAR AS THEY'RE CONCERNED, PEOPLE LIKE YOU AND I ARE AMERICA'S ENEMY.
I KNOW.
I THOUGHT POWER AND COMMUNICATIONS WERE DOWN.
THEY ARE. UNLESS YOU BUILD ONE OF THESE.
WHAT EXACTLY ARE YOU DOING?
WHAT DO YOU THINK I'M DOING, SOFIJA? I AM DEALING WITH THE HATE-MONGER AND HIS AMERICAN PANTHER. THEY'RE TAKING ADVANTAGE OF THE CHAOS, AND I WILL STOP THEM.
I MEAN, WHAT ARE YOU DOING HERE?
WE NEVER TALK ABOUT IT, BUT I KNOW WHO YOU ARE. AND YOU KNOW THAT, SO TALK TO ME. WHY ARE YOU EVEN IN HELL'S KITCHEN?
DAREDEVIL ASKED ME TO WATCH OVER HIS NEIGHBORHOOD. AND I HAD MY REASONS FOR SAYING YES.

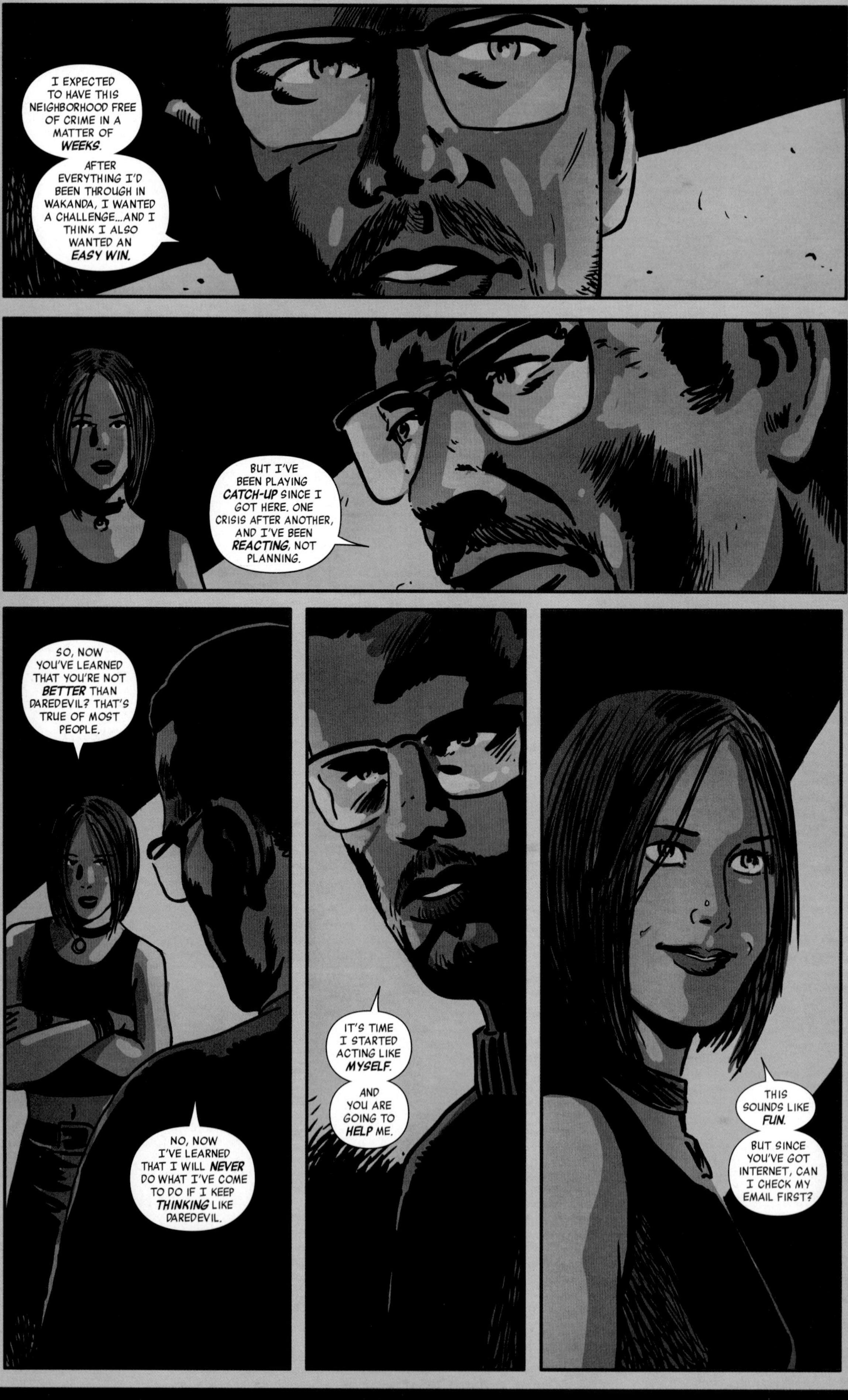
I EXPECTED TO HAVE THIS NEIGHBORHOOD FREE OF CRIME IN A MATTER OF WEEKS.
AFTER EVERYTHING I'D BEEN THROUGH IN WAKANDA, I WANTED A CHALLENGE...AND I THINK I ALSO WANTED AN EASY WIN.
BUT I'VE BEEN PLAYING CATCH-UP SINCE I GOT HERE. ONE CRISIS AFTER ANOTHER, AND I'VE BEEN REACTING, NOT PLANNING.
SO, NOW YOU'VE LEARNED THAT YOU'RE NOT BETTER THAN DAREDEVIL? THAT'S TRUE OF MOST PEOPLE.
NO, NOW I'VE LEARNED THAT I WILL NEVER DO WHAT I'VE COME TO DO IF I KEEP THINKING LIKE DAREDEVIL.
IT'S TIME I STARTED ACTING LIKE MYSELF.
AND YOU ARE GOING TO HELP ME.
THIS SOUNDS LIKE FUN.
BUT SINCE YOU'VE GOT INTERNET, CAN I CHECK MY EMAIL FIRST?

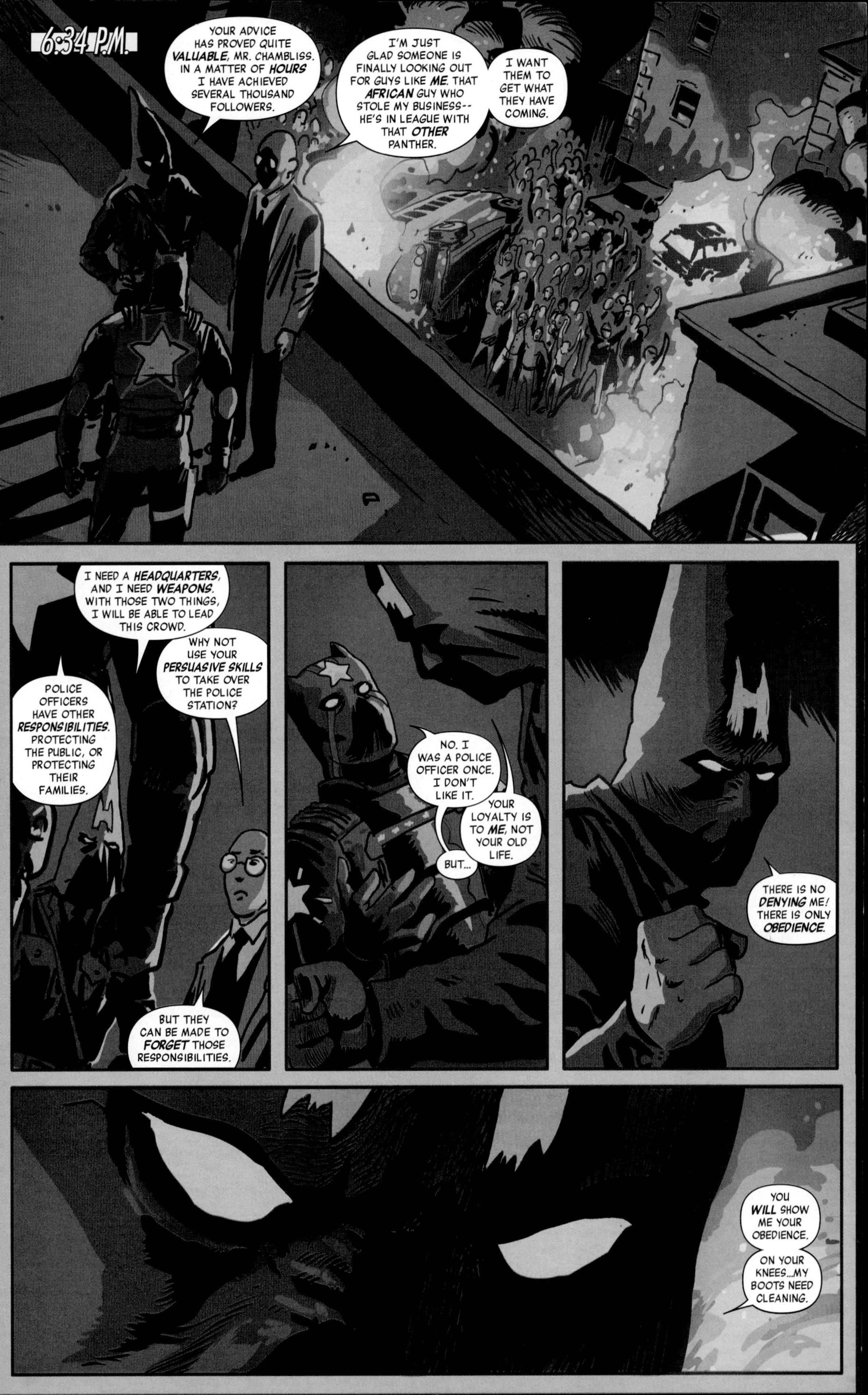
6:34 P.M.
YOUR ADVICE HAS PROVED QUITE VALUABLE, MR. CHAMBLISS. IN A MATTER OF HOURS I HAVE ACHIEVED SEVERAL THOUSAND FOLLOWERS.
I'M JUST GLAD SOMEONE IS FINALLY LOOKING OUT FOR GUYS LIKE ME. THAT AFRICAN GUY WHO STOLE MY BUSINESS-- HE'S IN LEAGUE WITH THAT OTHER PANTHER.
I WANT THEM TO GET WHAT THEY HAVE COMING.
I NEED A HEADQUARTERS, AND I NEED WEAPONS. WITH THOSE TWO THINGS, I WILL BE ABLE TO LEAD THIS CROWD.
WHY NOT USE YOUR PERSUASIVE SKILLS TO TAKE OVER THE POLICE STATION?
POLICE OFFICERS HAVE OTHER RESPONSIBILITIES. PROTECTING THE PUBLIC, OR PROTECTING THEIR FAMILIES.
BUT THEY CAN BE MADE TO FORGET THOSE RESPONSIBILITIES.
NO. I WAS A POLICE OFFICER ONCE. I DON'T LIKE IT.
BUT...
YOUR LOYALTY IS TO ME, NOT YOUR OLD LIFE.
THERE IS NO DENYING ME! THERE IS ONLY OBEDIENCE.
YOU WILL SHOW ME YOUR OBEDIENCE.
ON YOUR KNEES...MY BOOTS NEED CLEANING.

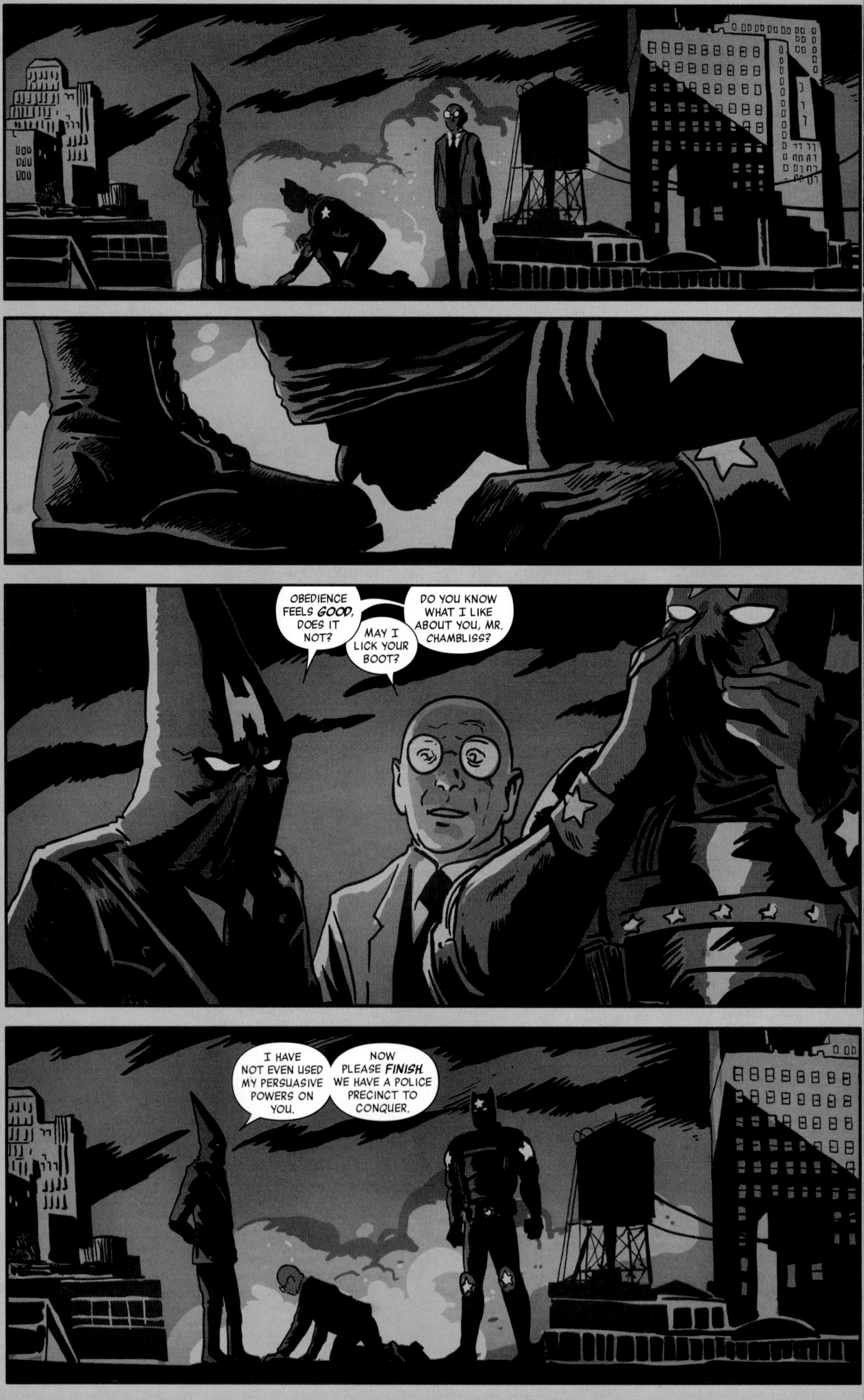
OBEDIENCE FEELS **GOOD**, DOES IT NOT?
DO YOU KNOW WHAT I LIKE ABOUT YOU, MR. CHAMBLISS?
MAY I LICK YOUR BOOT?
I HAVE NOT EVEN USED MY PERSUASIVE POWERS ON YOU.
NOW PLEASE **FINISH**. WE HAVE A POLICE PRECINCT TO CONQUER.

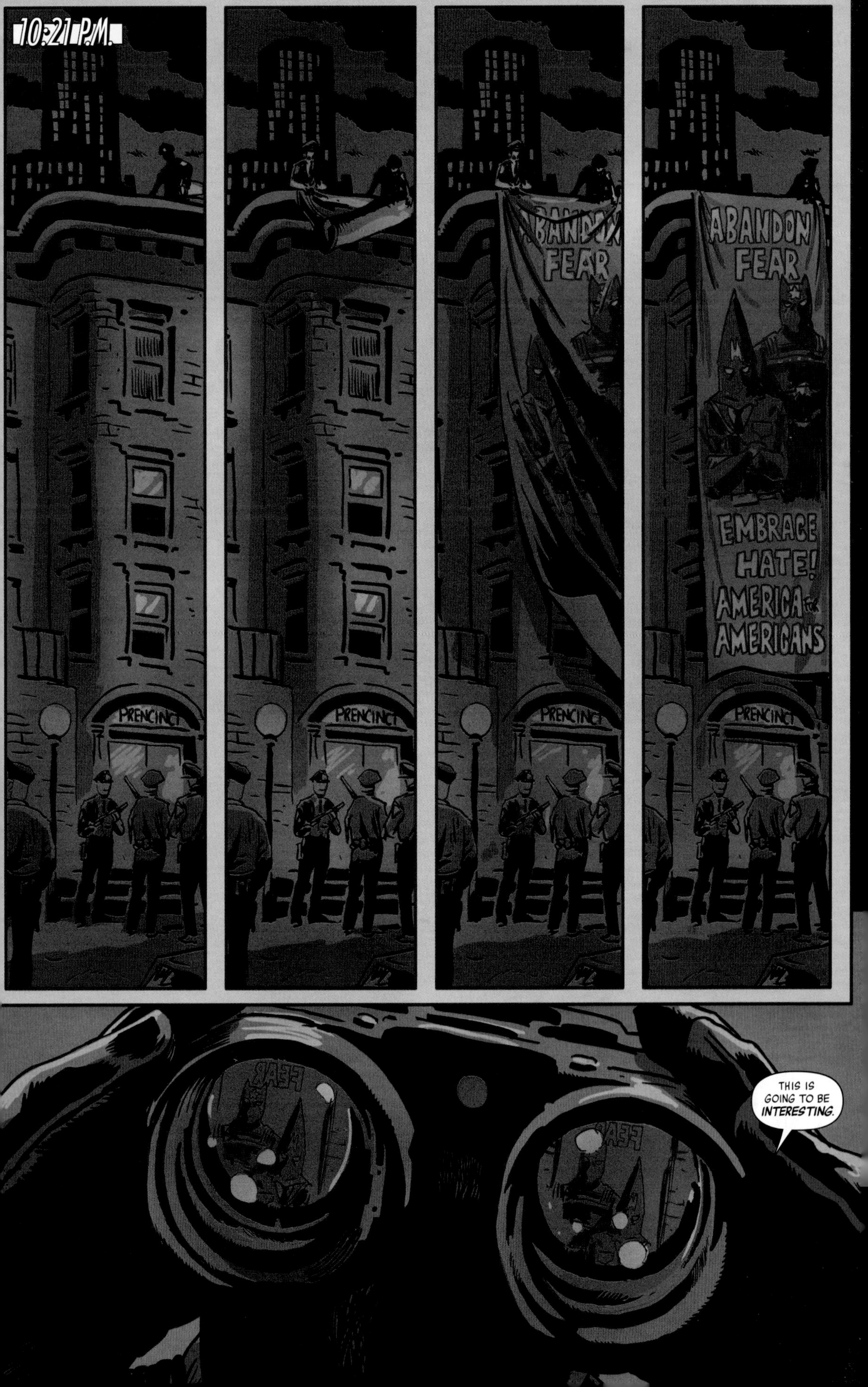
10:21 P.M.
PRENCINCT
ABANDON FEAR
EMBRACE HATE!
AMERICA
AMERICANS
THIS IS GOING TO BE INTERESTING.

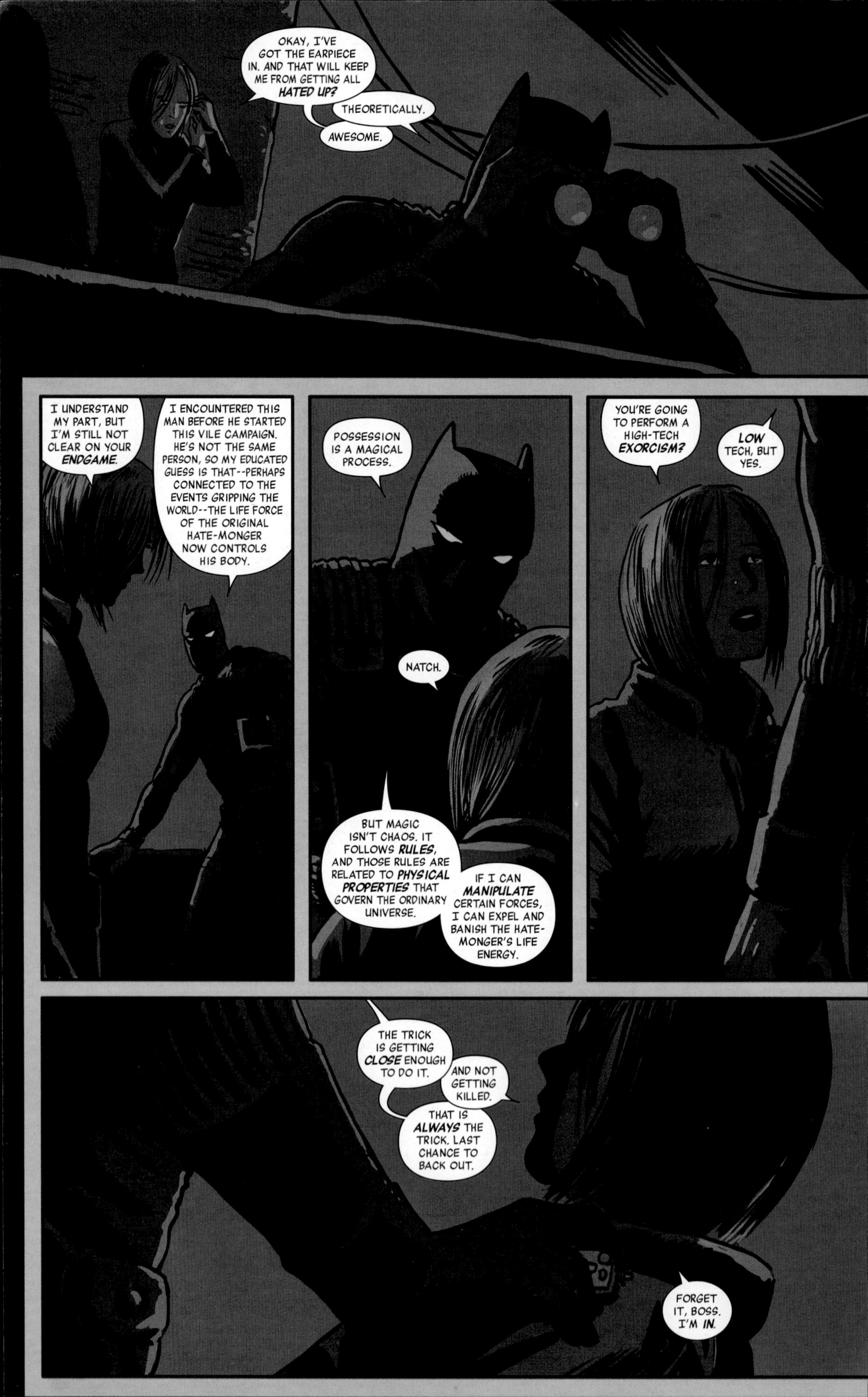
OKAY, I'VE GOT THE EARPIECE IN. AND THAT WILL KEEP ME FROM GETTING ALL HATED UP?
THEORETICALLY.
AWESOME.
I UNDERSTAND MY PART, BUT I'M STILL NOT CLEAR ON YOUR ENDGAME.
I ENCOUNTERED THIS MAN BEFORE HE STARTED THIS VILE CAMPAIGN. HE'S NOT THE SAME PERSON, SO MY EDUCATED GUESS IS THAT--PERHAPS CONNECTED TO THE EVENTS GRIPPING THE WORLD--THE LIFE FORCE OF THE ORIGINAL HATE-MONGER NOW CONTROLS HIS BODY.
POSSESSION IS A MAGICAL PROCESS.
NATCH.
BUT MAGIC ISN'T CHAOS. IT FOLLOWS RULES, AND THOSE RULES ARE RELATED TO PHYSICAL PROPERTIES THAT GOVERN THE ORDINARY UNIVERSE.
IF I CAN MANIPULATE CERTAIN FORCES, I CAN EXPEL AND BANISH THE HATE-MONGER'S LIFE ENERGY.
YOU'RE GOING TO PERFORM A HIGH-TECH EXORCISM?
LOW TECH, BUT YES.
THE TRICK IS GETTING CLOSE ENOUGH TO DO IT.
AND NOT GETTING KILLED.
THAT IS ALWAYS THE TRICK. LAST CHANCE TO BACK OUT.
FORGET IT, BOSS. I'M IN.

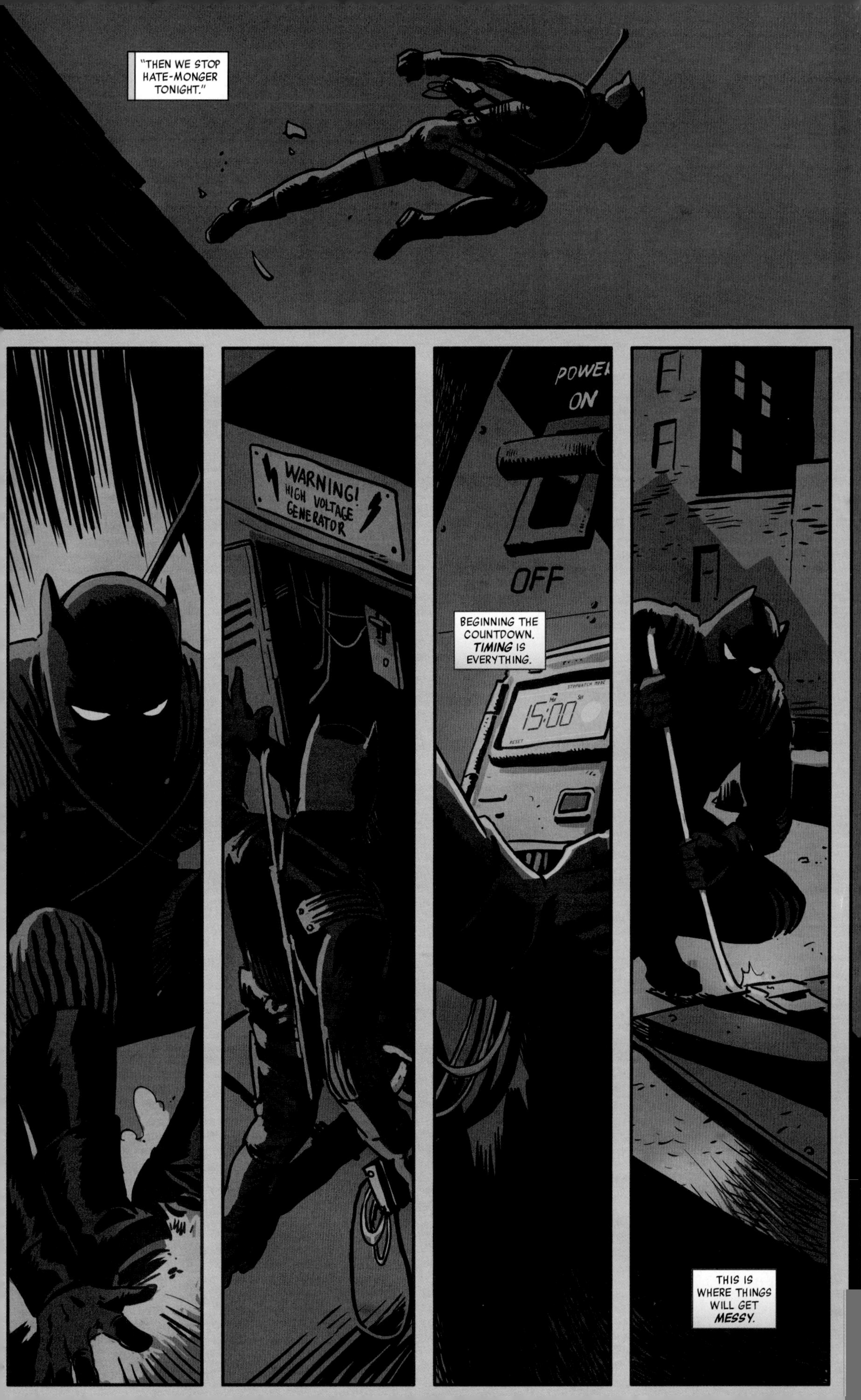
"THEN WE STOP HATE-MONGER TONIGHT."
WARNING! HIGH VOLTAGE GENERATOR
ON
OFF
BEGINNING THE COUNTDOWN. *TIMING* IS EVERYTHING.
15:00
THIS IS WHERE THINGS WILL GET *MESSY*.

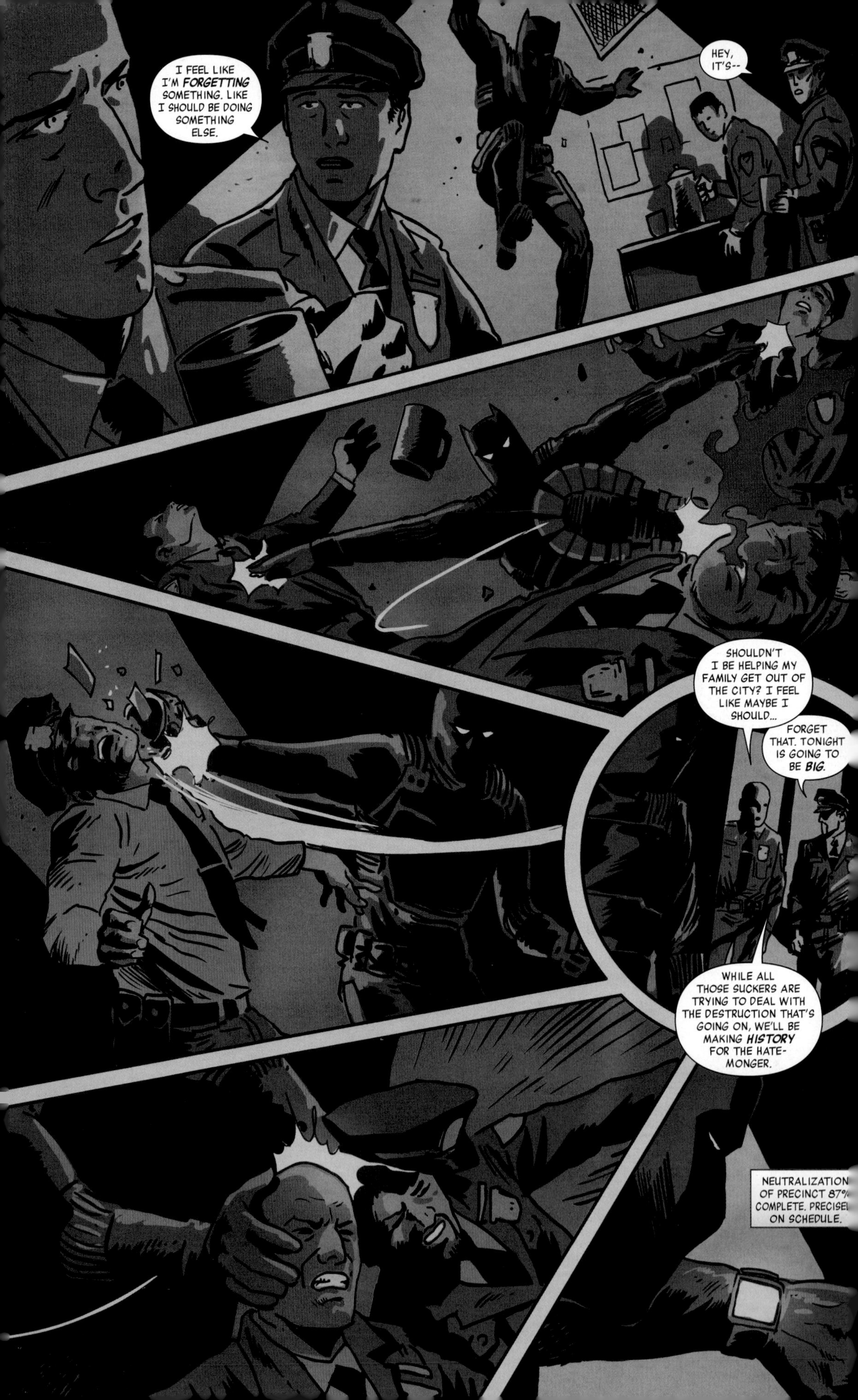
I FEEL LIKE I'M FORGETTING SOMETHING. LIKE I SHOULD BE DOING SOMETHING ELSE.
HEY, IT'S--
SHOULDN'T I BE HELPING MY FAMILY GET OUT OF THE CITY? I FEEL LIKE MAYBE I SHOULD...
FORGET THAT. TONIGHT IS GOING TO BE BIG.
WHILE ALL THOSE SUCKERS ARE TRYING TO DEAL WITH THE DESTRUCTION THAT'S GOING ON, WE'LL BE MAKING HISTORY FOR THE HATE-MONGER.
NEUTRALIZATION OF PRECINCT 87% COMPLETE. PRECISEL ON SCHEDULE.

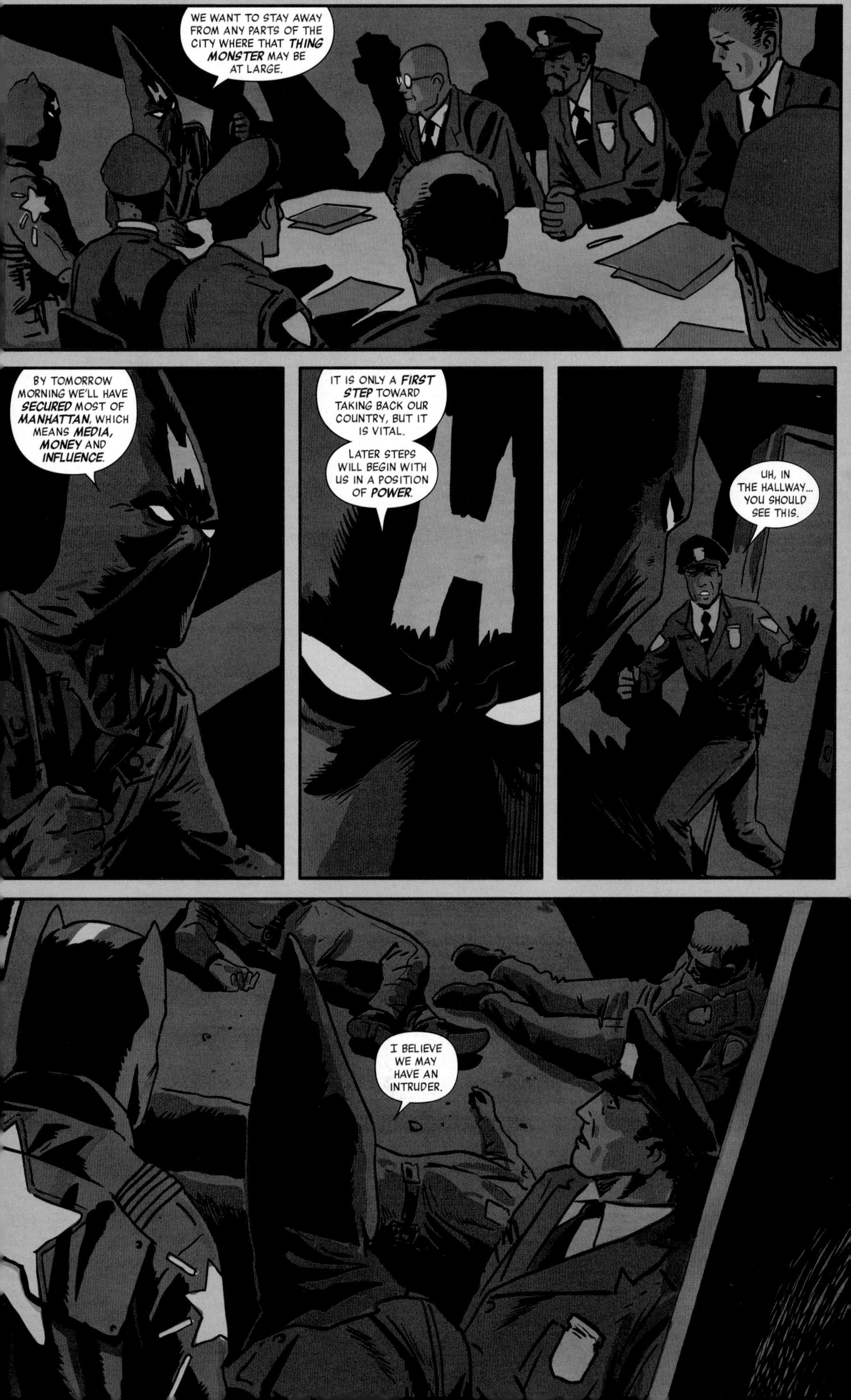
WE WANT TO STAY AWAY FROM ANY PARTS OF THE CITY WHERE THAT THING MONSTER MAY BE AT LARGE.
BY TOMORROW MORNING WE'LL HAVE SECURED MOST OF MANHATTAN, WHICH MEANS MEDIA, MONEY AND INFLUENCE.
IT IS ONLY A FIRST STEP TOWARD TAKING BACK OUR COUNTRY, BUT IT IS VITAL.
LATER STEPS WILL BEGIN WITH US IN A POSITION OF POWER.
UH, IN THE HALLWAY... YOU SHOULD SEE THIS.
I BELIEVE WE MAY HAVE AN INTRUDER.

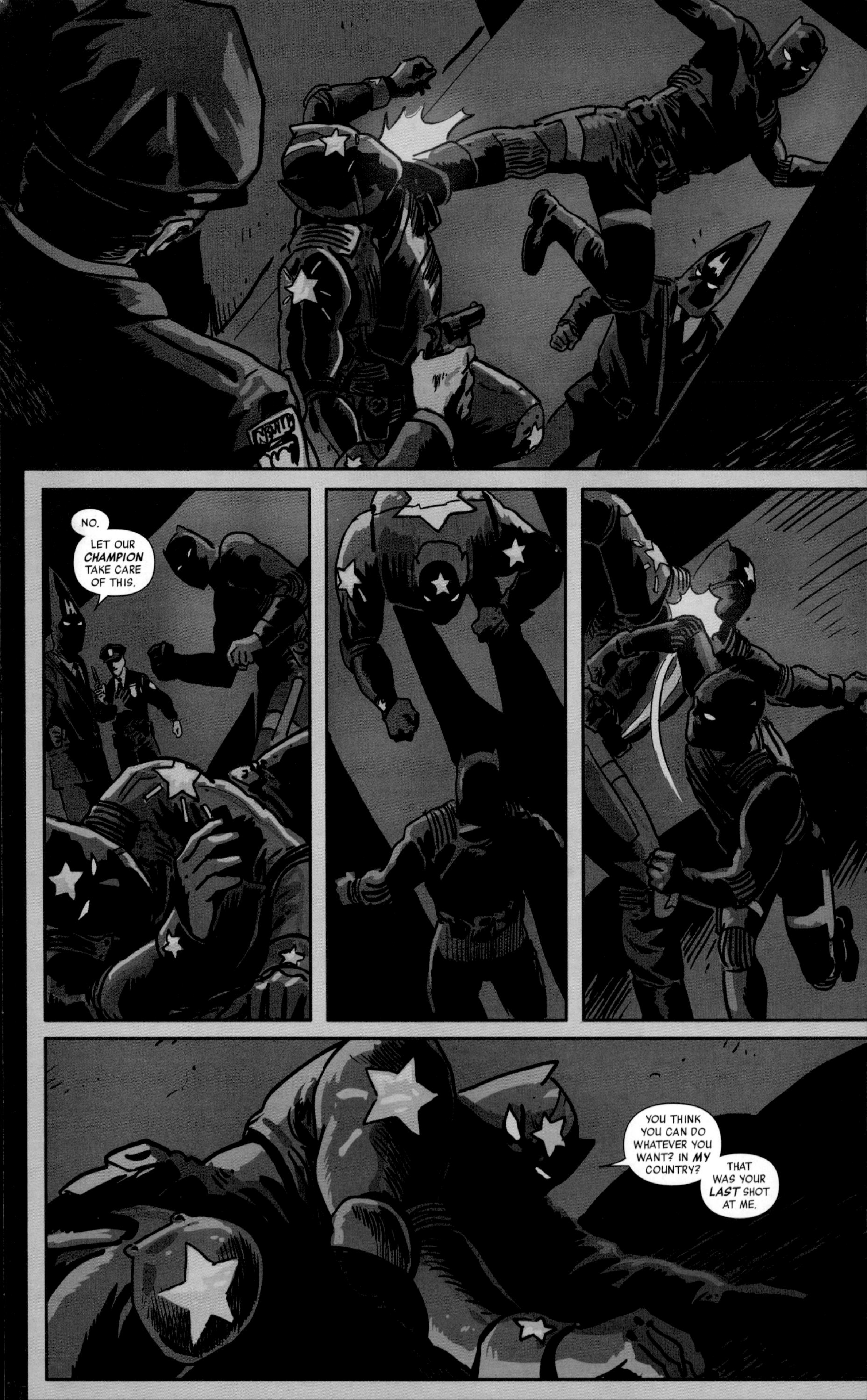

NO.
LET OUR CHAMPION TAKE CARE OF THIS.
YOU THINK YOU CAN DO WHATEVER YOU WANT? IN MY COUNTRY?
THAT WAS YOUR LAST SHOT AT ME.

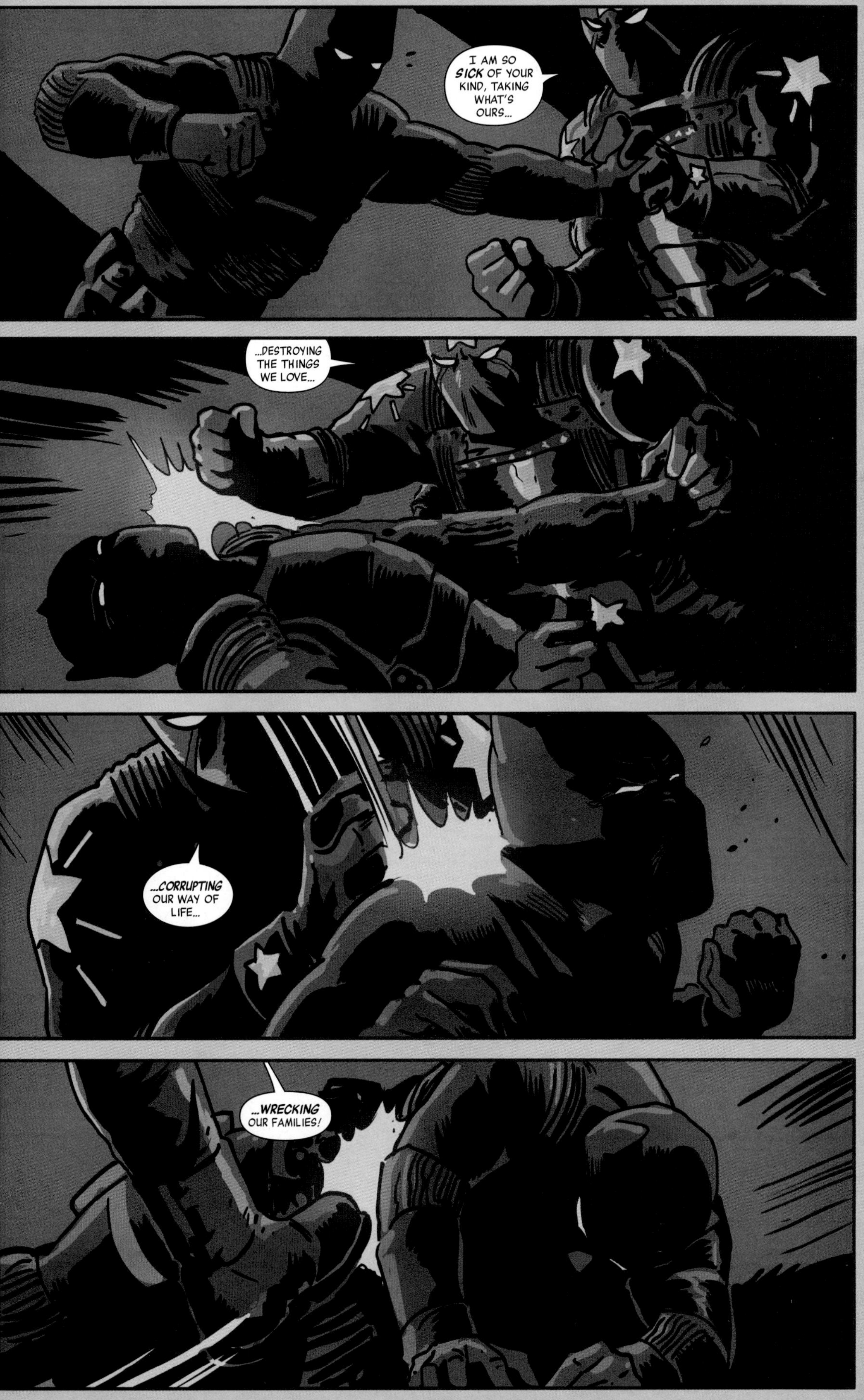
I AM SO SICK OF YOUR KIND, TAKING WHAT'S OURS...
...DESTROYING THE THINGS WE LOVE...
...CORRUPTING OUR WAY OF LIFE...
...WRECKING OUR FAMILIES!

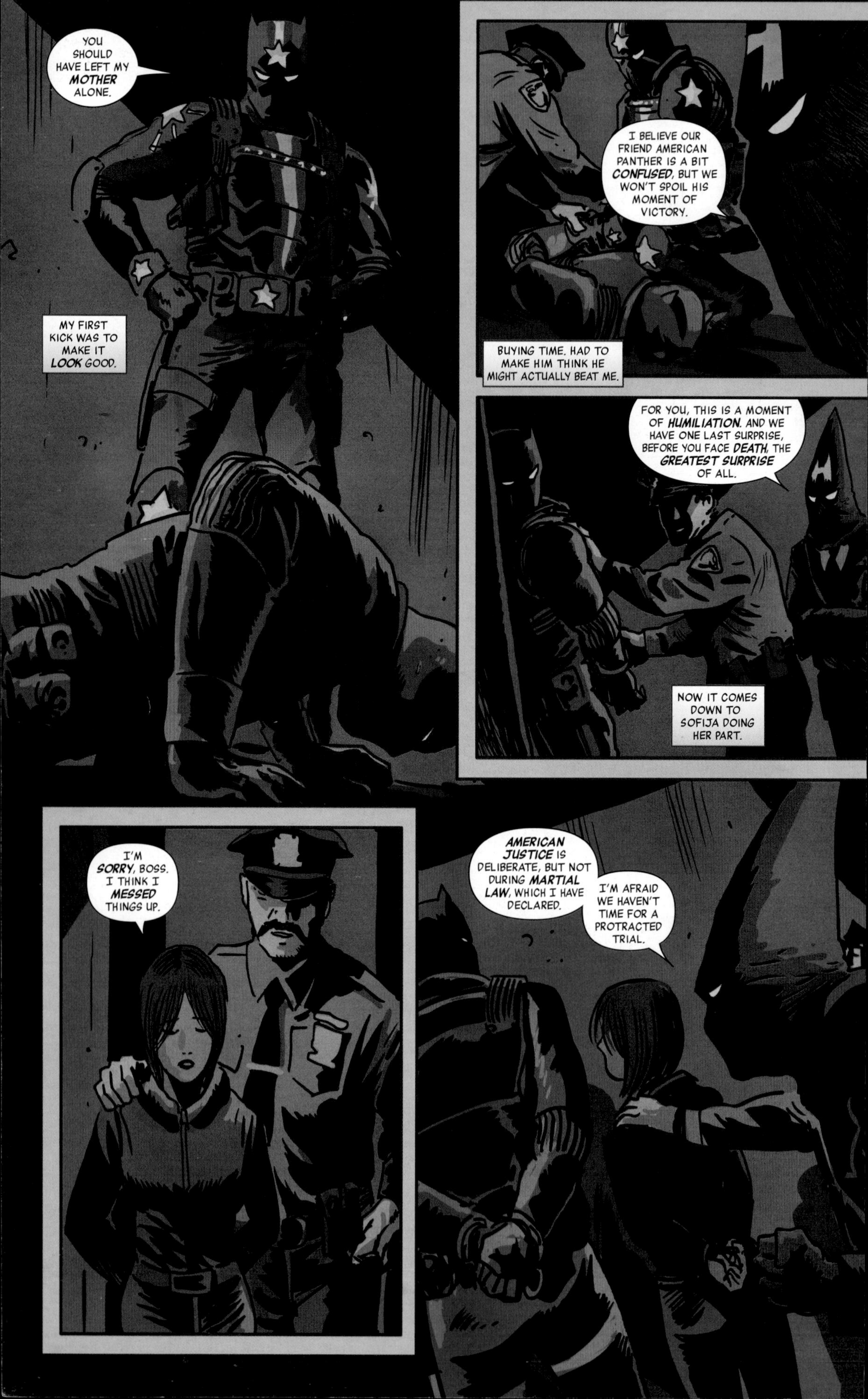
YOU SHOULD HAVE LEFT MY MOTHER ALONE.
MY FIRST KICK WAS TO MAKE IT LOOK GOOD.
I BELIEVE OUR FRIEND AMERICAN PANTHER IS A BIT CONFUSED, BUT WE WON'T SPOIL HIS MOMENT OF VICTORY.
BUYING TIME. HAD TO MAKE HIM THINK HE MIGHT ACTUALLY BEAT ME.
FOR YOU, THIS IS A MOMENT OF HUMILIATION. AND WE HAVE ONE LAST SURPRISE, BEFORE YOU FACE DEATH, THE GREATEST SURPRISE OF ALL.
NOW IT COMES DOWN TO SOFIJA DOING HER PART.
I'M SORRY, BOSS. I THINK I MESSED THINGS UP.
AMERICAN JUSTICE IS DELIBERATE, BUT NOT DURING MARTIAL LAW, WHICH I HAVE DECLARED.
I'M AFRAID WE HAVEN'T TIME FOR A PROTRACTED TRIAL.

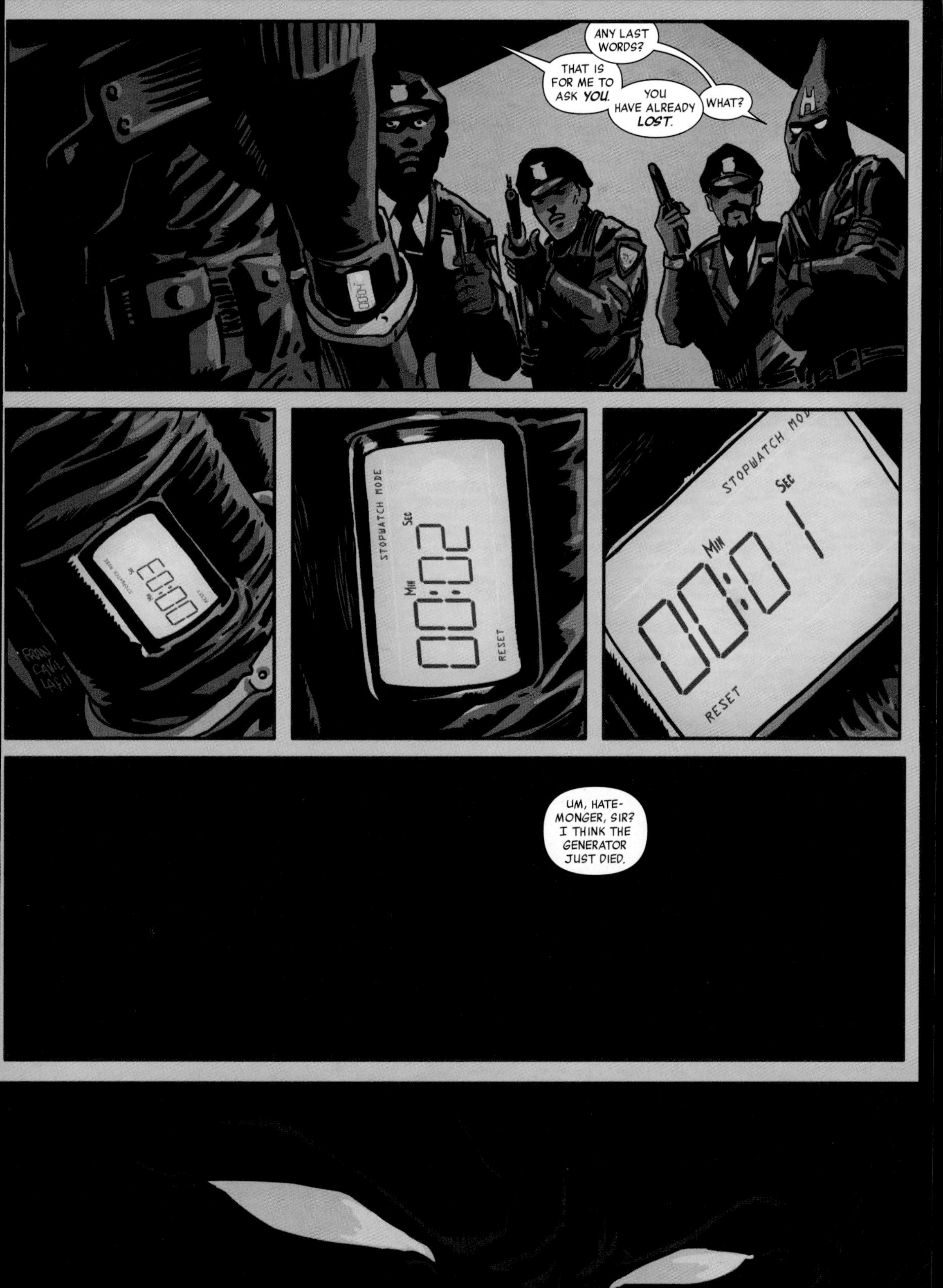
ANY LAST WORDS?
THAT IS FOR ME TO ASK ***YOU***.
YOU HAVE ALREADY ***LOST***.
WHAT?
STOPWATCH MODE
MIN
SEC
00:02
RESET
STOPWATCH MODE
MIN
SEC
00:01
RESET
UM, HATE-MONGER, SIR? I THINK THE GENERATOR JUST DIED.

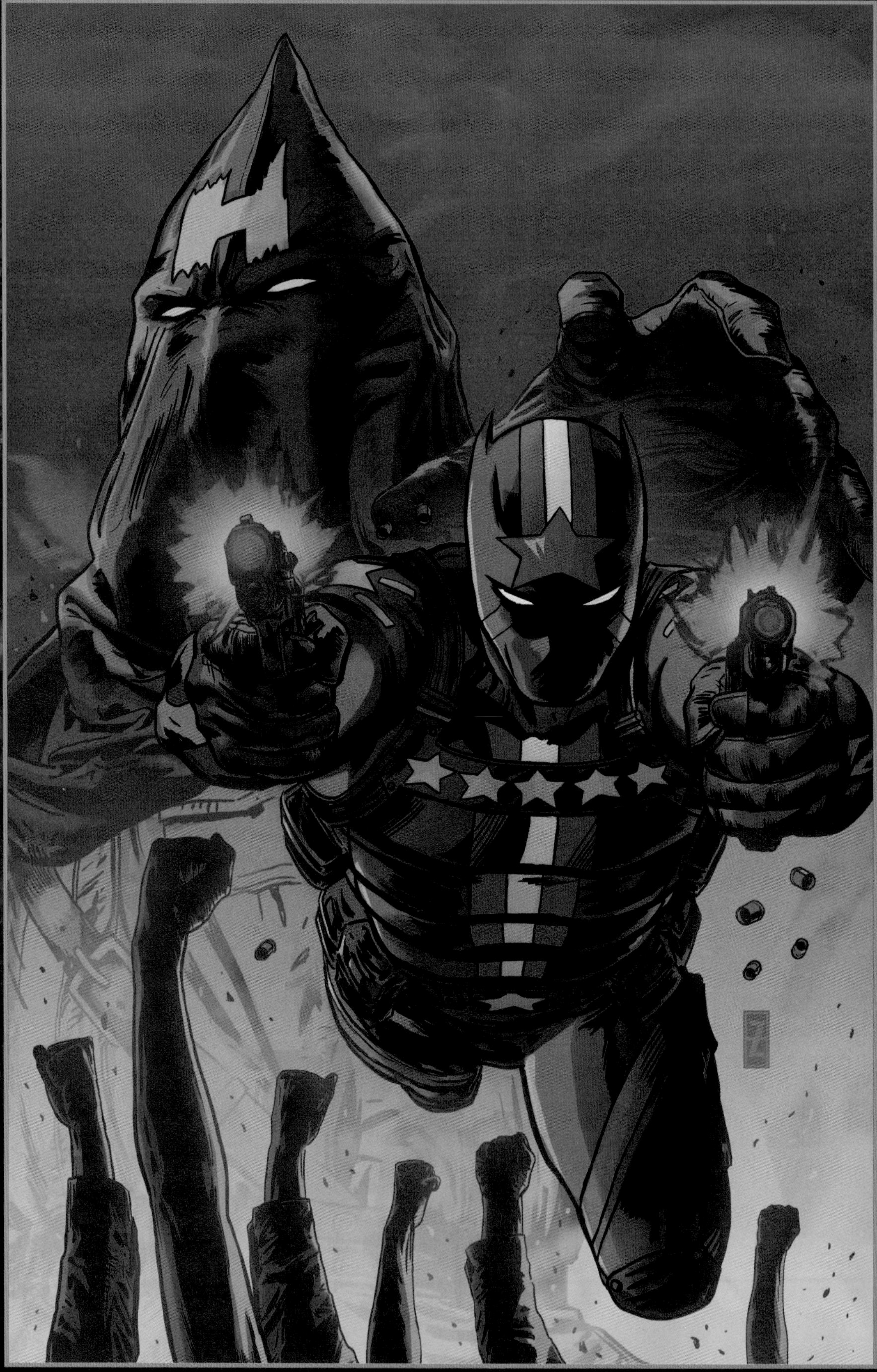

BLACK PANTHER:
THE MAN WITHOUT FEAR #523

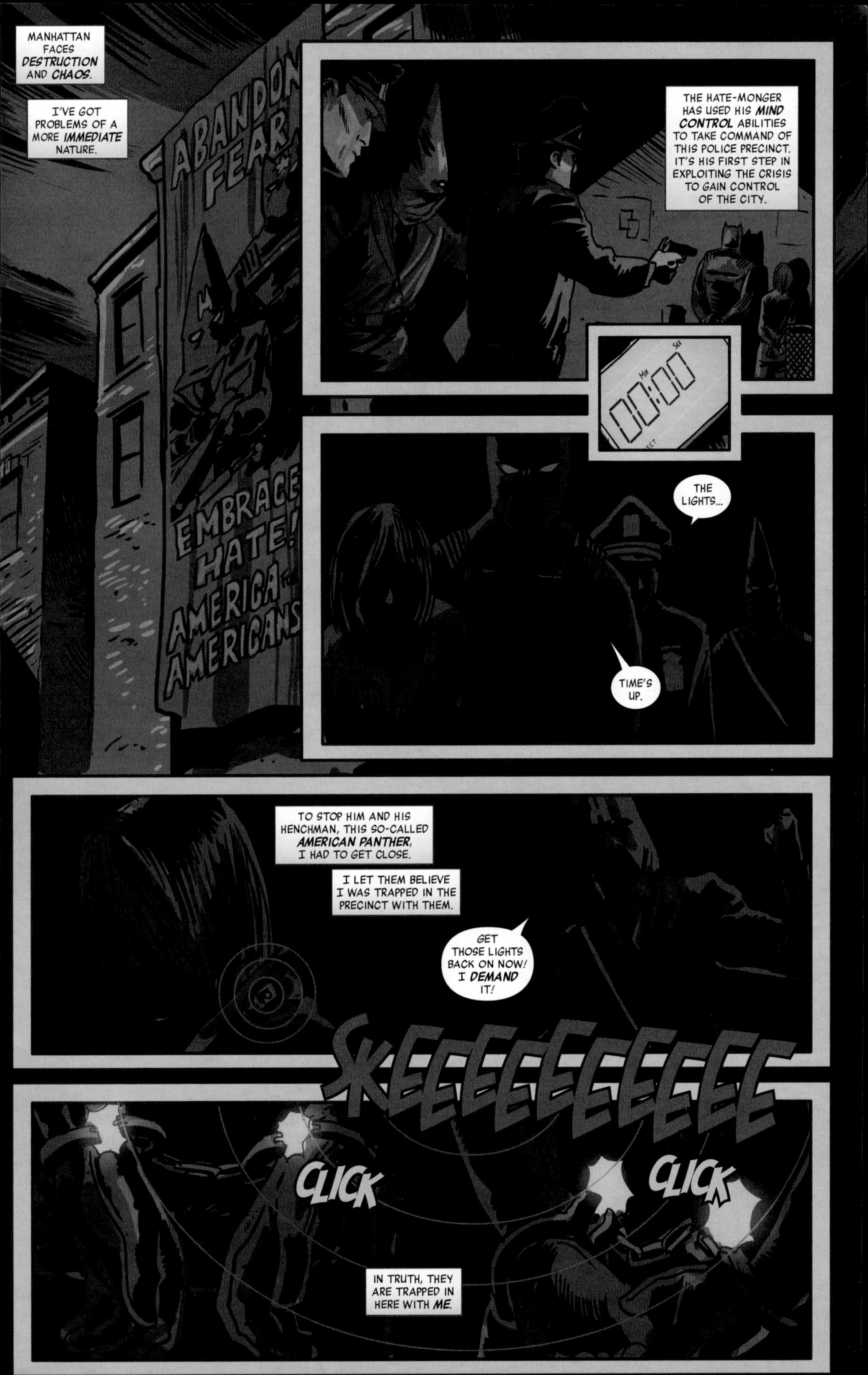

MANHATTAN FACES DESTRUCTION AND CHAOS.
I'VE GOT PROBLEMS OF A MORE IMMEDIATE NATURE.
ABANDON FEAR
EMBRACE HATE!
AMERICA FOR AMERICANS
THE HATE-MONGER HAS USED HIS MIND CONTROL ABILITIES TO TAKE COMMAND OF THIS POLICE PRECINCT. IT'S HIS FIRST STEP IN EXPLOITING THE CRISIS TO GAIN CONTROL OF THE CITY.
00:00
THE LIGHTS...
TIME'S UP.
TO STOP HIM AND HIS HENCHMAN, THIS SO-CALLED AMERICAN PANTHER, I HAD TO GET CLOSE.
I LET THEM BELIEVE I WAS TRAPPED IN THE PRECINCT WITH THEM.
GET THOSE LIGHTS BACK ON NOW! I DEMAND IT!
SKEEEEEEEEEEE
CLICK
CLICK
IN TRUTH, THEY ARE TRAPPED IN HERE WITH ME.

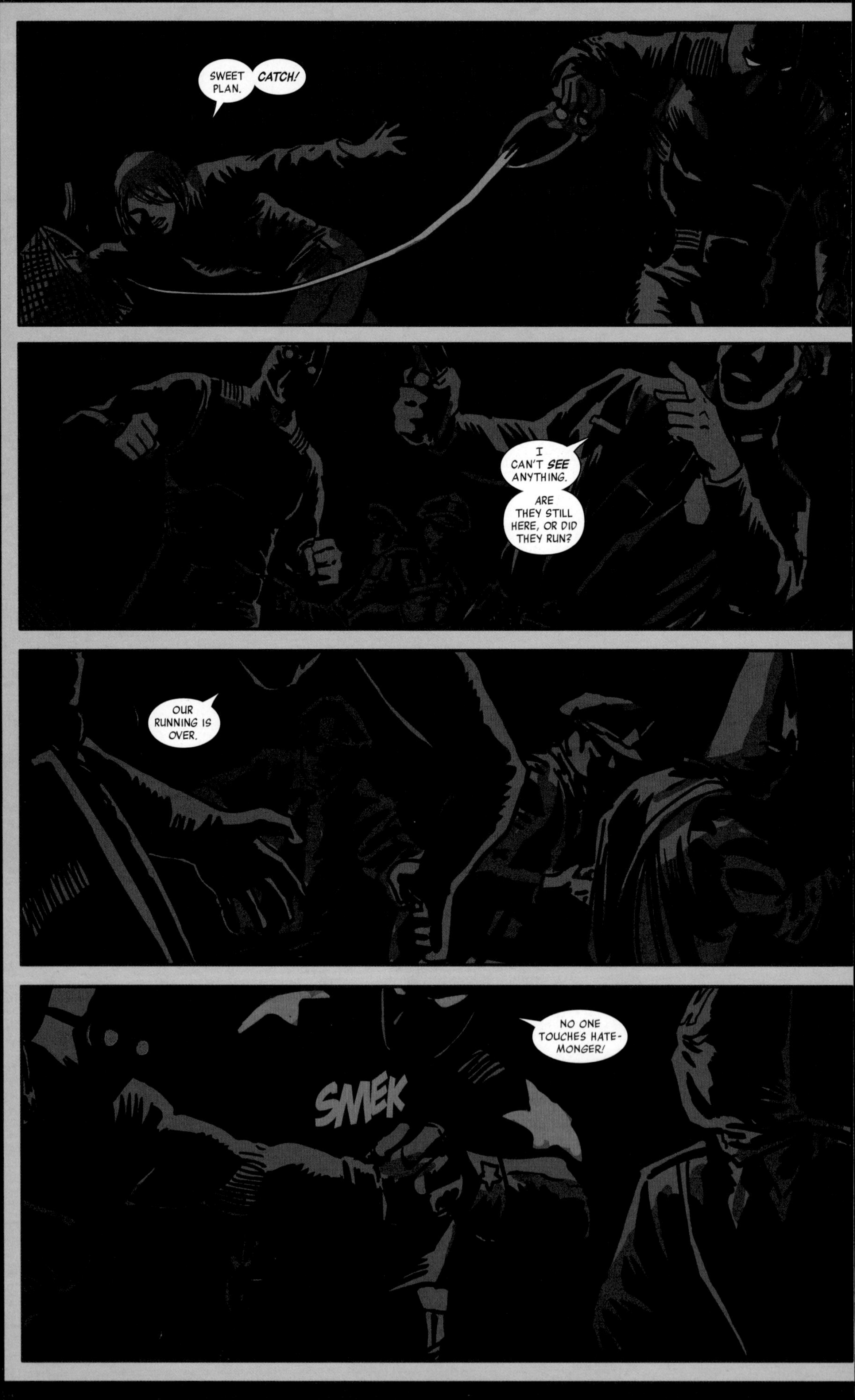
SWEET PLAN.
CATCH!
I CAN'T SEE ANYTHING.
ARE THEY STILL HERE, OR DID THEY RUN?
OUR RUNNING IS OVER.
NO ONE TOUCHES HATE-MONGER!
SMEK

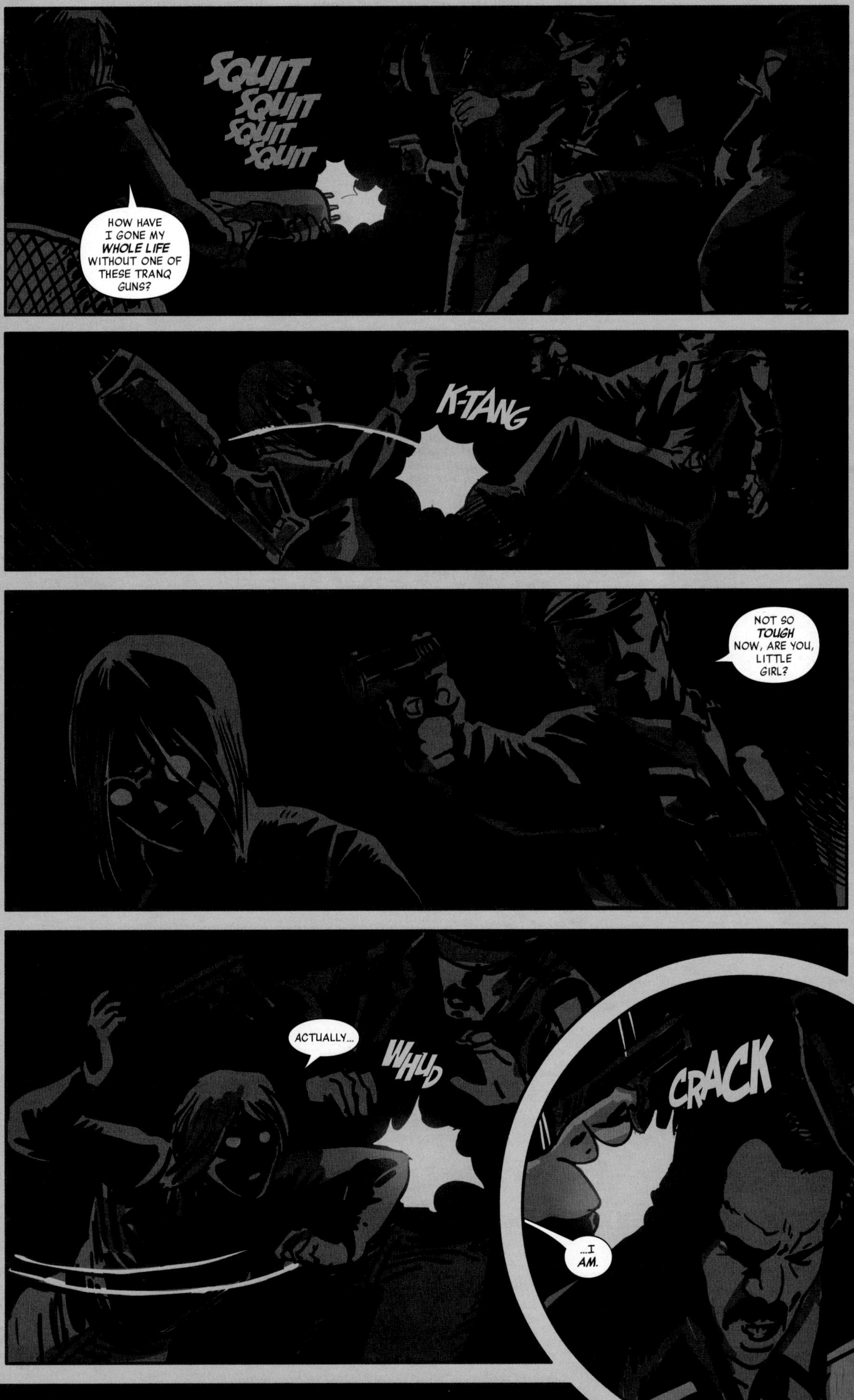

SQUIT SQUIT SQUIT SQUIT
HOW HAVE I GONE MY WHOLE LIFE WITHOUT ONE OF THESE TRANQ GUNS?
K-TANG
NOT SO TOUGH NOW, ARE YOU, LITTLE GIRL?
ACTUALLY...
WHUD
CRACK
...I AM.

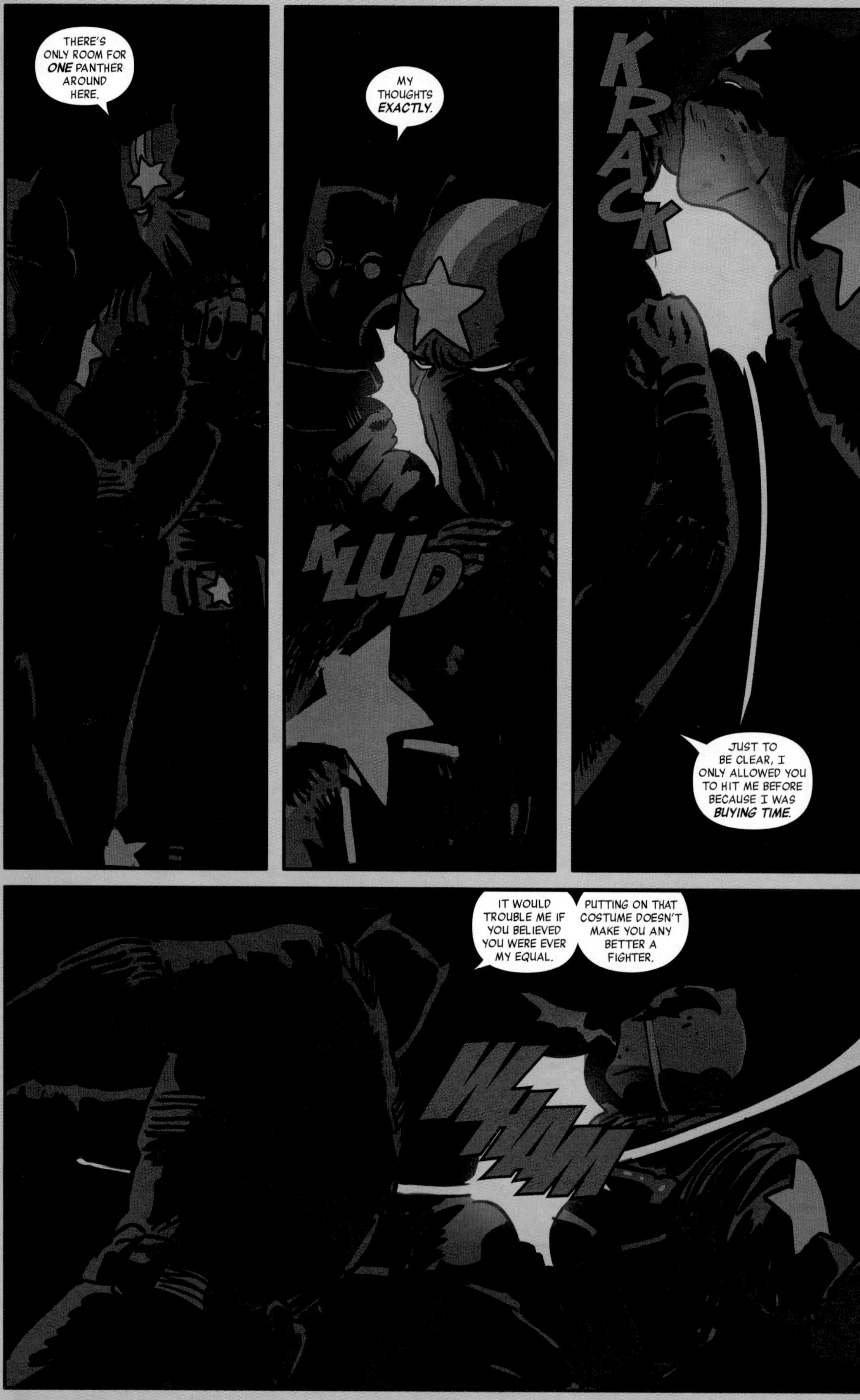
THERE'S ONLY ROOM FOR ONE PANTHER AROUND HERE.
MY THOUGHTS EXACTLY.
KLUD
KRACK
JUST TO BE CLEAR, I ONLY ALLOWED YOU TO HIT ME BEFORE BECAUSE I WAS BUYING TIME.
PUTTING ON THAT COSTUME DOESN'T MAKE YOU ANY BETTER A FIGHTER.
IT WOULD TROUBLE ME IF YOU BELIEVED YOU WERE EVER MY EQUAL.
WHAM

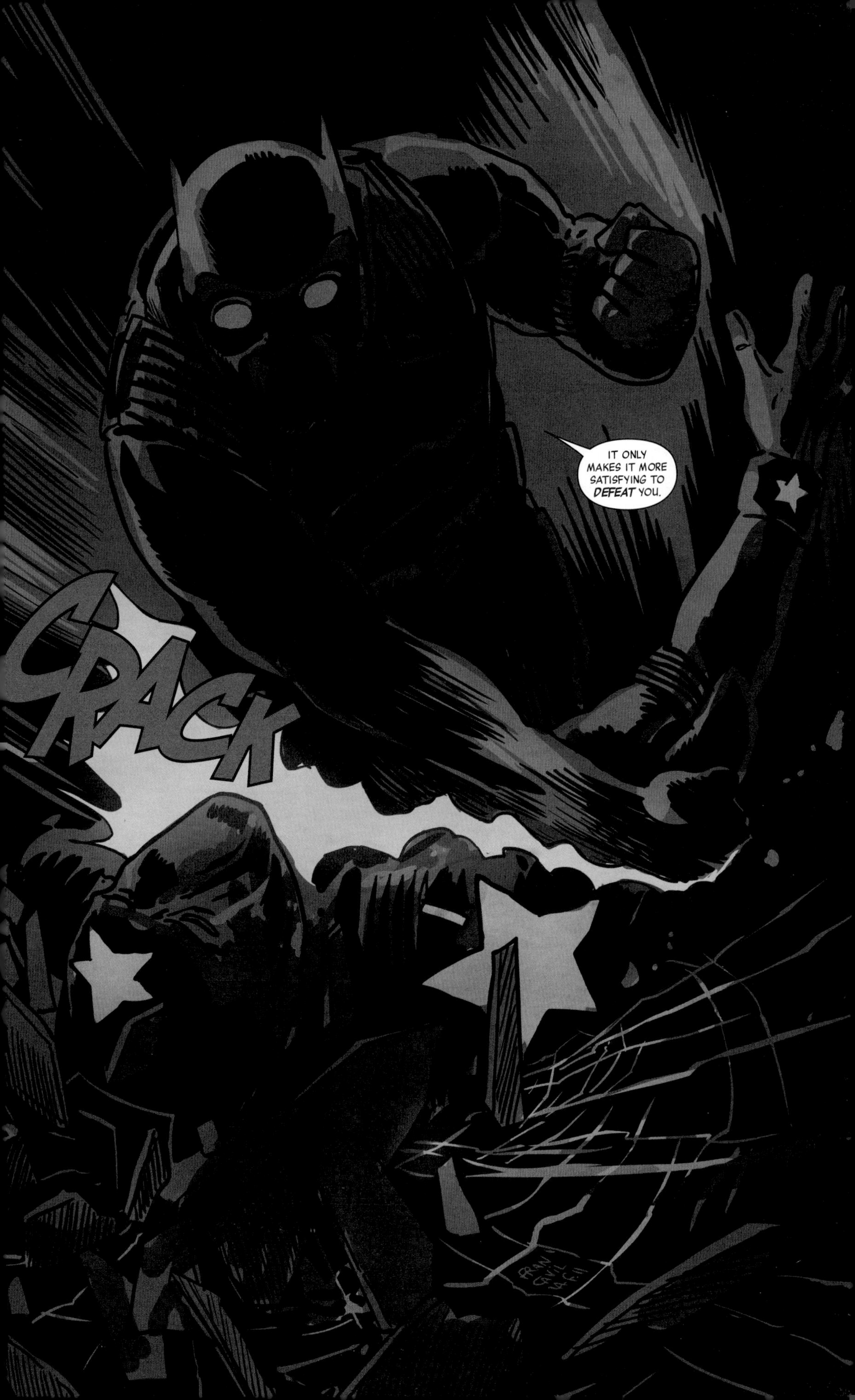
IT ONLY MAKES IT MORE SATISFYING TO *DEFEAT* YOU.
CRACK

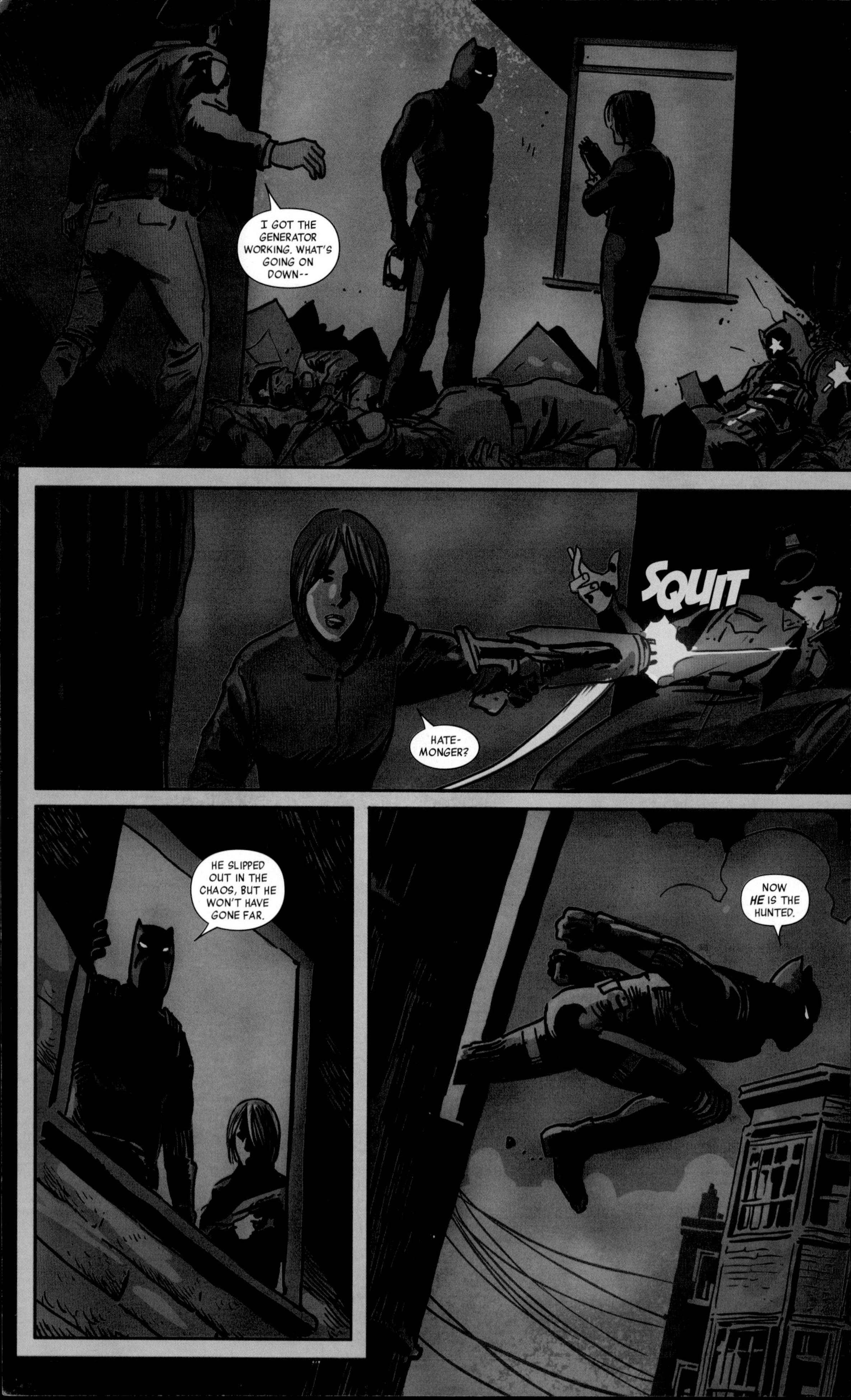
I GOT THE GENERATOR WORKING. WHAT'S GOING ON DOWN--
SQUIT
HATE-MONGER?
HE SLIPPED OUT IN THE CHAOS, BUT HE WON'T HAVE GONE FAR.
NOW HE IS THE HUNTED.

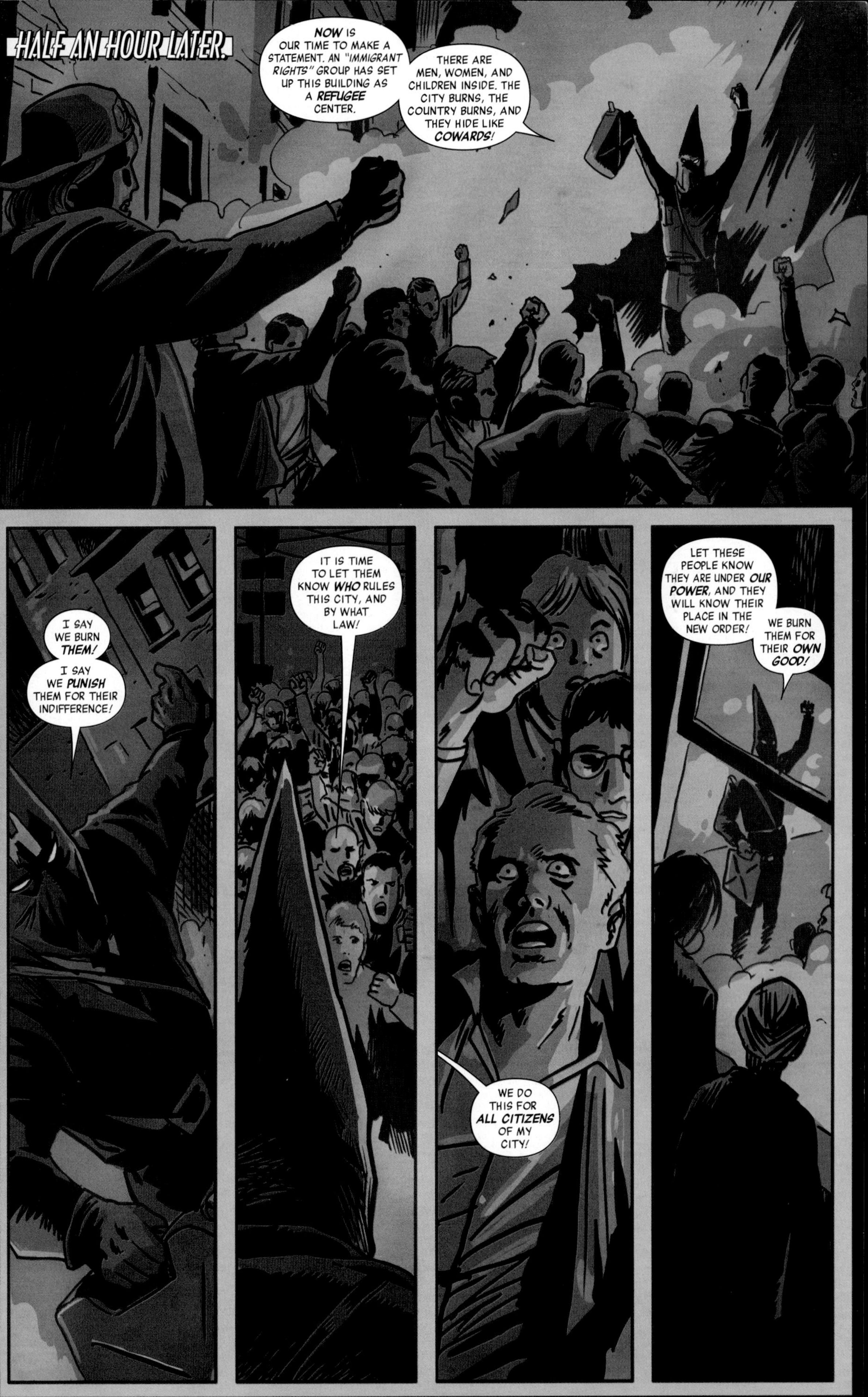
HALF AN HOUR LATER.
NOW IS OUR TIME TO MAKE A STATEMENT. AN "IMMIGRANT RIGHTS" GROUP HAS SET UP THIS BUILDING AS A REFUGEE CENTER.
THERE ARE MEN, WOMEN, AND CHILDREN INSIDE. THE CITY BURNS, THE COUNTRY BURNS, AND THEY HIDE LIKE COWARDS!
I SAY WE BURN THEM!
I SAY WE PUNISH THEM FOR THEIR INDIFFERENCE!
IT IS TIME TO LET THEM KNOW WHO RULES THIS CITY, AND BY WHAT LAW!
WE DO THIS FOR ALL CITIZENS OF MY CITY!
LET THESE PEOPLE KNOW THEY ARE UNDER OUR POWER, AND THEY WILL KNOW THEIR PLACE IN THE NEW ORDER!
WE BURN THEM FOR THEIR OWN GOOD!

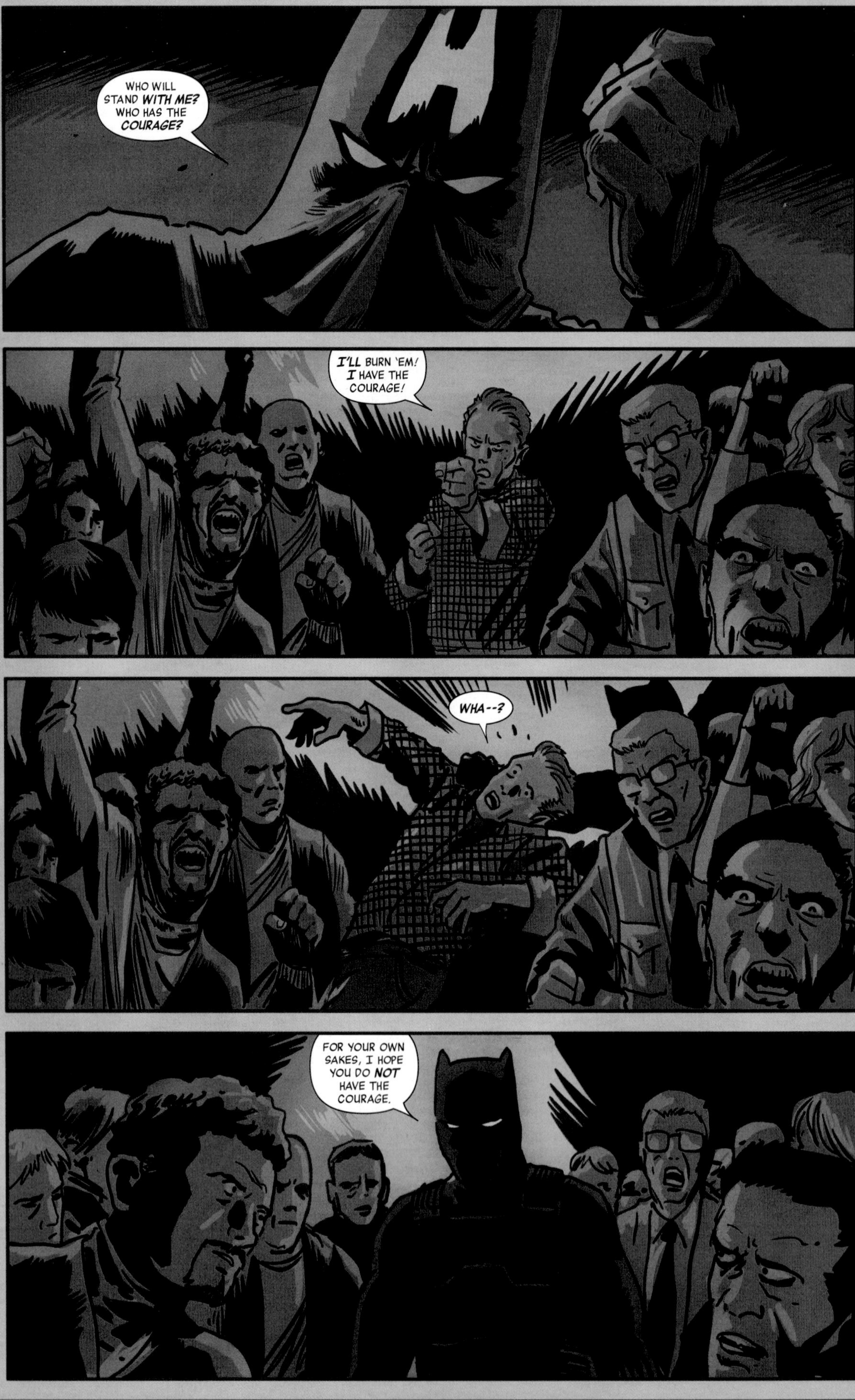

WHO WILL STAND WITH ME? WHO HAS THE COURAGE?
I'LL BURN 'EM! I HAVE THE COURAGE!
WHA--?
FOR YOUR OWN SAKES, I HOPE YOU DO NOT HAVE THE COURAGE.

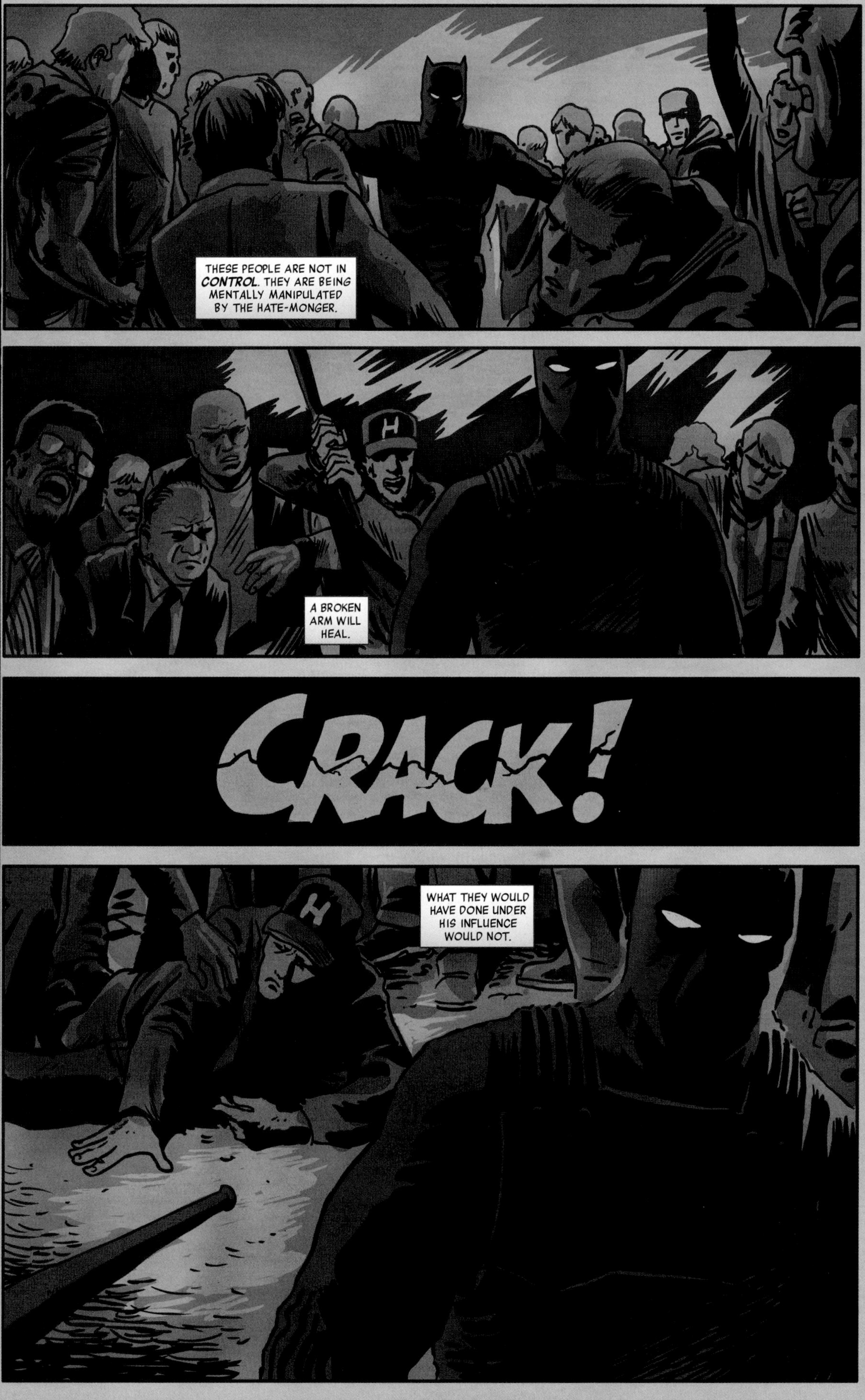
THESE PEOPLE ARE NOT IN CONTROL. THEY ARE BEING MENTALLY MANIPULATED BY THE HATE-MONGER.
A BROKEN ARM WILL HEAL.
CRACK!
WHAT THEY WOULD HAVE DONE UNDER HIS INFLUENCE WOULD NOT.

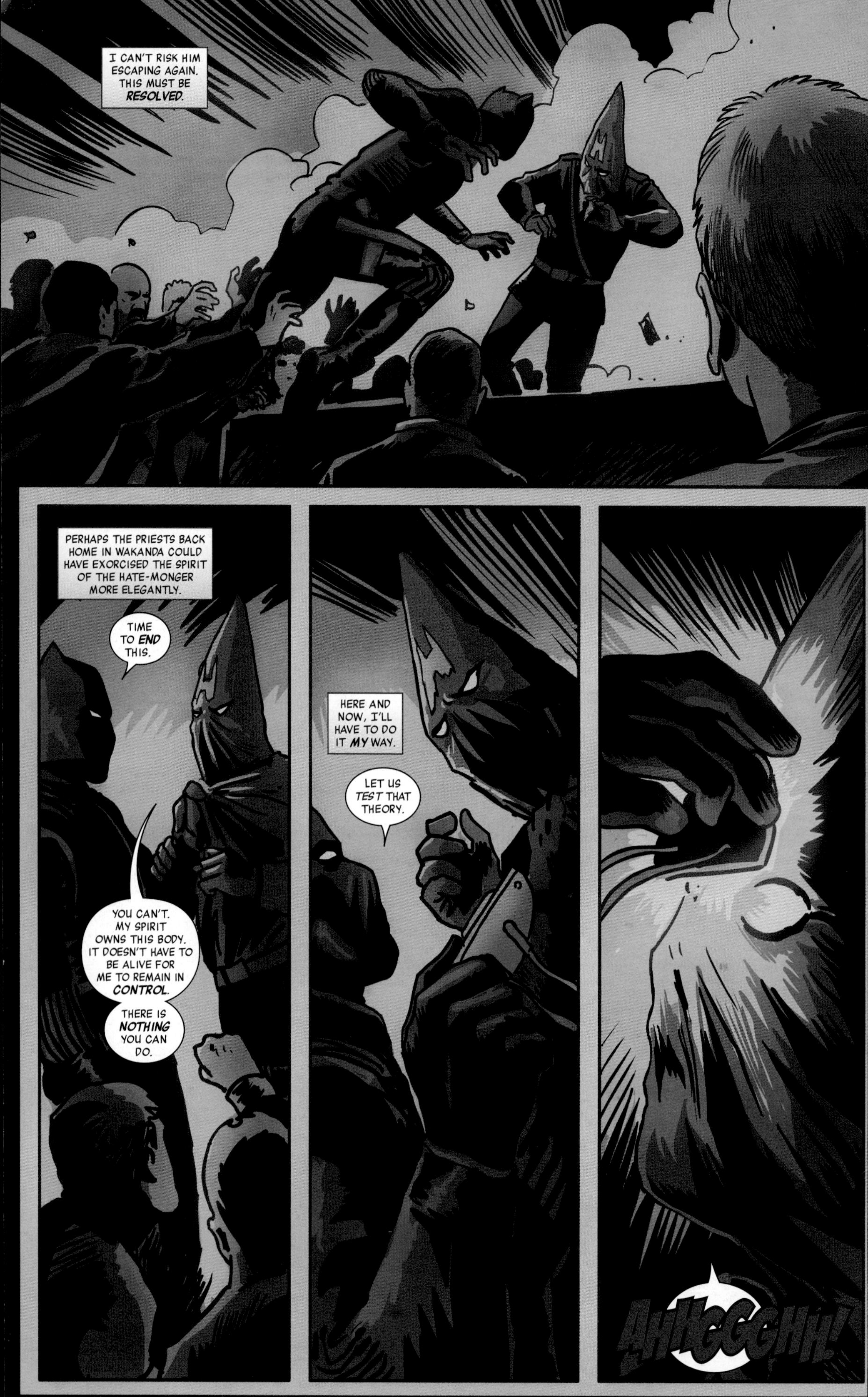
I CAN'T RISK HIM ESCAPING AGAIN. THIS MUST BE *RESOLVED*.
PERHAPS THE PRIESTS BACK HOME IN WAKANDA COULD HAVE EXORCISED THE SPIRIT OF THE HATE-MONGER MORE ELEGANTLY.
TIME TO *END* THIS.
YOU CAN'T. MY SPIRIT OWNS THIS BODY. IT DOESN'T HAVE TO BE ALIVE FOR ME TO REMAIN IN *CONTROL*.
THERE IS *NOTHING* YOU CAN DO.
HERE AND NOW, I'LL HAVE TO DO IT *MY* WAY.
LET US *TEST* THAT THEORY.
AHHGGGHH!

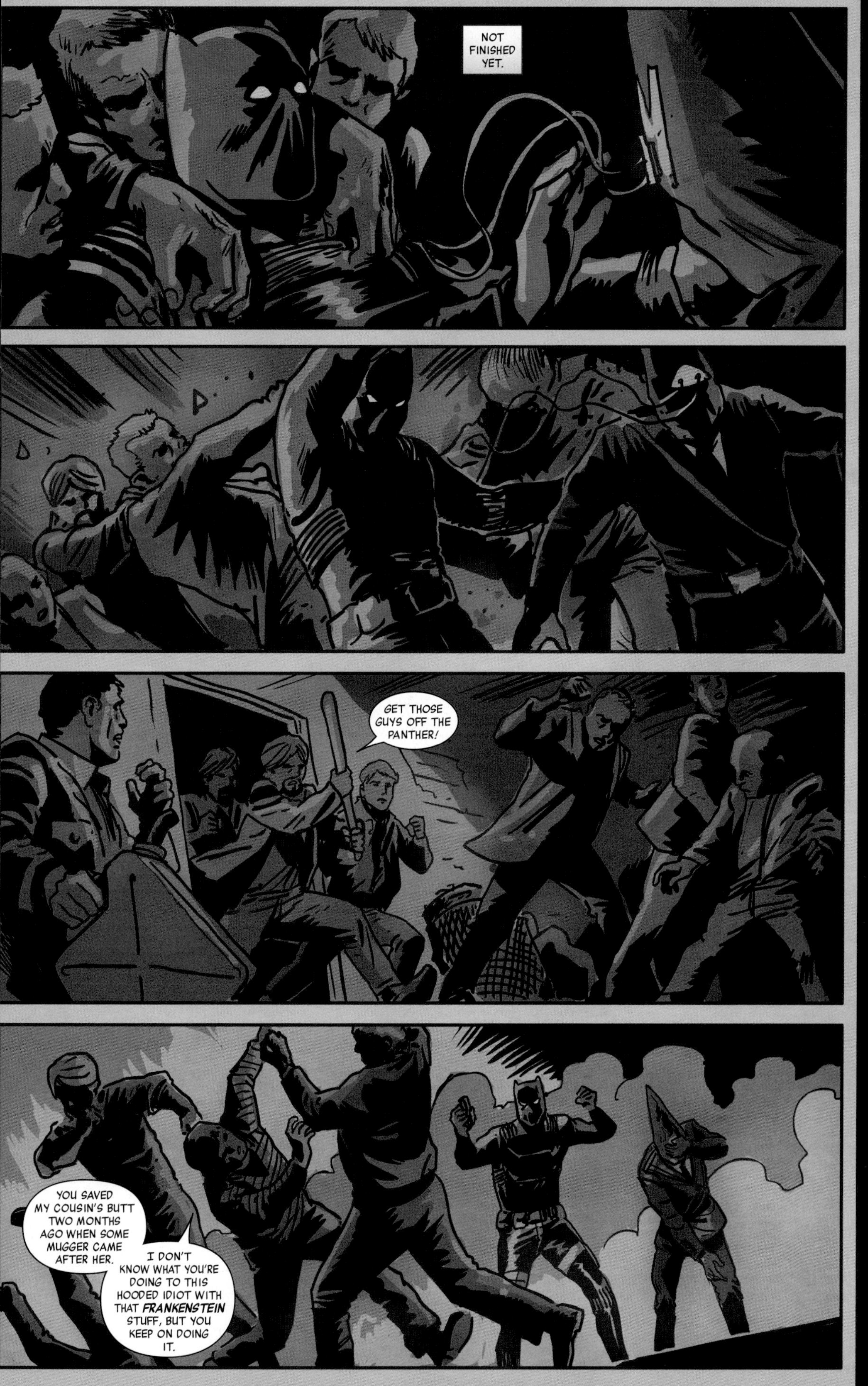
NOT FINISHED YET.
GET THOSE GUYS OFF THE PANTHER!
YOU SAVED MY COUSIN'S BUTT TWO MONTHS AGO WHEN SOME MUGGER CAME AFTER HER.
I DON'T KNOW WHAT YOU'RE DOING TO THIS HOODED IDIOT WITH THAT FRANKENSTEIN STUFF, BUT YOU KEEP ON DOING IT.

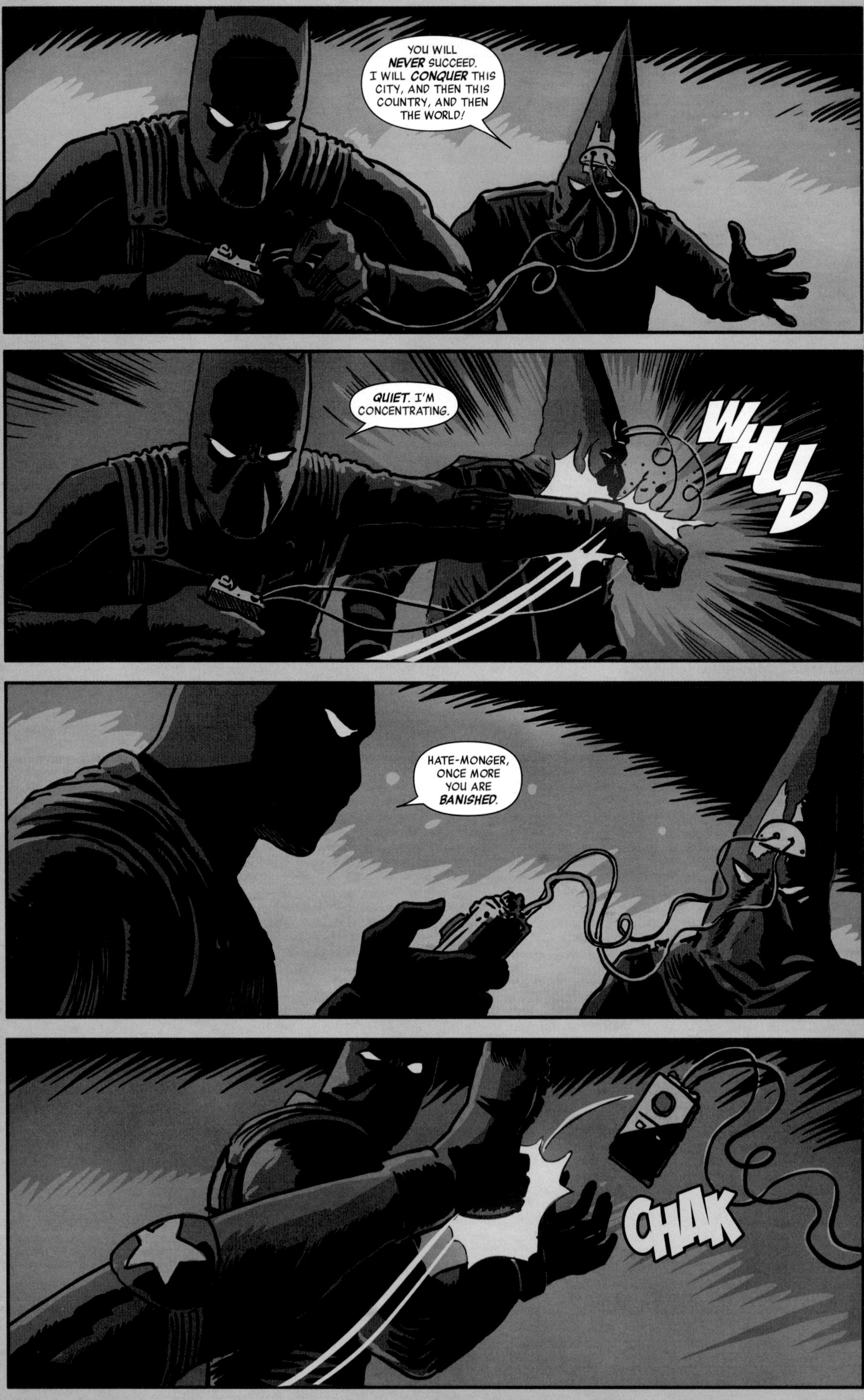

YOU WILL **NEVER** SUCCEED. I WILL **CONQUER** THIS CITY, AND THEN THIS COUNTRY, AND THEN THE WORLD!
QUIET. I'M CONCENTRATING.
WHUD
HATE-MONGER, ONCE MORE YOU ARE **BANISHED**.
CHAK

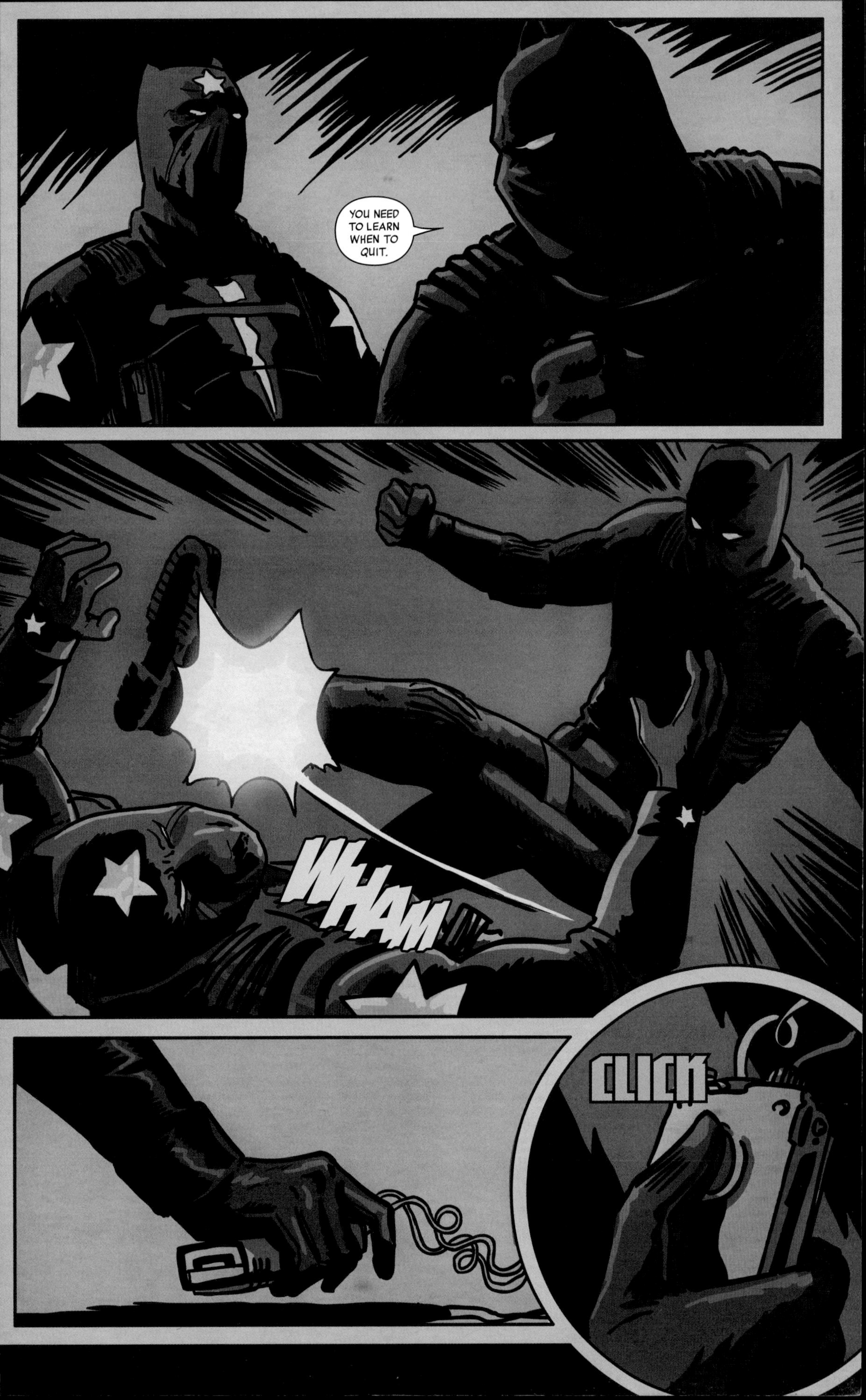
YOU NEED TO LEARN WHEN TO QUIT.
WHAM
CLICK

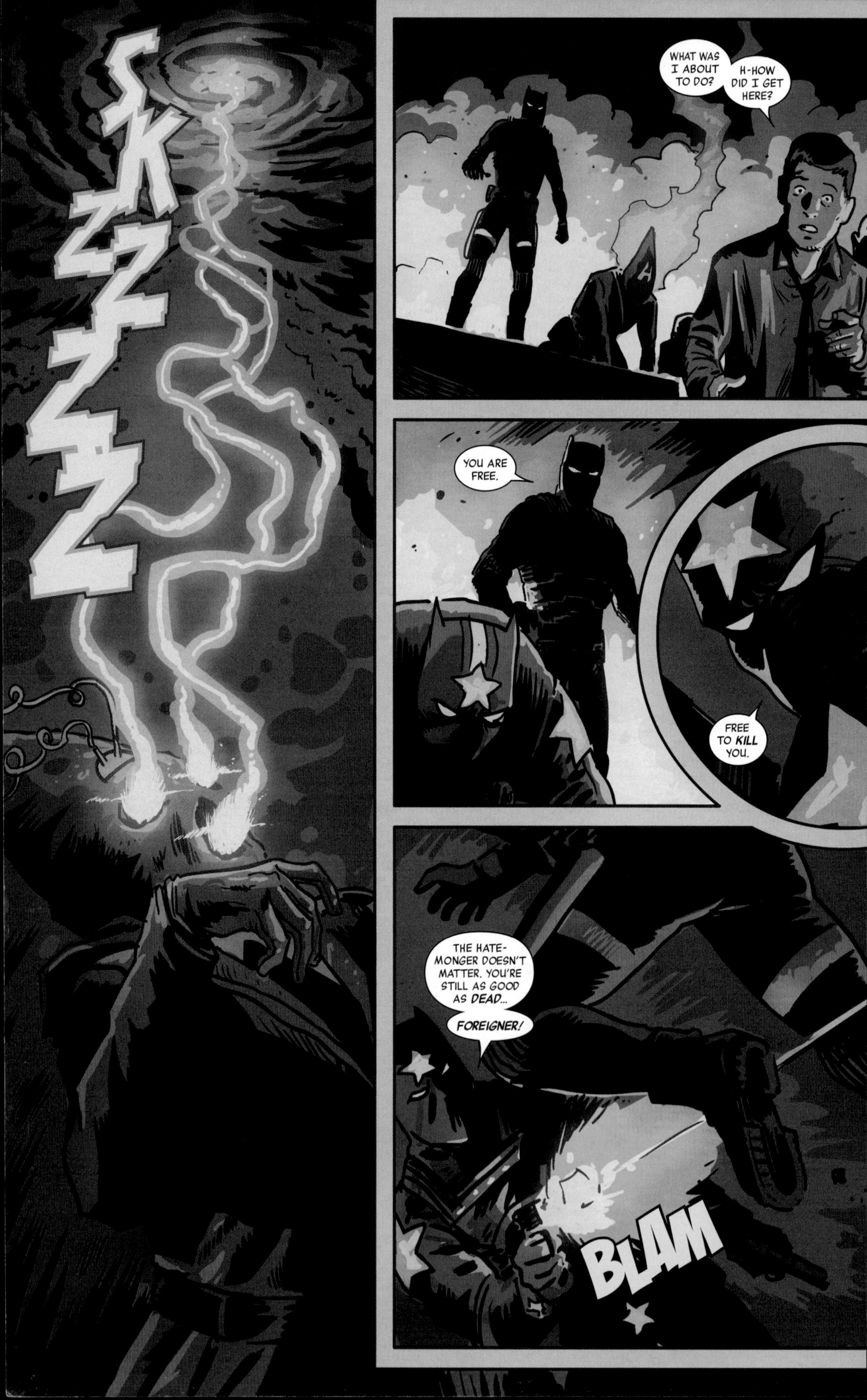
SKZZZZZ
WHAT WAS I ABOUT TO DO?
H-HOW DID I GET HERE?
YOU ARE FREE.
FREE TO KILL YOU.
THE HATE-MONGER DOESN'T MATTER. YOU'RE STILL AS GOOD AS DEAD...
FOREIGNER!
BLAM

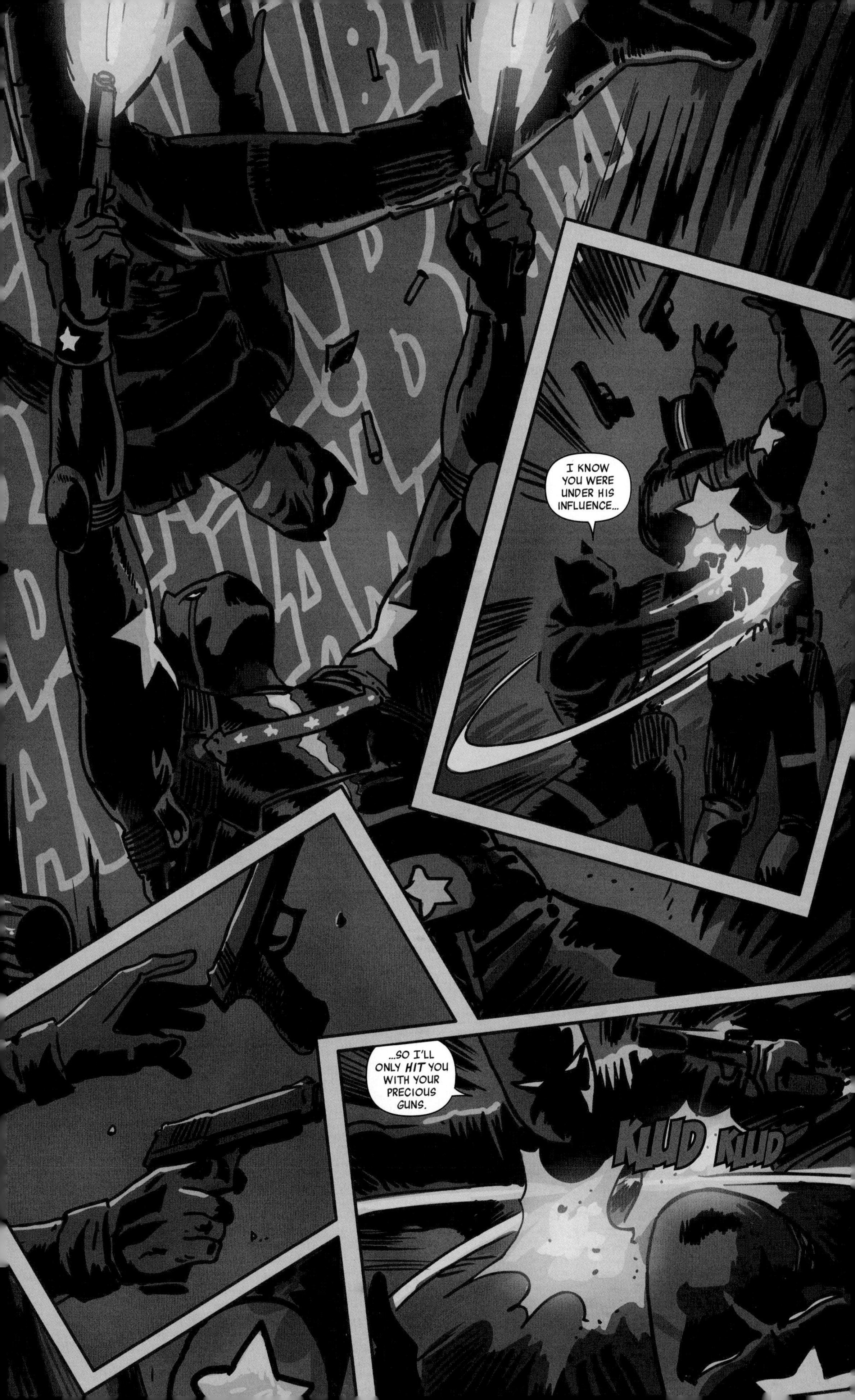

I KNOW YOU WERE UNDER HIS INFLUENCE...
...SO I'LL ONLY HIT YOU WITH YOUR PRECIOUS GUNS.
KLUD KLUD

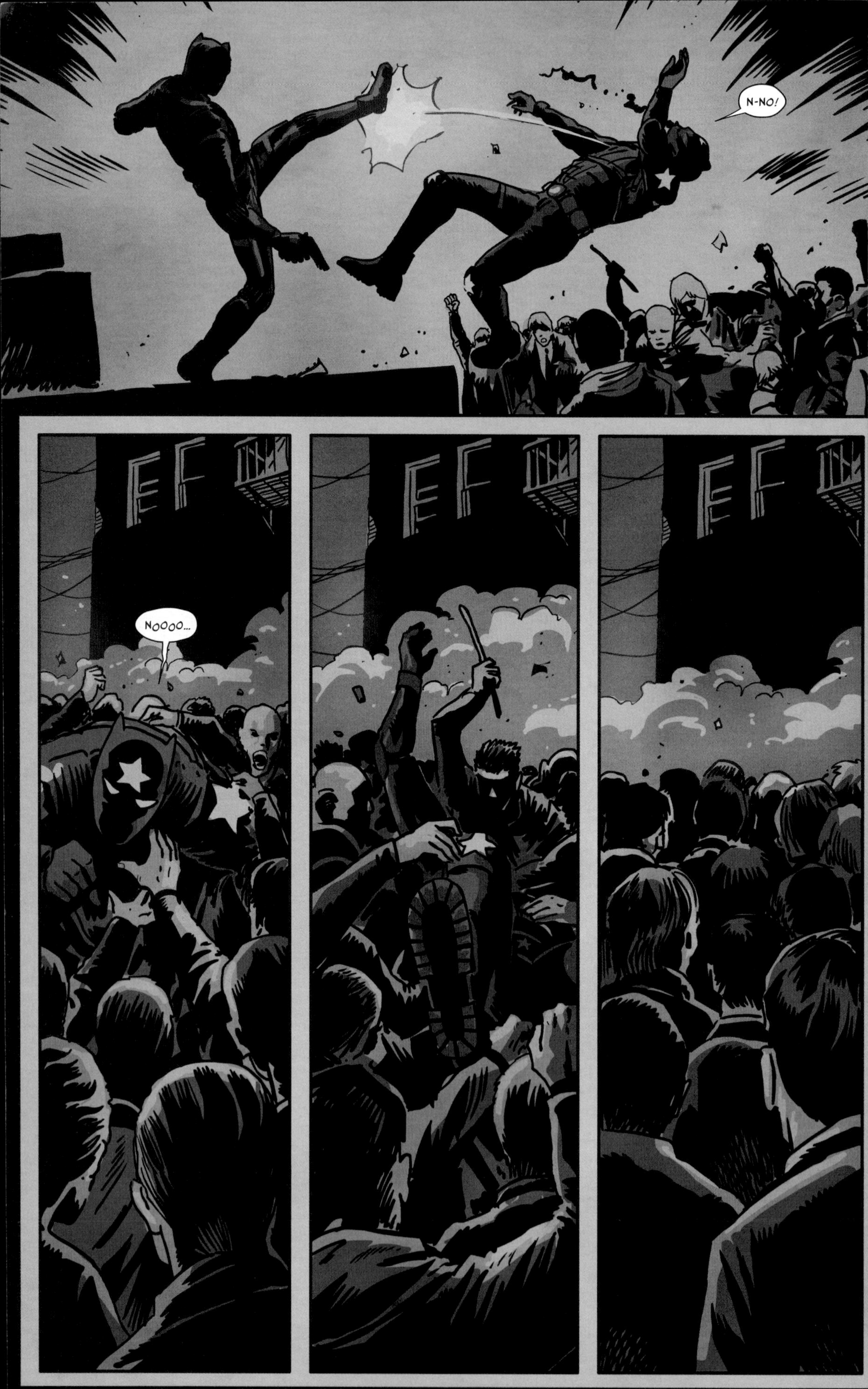
N-NO!
NOOOO...

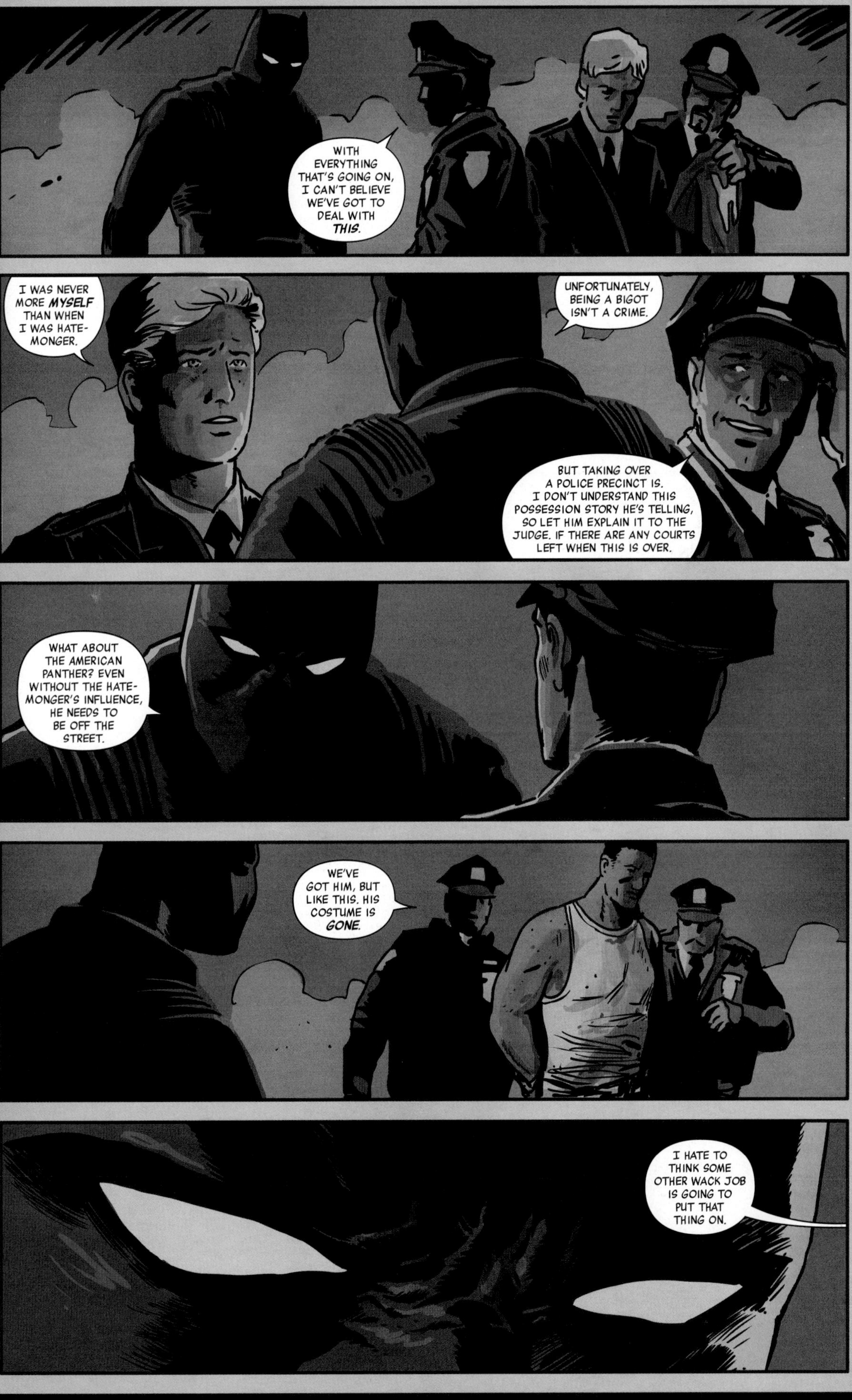
WITH EVERYTHING THAT'S GOING ON, I CAN'T BELIEVE WE'VE GOT TO DEAL WITH THIS.
I WAS NEVER MORE MYSELF THAN WHEN I WAS HATE-MONGER.
UNFORTUNATELY, BEING A BIGOT ISN'T A CRIME.
BUT TAKING OVER A POLICE PRECINCT IS. I DON'T UNDERSTAND THIS POSSESSION STORY HE'S TELLING, SO LET HIM EXPLAIN IT TO THE JUDGE. IF THERE ARE ANY COURTS LEFT WHEN THIS IS OVER.
WHAT ABOUT THE AMERICAN PANTHER? EVEN WITHOUT THE HATE-MONGER'S INFLUENCE, HE NEEDS TO BE OFF THE STREET.
WE'VE GOT HIM, BUT LIKE THIS. HIS COSTUME IS GONE.
I HATE TO THINK SOME OTHER WACK JOB IS GOING TO PUT THAT THING ON.

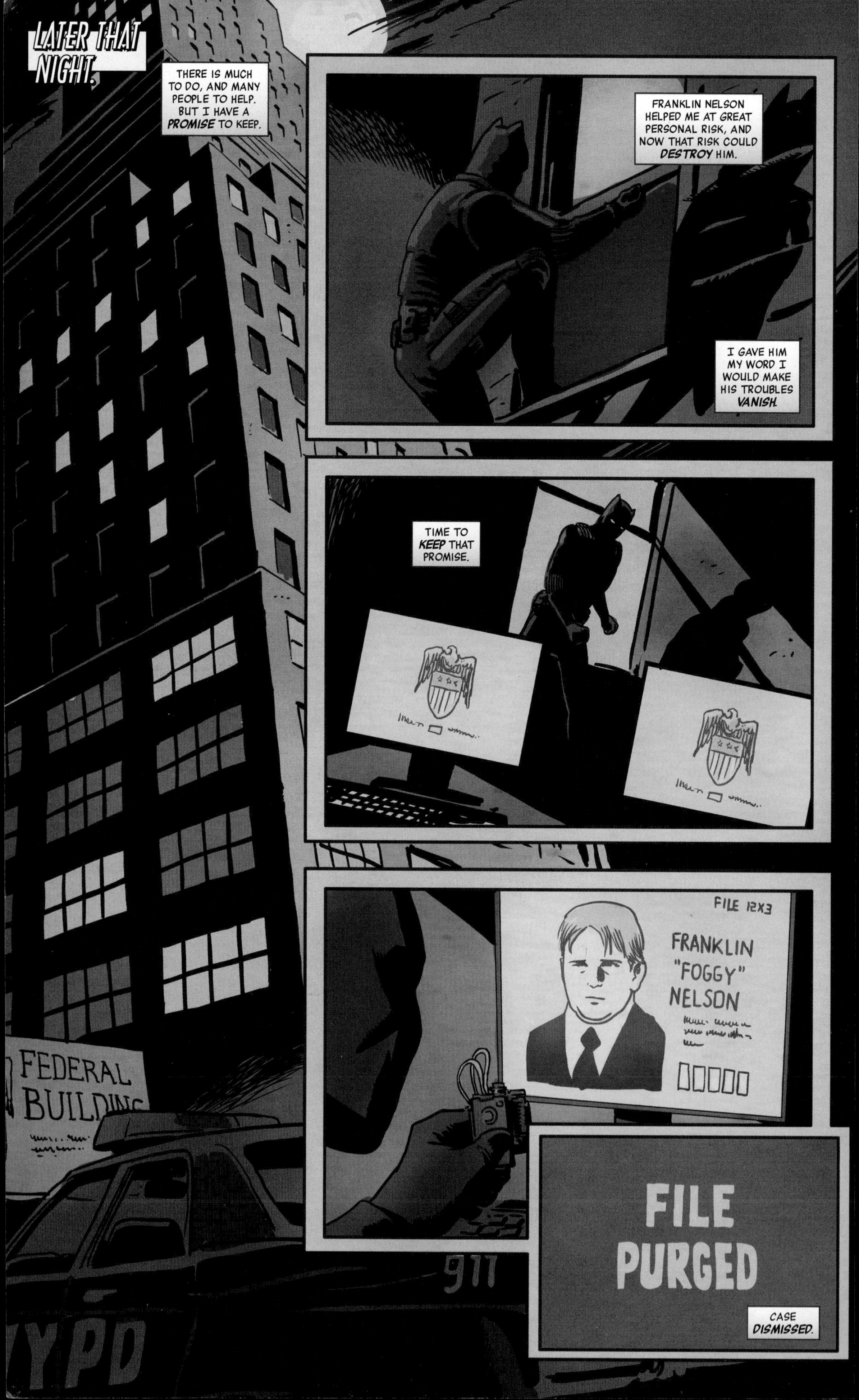
LATER THAT NIGHT.
THERE IS MUCH TO DO, AND MANY PEOPLE TO HELP. BUT I HAVE A PROMISE TO KEEP.
FRANKLIN NELSON HELPED ME AT GREAT PERSONAL RISK, AND NOW THAT RISK COULD DESTROY HIM.
I GAVE HIM MY WORD I WOULD MAKE HIS TROUBLES VANISH.
TIME TO KEEP THAT PROMISE.
FILE 12X3
FRANKLIN "FOGGY" NELSON
FILE PURGED
CASE DISMISSED.
FEDERAL BUILDING
911
NYPD

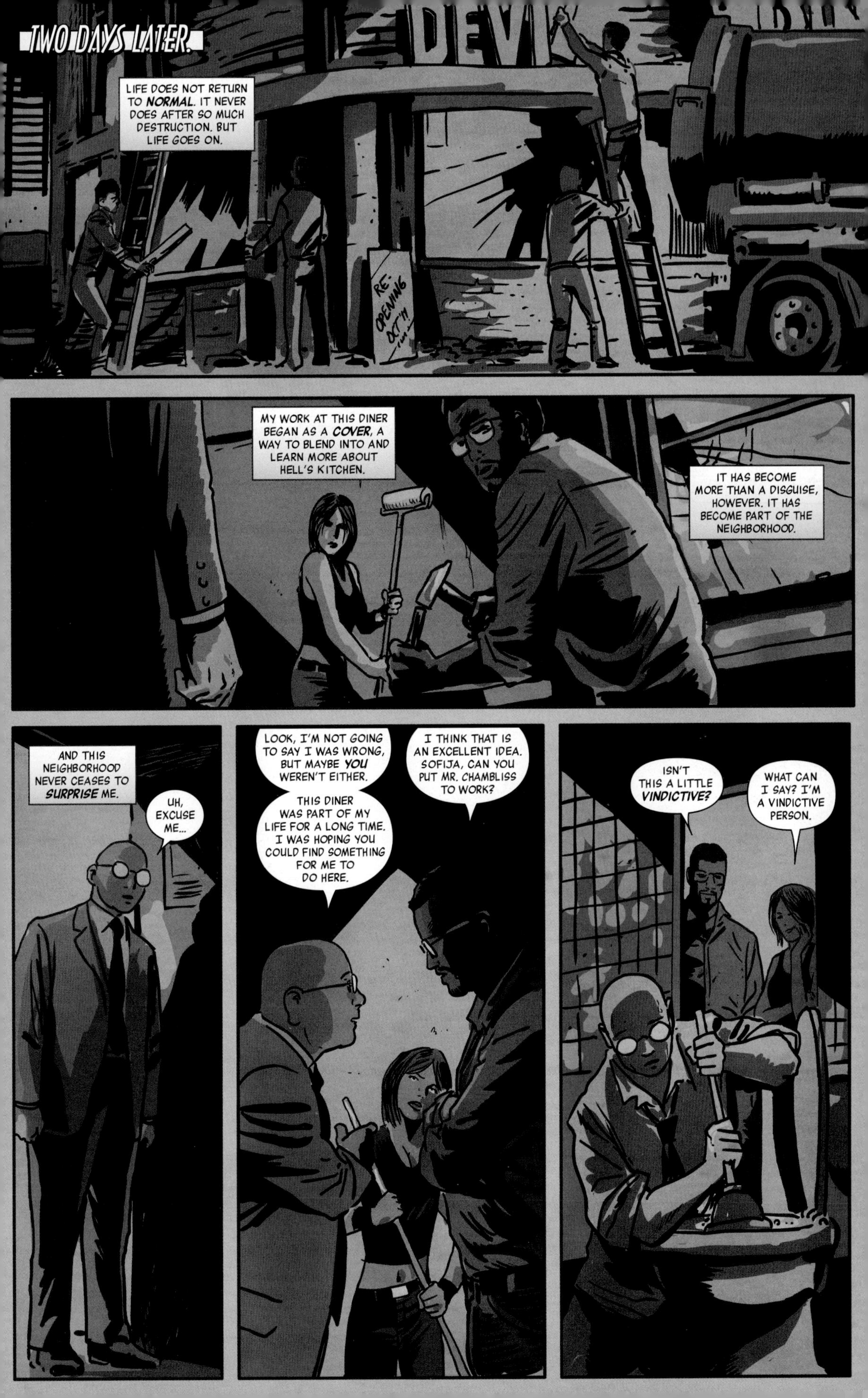
TWO DAYS LATER.
LIFE DOES NOT RETURN TO NORMAL. IT NEVER DOES AFTER SO MUCH DESTRUCTION. BUT LIFE GOES ON.
DEVI
RE-OPENING OCT '11
MY WORK AT THIS DINER BEGAN AS A COVER, A WAY TO BLEND INTO AND LEARN MORE ABOUT HELL'S KITCHEN.
IT HAS BECOME MORE THAN A DISGUISE, HOWEVER. IT HAS BECOME PART OF THE NEIGHBORHOOD.
AND THIS NEIGHBORHOOD NEVER CEASES TO SURPRISE ME.
UH, EXCUSE ME...
LOOK, I'M NOT GOING TO SAY I WAS WRONG, BUT MAYBE YOU WEREN'T EITHER.
THIS DINER WAS PART OF MY LIFE FOR A LONG TIME. I WAS HOPING YOU COULD FIND SOMETHING FOR ME TO DO HERE.
I THINK THAT IS AN EXCELLENT IDEA. SOFIJA, CAN YOU PUT MR. CHAMBLISS TO WORK?
ISN'T THIS A LITTLE VINDICTIVE?
WHAT CAN I SAY? I'M A VINDICTIVE PERSON.

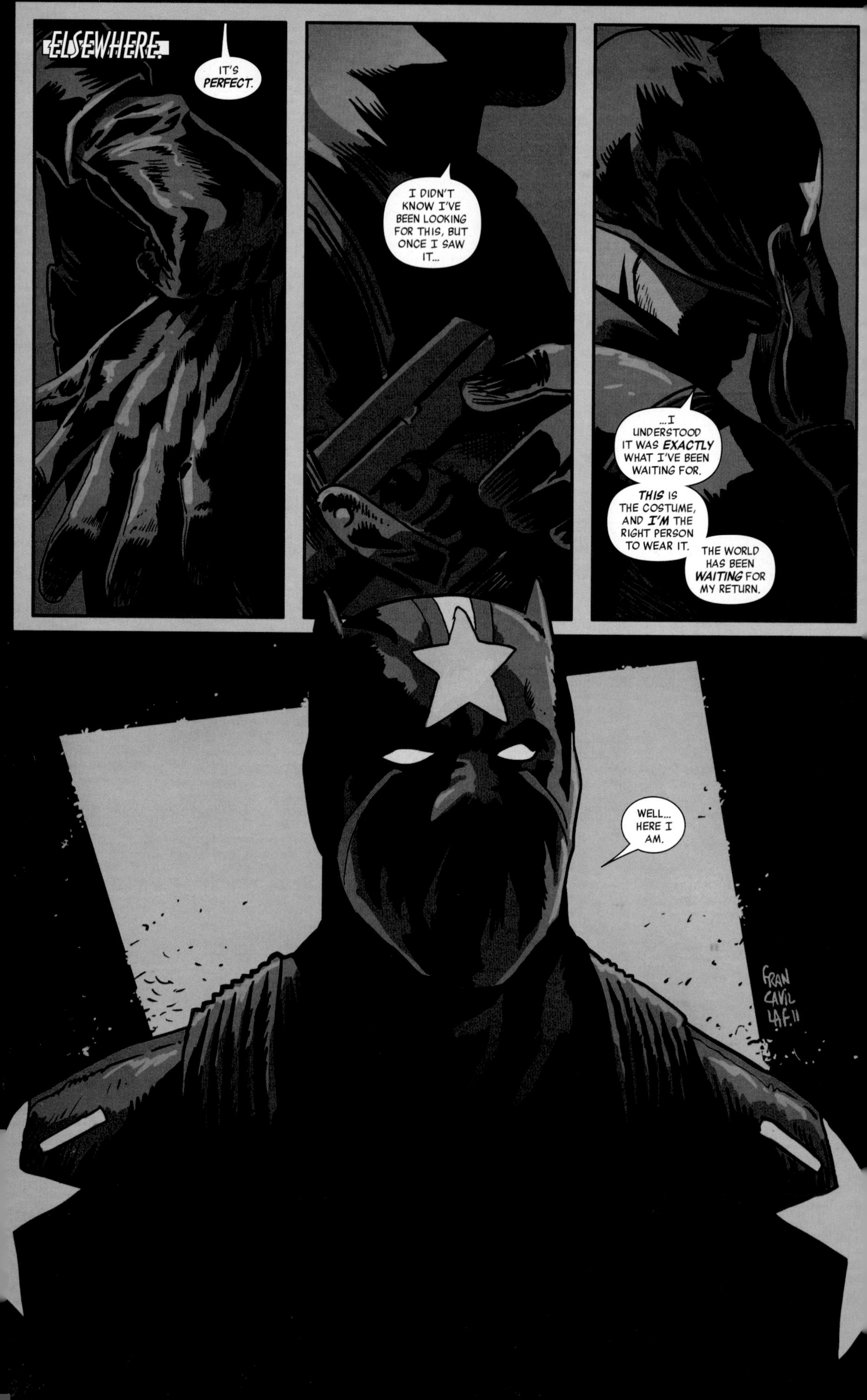
ELSEWHERE.
IT'S PERFECT.
I DIDN'T KNOW I'VE BEEN LOOKING FOR THIS, BUT ONCE I SAW IT...
...I UNDERSTOOD IT WAS EXACTLY WHAT I'VE BEEN WAITING FOR.
THIS IS THE COSTUME, AND I'M THE RIGHT PERSON TO WEAR IT.
THE WORLD HAS BEEN WAITING FOR MY RETURN.
WELL... HERE I AM.
FRAN CAVIL LAF.11

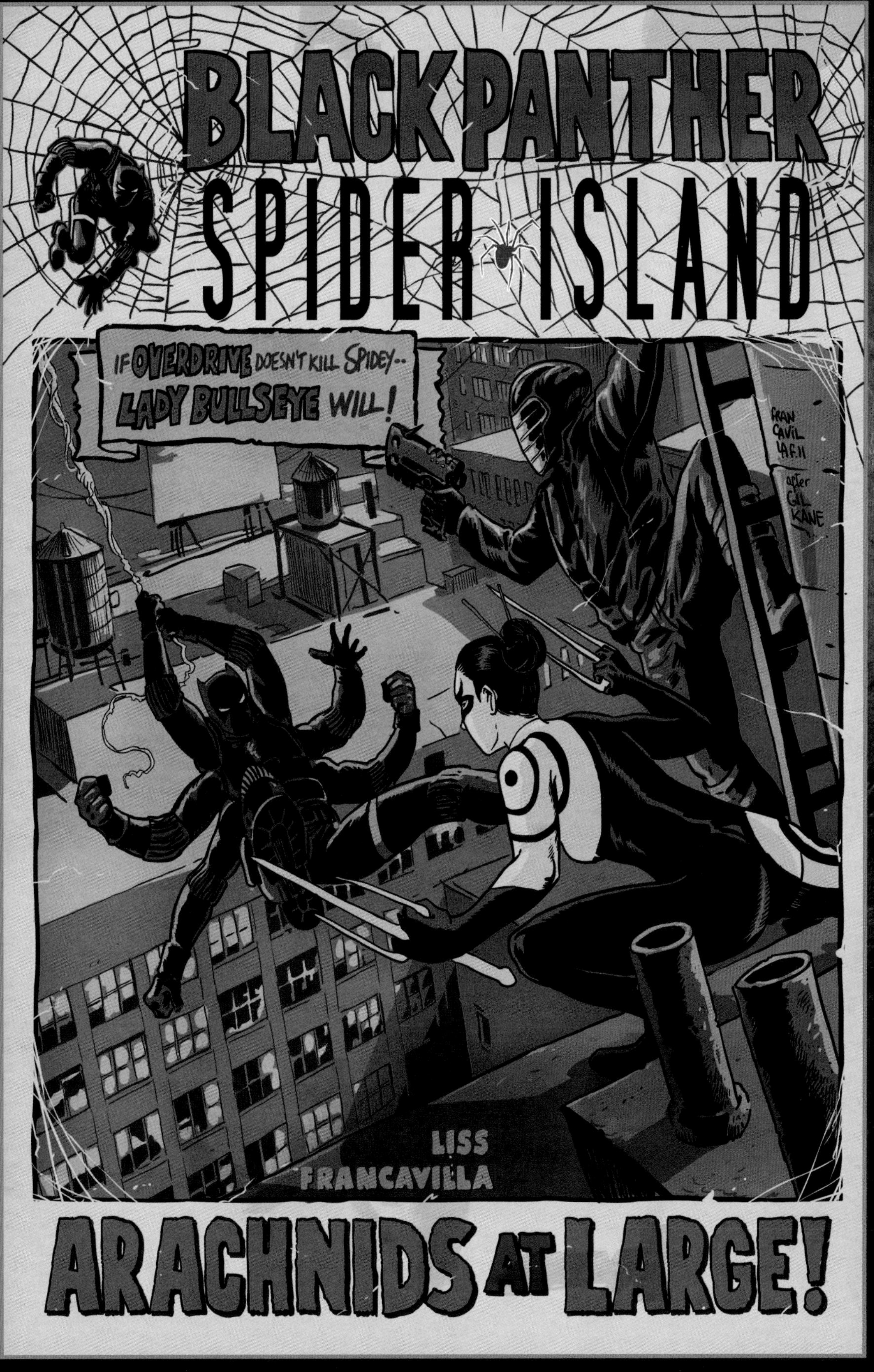
BLACK PANTHER
SPIDER ISLAND
IF OVERDRIVE DOESN'T KILL SPIDEY--
LADY BULLSEYE WILL!
FRAN CAVIL 14.F.11
after GIL KANE
LISS
FRANCAVILLA
ARACHNIDS AT LARGE!

BLACK PANTHER:
THE MOST DANGEROUS MAN ALIVE #524

SPIDER-ISLAND
BLACK PANTHER:
THE MOST DANGEROUS MAN ALIVE!

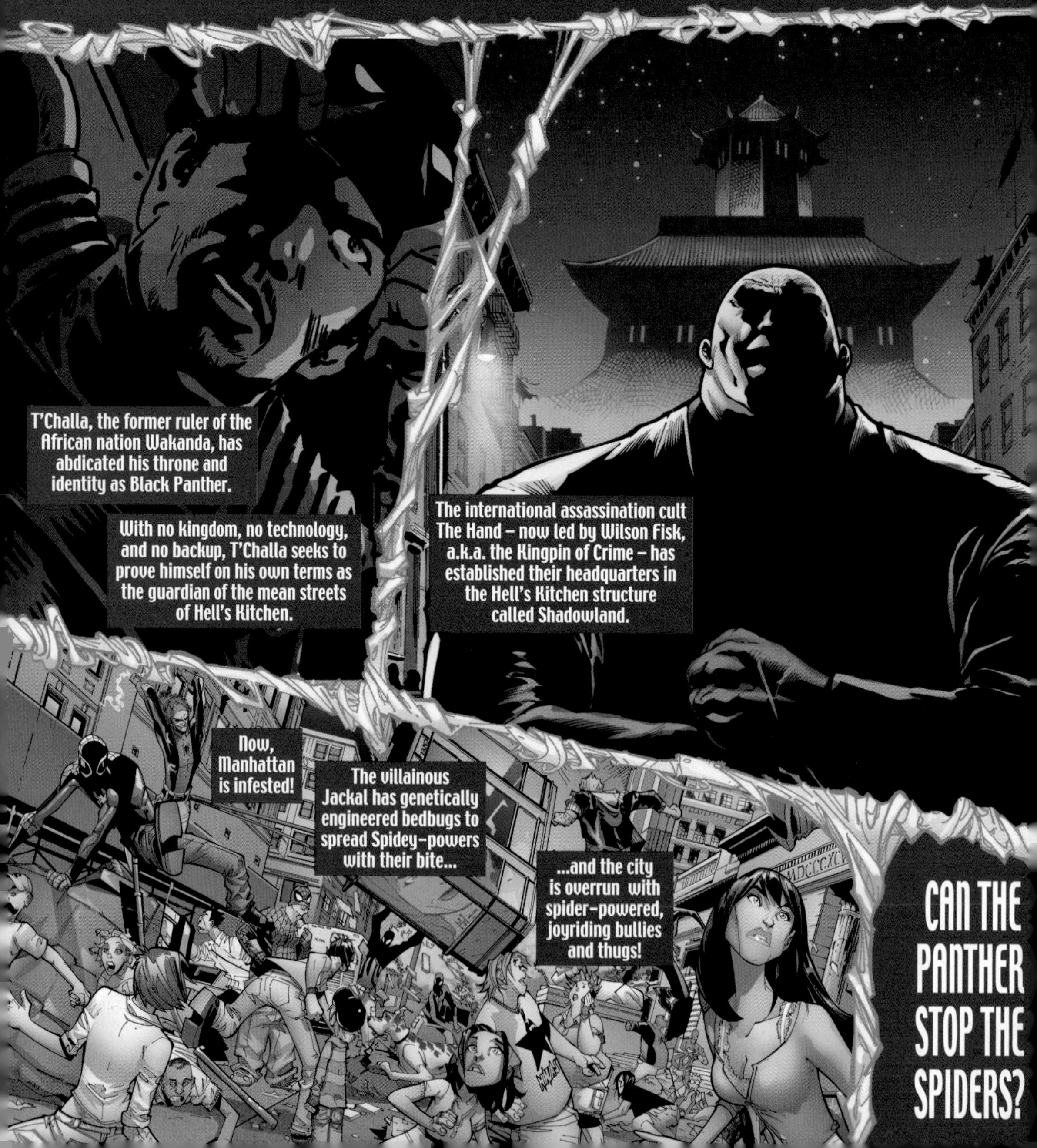
T'Challa, the former ruler of the African nation Wakanda, has abdicated his throne and identity as Black Panther.
With no kingdom, no technology, and no backup, T'Challa seeks to prove himself on his own terms as the guardian of the mean streets of Hell's Kitchen.
The international assassination cult The Hand – now led by Wilson Fisk, a.k.a. the Kingpin of Crime – has established their headquarters in the Hell's Kitchen structure called Shadowland.
Now, Manhattan is infested!
The villainous Jackal has genetically engineered bedbugs to spread Spidey-powers with their bite...
...and the city is overrun with spider-powered, joyriding bullies and thugs!
CAN THE PANTHER STOP THE SPIDERS?

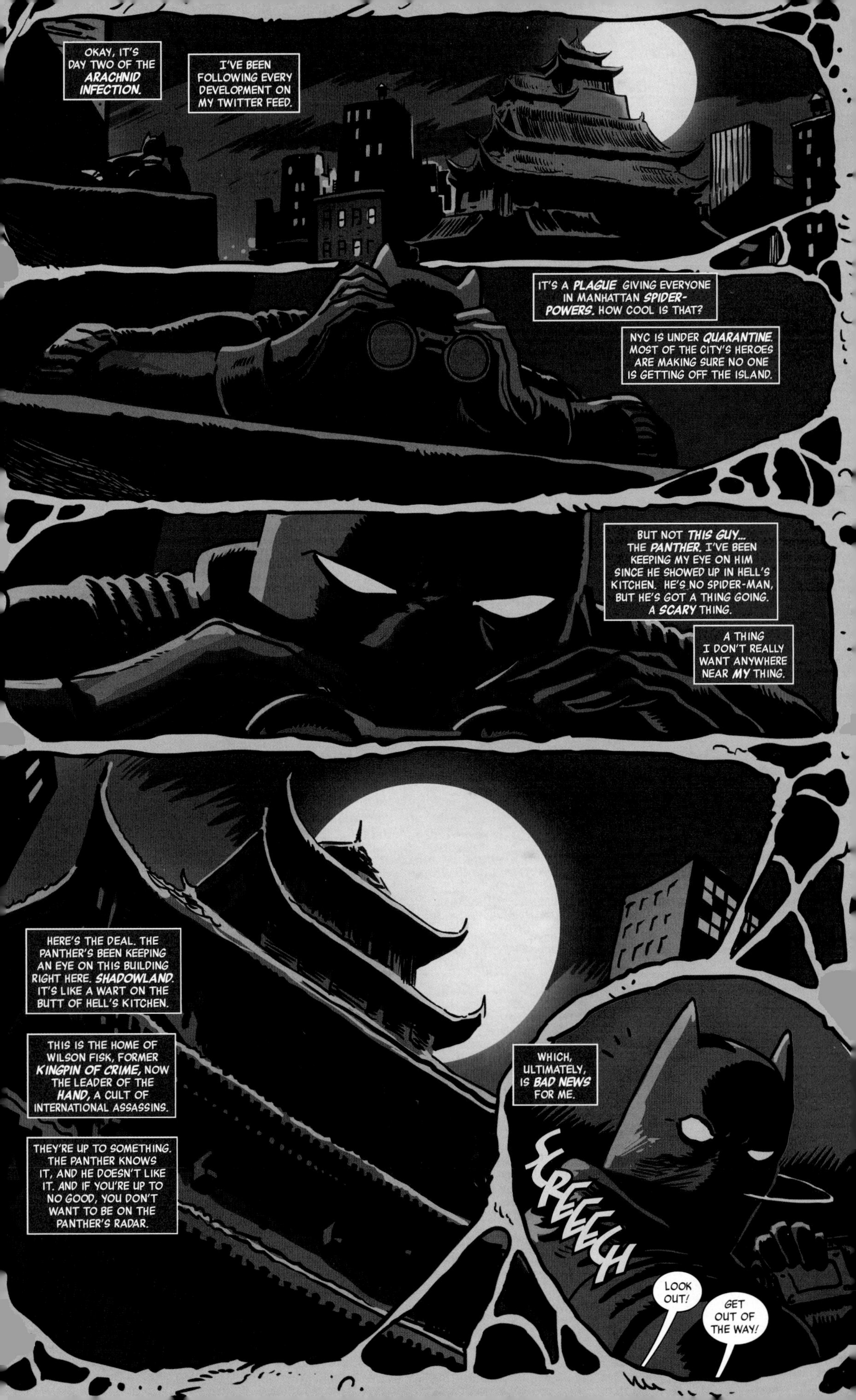
OKAY, IT'S DAY TWO OF THE ARACHNID INFECTION.
I'VE BEEN FOLLOWING EVERY DEVELOPMENT ON MY TWITTER FEED.
IT'S A PLAGUE GIVING EVERYONE IN MANHATTAN SPIDER-POWERS. HOW COOL IS THAT?
NYC IS UNDER QUARANTINE. MOST OF THE CITY'S HEROES ARE MAKING SURE NO ONE IS GETTING OFF THE ISLAND.
BUT NOT THIS GUY... THE PANTHER. I'VE BEEN KEEPING MY EYE ON HIM SINCE HE SHOWED UP IN HELL'S KITCHEN. HE'S NO SPIDER-MAN, BUT HE'S GOT A THING GOING. A SCARY THING.
A THING I DON'T REALLY WANT ANYWHERE NEAR MY THING.
HERE'S THE DEAL. THE PANTHER'S BEEN KEEPING AN EYE ON THIS BUILDING RIGHT HERE. SHADOWLAND. IT'S LIKE A WART ON THE BUTT OF HELL'S KITCHEN.
THIS IS THE HOME OF WILSON FISK, FORMER KINGPIN OF CRIME, NOW THE LEADER OF THE HAND, A CULT OF INTERNATIONAL ASSASSINS.
THEY'RE UP TO SOMETHING. THE PANTHER KNOWS IT, AND HE DOESN'T LIKE IT. AND IF YOU'RE UP TO NO GOOD, YOU DON'T WANT TO BE ON THE PANTHER'S RADAR.
WHICH, ULTIMATELY, IS BAD NEWS FOR ME.
SCREEECH
LOOK OUT!
GET OUT OF THE WAY!

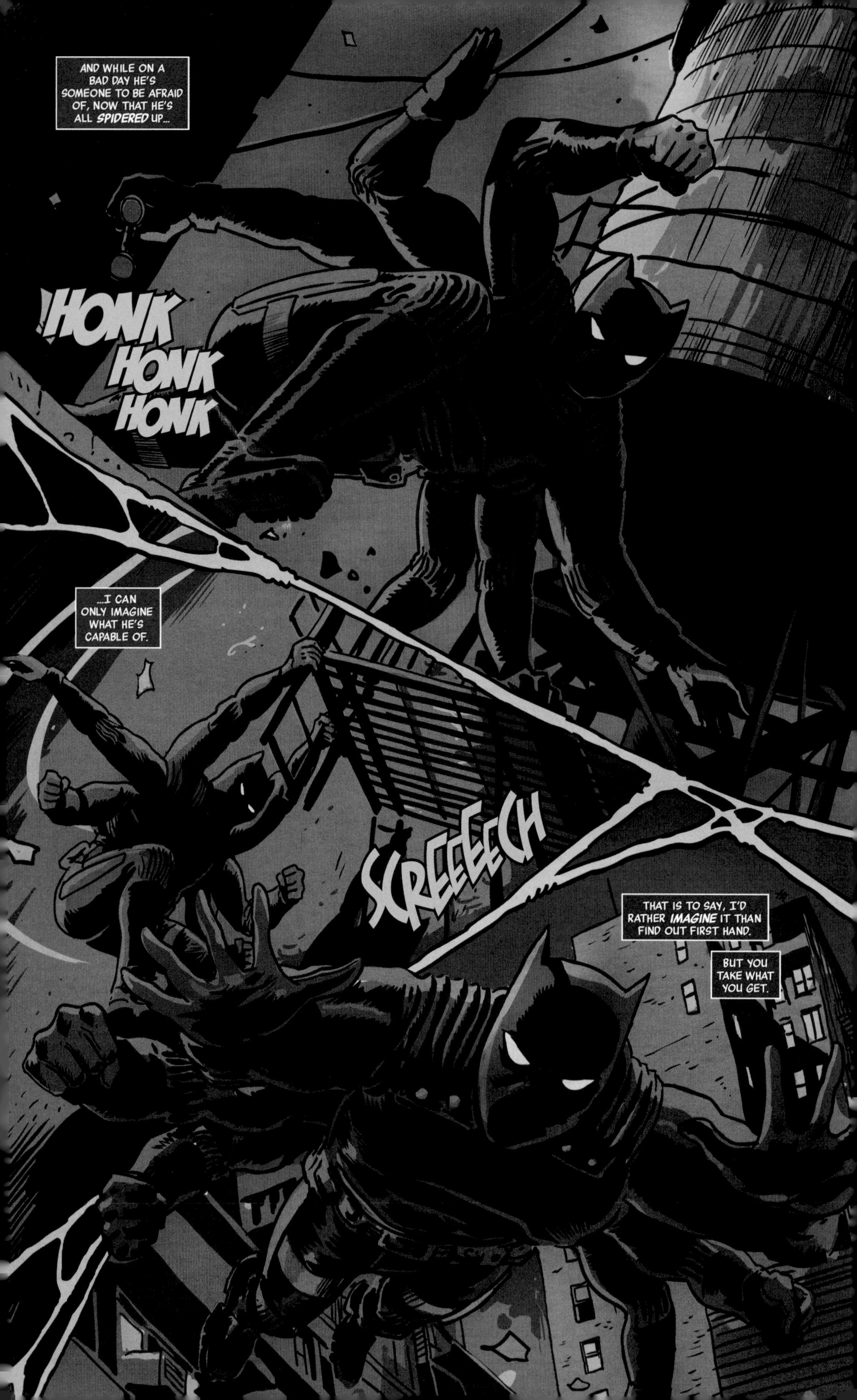

AND WHILE ON A BAD DAY HE'S SOMEONE TO BE AFRAID OF, NOW THAT HE'S ALL SPIDERED UP...
HONK HONK HONK
...I CAN ONLY IMAGINE WHAT HE'S CAPABLE OF.
SCREEEECH
THAT IS TO SAY, I'D RATHER IMAGINE IT THAN FIND OUT FIRST HAND.
BUT YOU TAKE WHAT YOU GET.

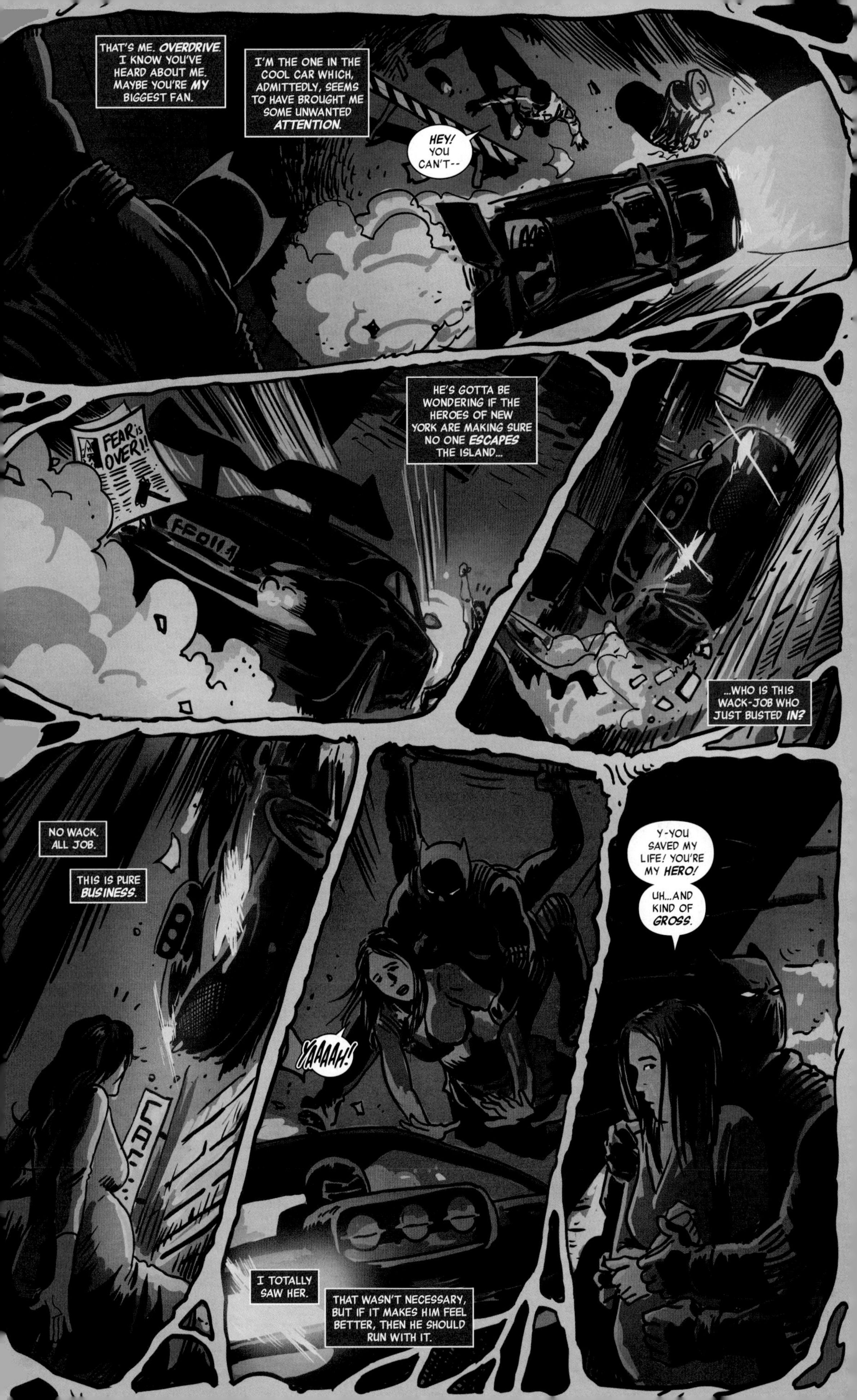
THAT'S ME. OVERDRIVE. I KNOW YOU'VE HEARD ABOUT ME. MAYBE YOU'RE MY BIGGEST FAN.
I'M THE ONE IN THE COOL CAR WHICH, ADMITTEDLY, SEEMS TO HAVE BROUGHT ME SOME UNWANTED ATTENTION.
HEY! YOU CAN'T--
FEAR is OVER!!
HE'S GOTTA BE WONDERING IF THE HEROES OF NEW YORK ARE MAKING SURE NO ONE ESCAPES THE ISLAND...
...WHO IS THIS WACK-JOB WHO JUST BUSTED IN?
NO WACK. ALL JOB.
THIS IS PURE BUSINESS.
YAAAAH!
I TOTALLY SAW HER.
THAT WASN'T NECESSARY, BUT IF IT MAKES HIM FEEL BETTER, THEN HE SHOULD RUN WITH IT.
Y-YOU SAVED MY LIFE! YOU'RE MY HERO!
UH...AND KIND OF GROSS.

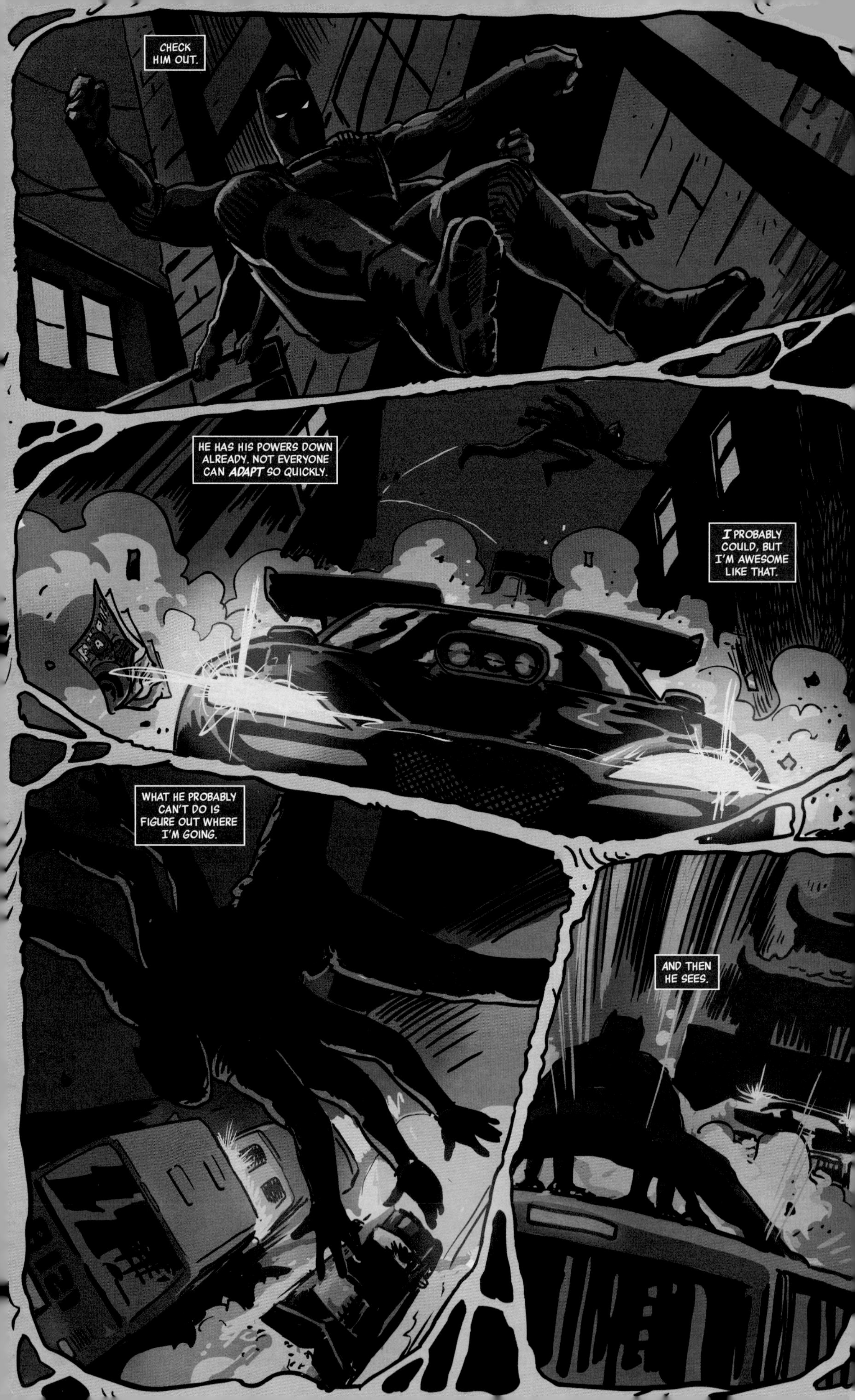
CHECK HIM OUT.
HE HAS HIS POWERS DOWN ALREADY. NOT EVERYONE CAN ADAPT SO QUICKLY.
I PROBABLY COULD, BUT I'M AWESOME LIKE THAT.
WHAT HE PROBABLY CAN'T DO IS FIGURE OUT WHERE I'M GOING.
AND THEN HE SEES.

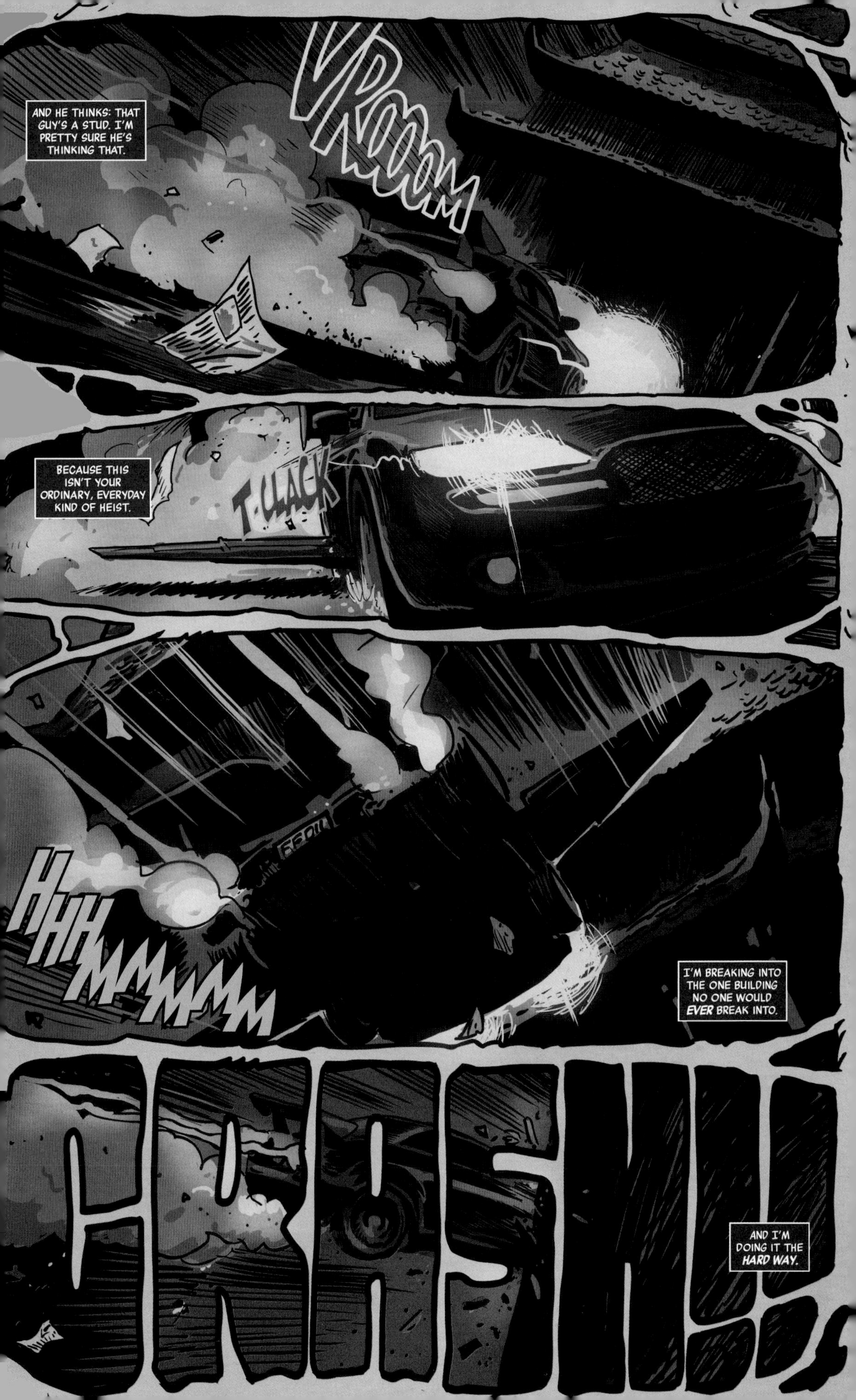
AND HE THINKS: THAT GUY'S A STUD. I'M PRETTY SURE HE'S THINKING THAT.
VROOOOM
BECAUSE THIS ISN'T YOUR ORDINARY, EVERYDAY KIND OF HEIST.
T-CLACK
HHHMMMMMM
I'M BREAKING INTO THE ONE BUILDING NO ONE WOULD *EVER* BREAK INTO.
CRRASH!!
AND I'M DOING IT THE *HARD WAY*.

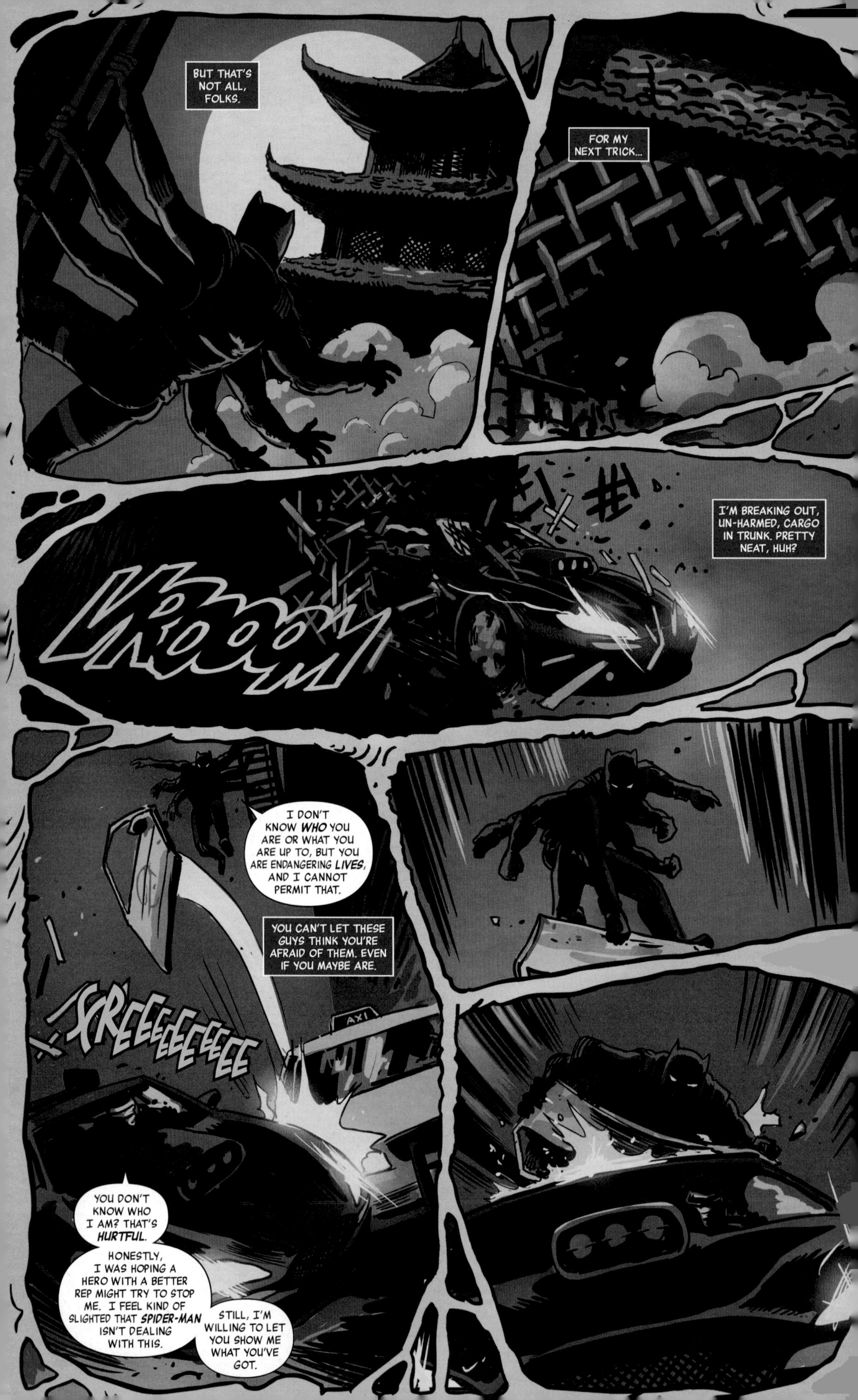

BUT THAT'S NOT ALL, FOLKS.
FOR MY NEXT TRICK...
KROOOM
I'M BREAKING OUT, UN-HARMED, CARGO IN TRUNK. PRETTY NEAT, HUH?
I DON'T KNOW WHO YOU ARE OR WHAT YOU ARE UP TO, BUT YOU ARE ENDANGERING LIVES, AND I CANNOT PERMIT THAT.
YOU CAN'T LET THESE GUYS THINK YOU'RE AFRAID OF THEM. EVEN IF YOU MAYBE ARE.
SCREEEEEEEEEE
TAXI
YOU DON'T KNOW WHO I AM? THAT'S HURTFUL.
HONESTLY, I WAS HOPING A HERO WITH A BETTER REP MIGHT TRY TO STOP ME. I FEEL KIND OF SLIGHTED THAT SPIDER-MAN ISN'T DEALING WITH THIS.
STILL, I'M WILLING TO LET YOU SHOW ME WHAT YOU'VE GOT.

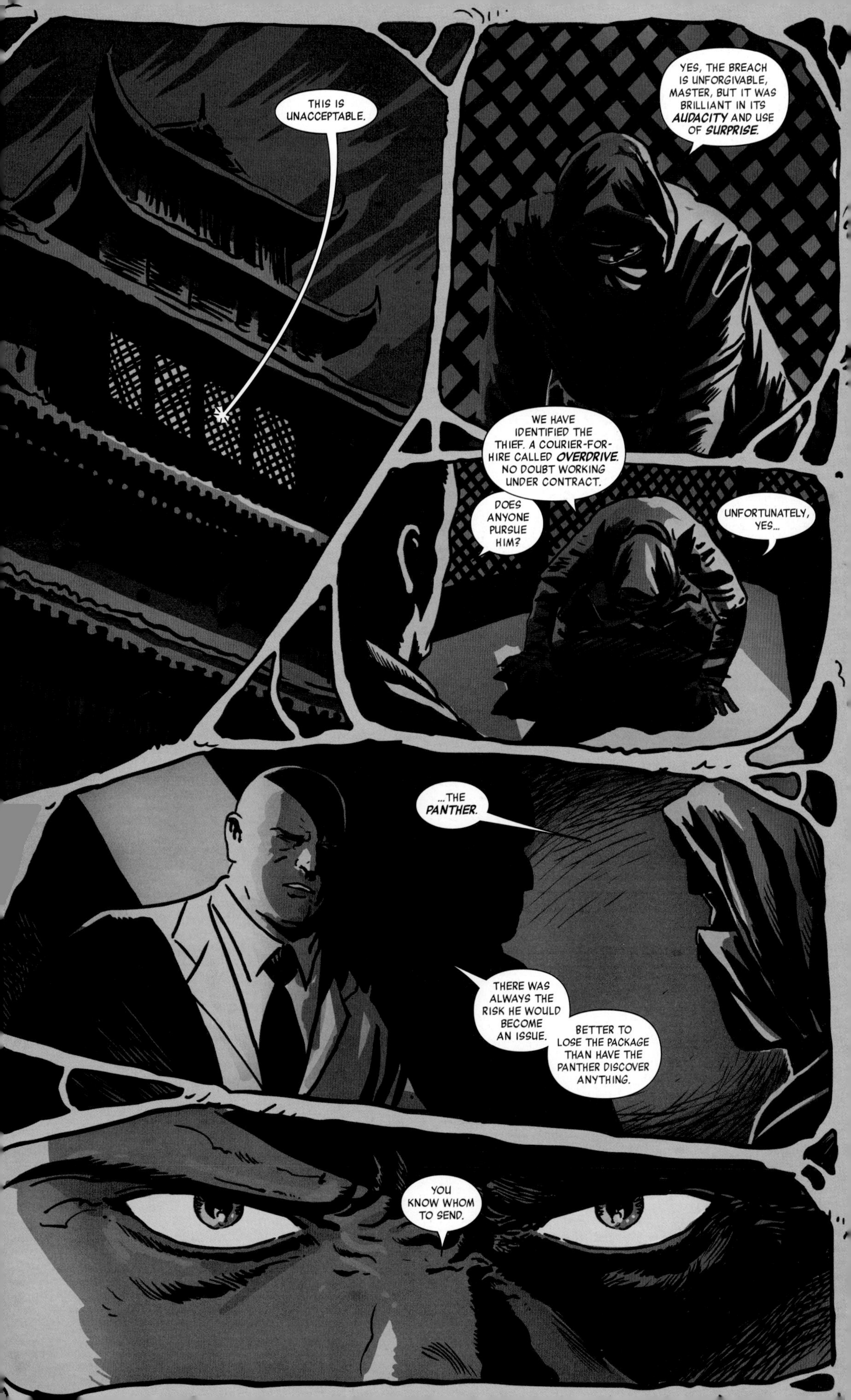
THIS IS UNACCEPTABLE.
YES, THE BREACH IS UNFORGIVABLE, MASTER, BUT IT WAS BRILLIANT IN ITS AUDACITY AND USE OF SURPRISE.
WE HAVE IDENTIFIED THE THIEF. A COURIER-FOR-HIRE CALLED OVERDRIVE. NO DOUBT WORKING UNDER CONTRACT.
DOES ANYONE PURSUE HIM?
UNFORTUNATELY, YES...
...THE PANTHER.
THERE WAS ALWAYS THE RISK HE WOULD BECOME AN ISSUE.
BETTER TO LOSE THE PACKAGE THAN HAVE THE PANTHER DISCOVER ANYTHING.
YOU KNOW WHOM TO SEND.

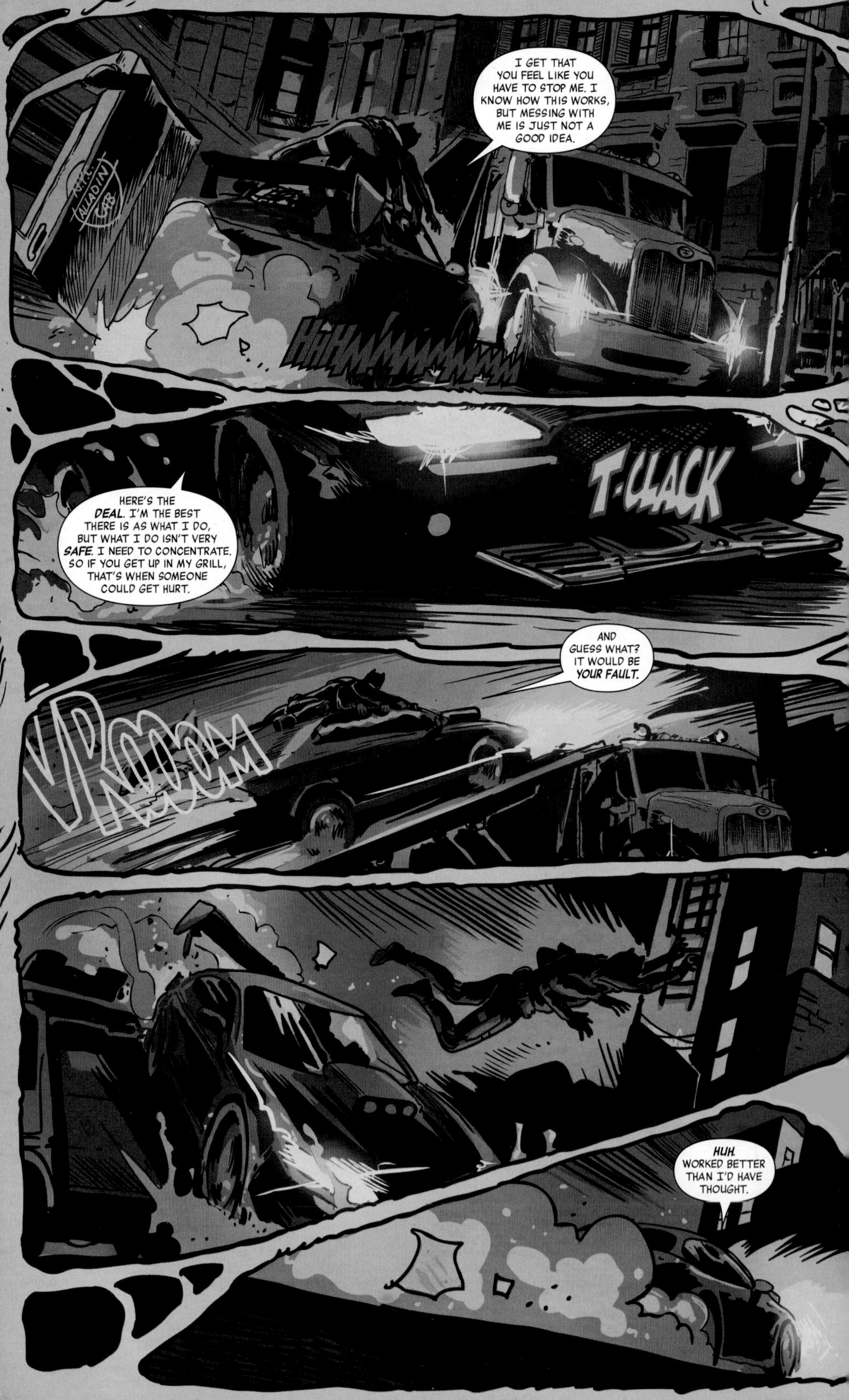
I GET THAT YOU FEEL LIKE YOU HAVE TO STOP ME. I KNOW HOW THIS WORKS, BUT MESSING WITH ME IS JUST NOT A GOOD IDEA.
ALLADIN CAB
HHHMMMMMMMMM
T-CLACK
HERE'S THE DEAL. I'M THE BEST THERE IS AS WHAT I DO, BUT WHAT I DO ISN'T VERY SAFE. I NEED TO CONCENTRATE. SO IF YOU GET UP IN MY GRILL, THAT'S WHEN SOMEONE COULD GET HURT.
AND GUESS WHAT? IT WOULD BE YOUR FAULT.
VROOOOM
HUH. WORKED BETTER THAN I'D HAVE THOUGHT.

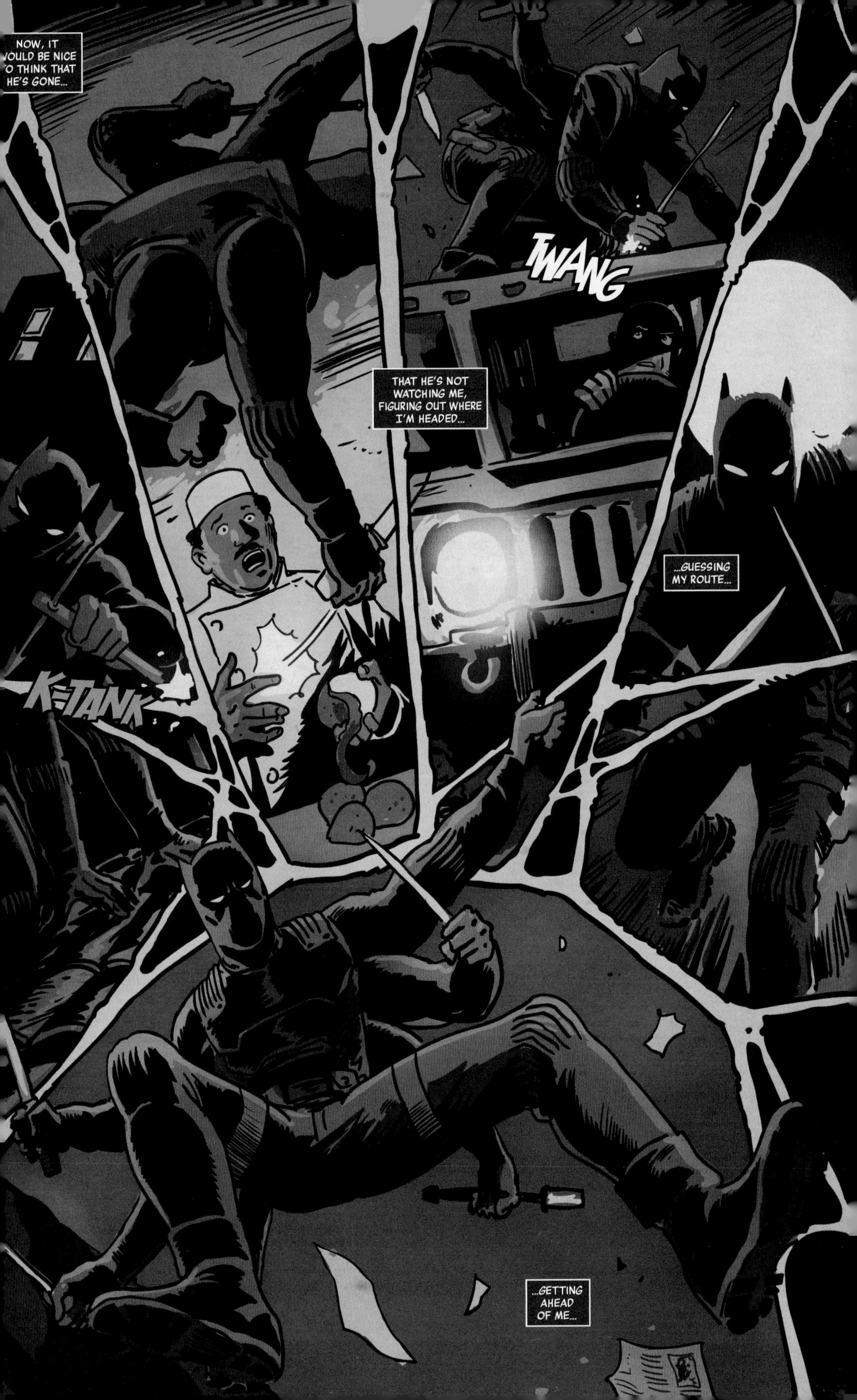
NOW, IT WOULD BE NICE TO THINK THAT HE'S GONE...
TWANG
THAT HE'S NOT WATCHING ME, FIGURING OUT WHERE I'M HEADED...
...GUESSING MY ROUTE...
K-TANK
...GETTING AHEAD OF ME...

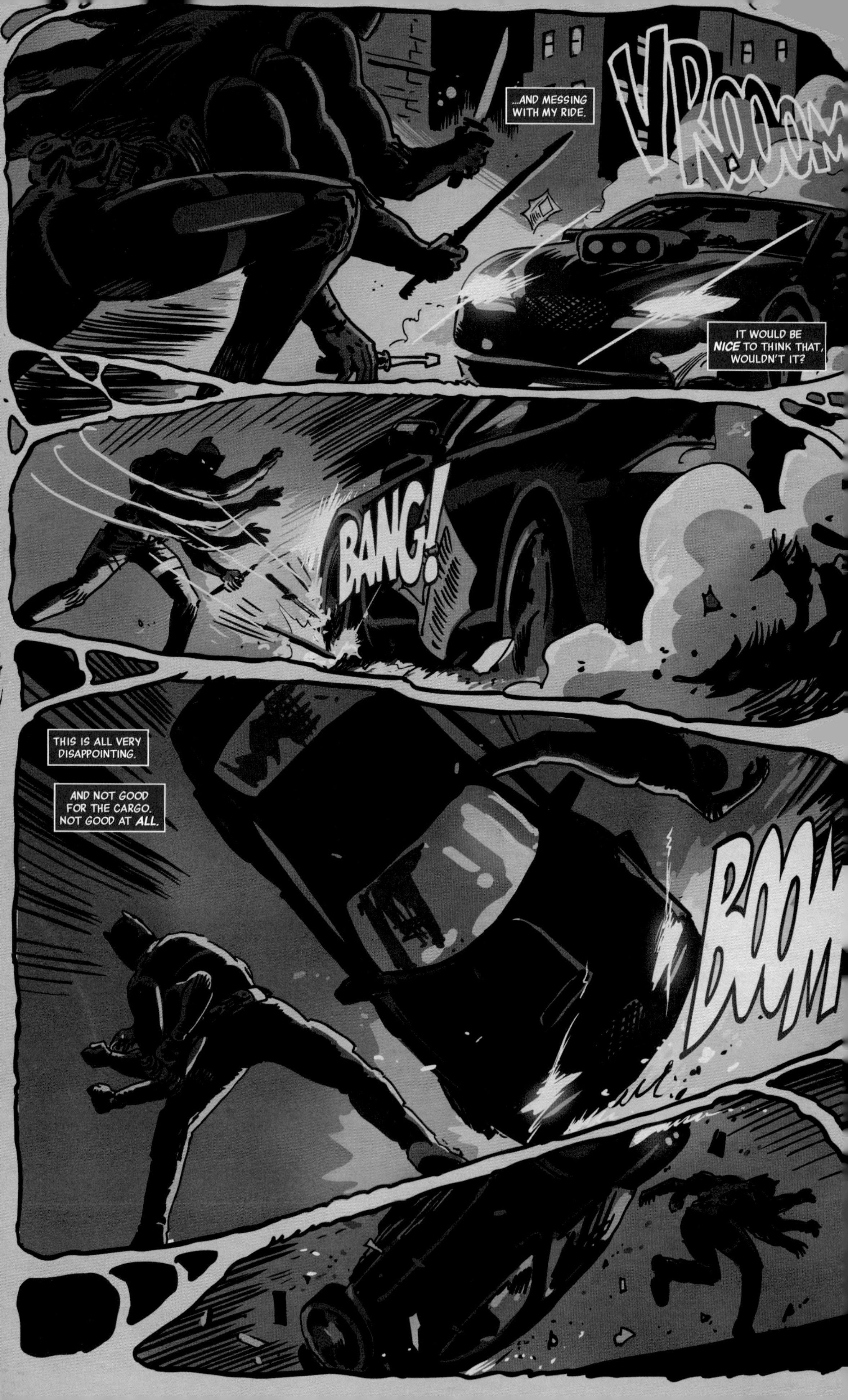

...AND MESSING WITH MY RIDE.
VROOOM
IT WOULD BE NICE TO THINK THAT, WOULDN'T IT?
BANG!
THIS IS ALL VERY DISAPPOINTING.
AND NOT GOOD FOR THE CARGO. NOT GOOD AT ALL.
BOOM

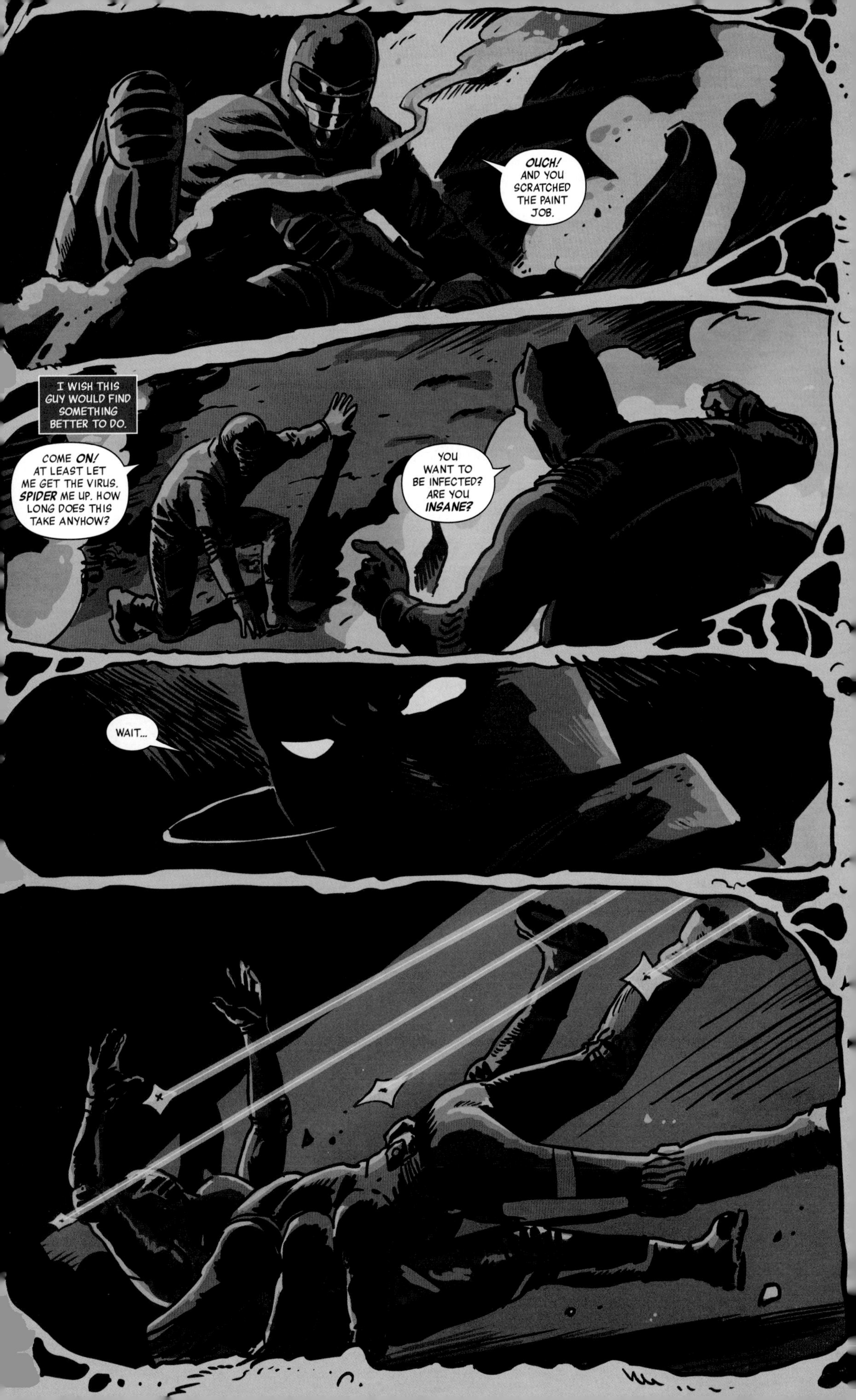
OUCH! AND YOU SCRATCHED THE PAINT JOB.
I WISH THIS GUY WOULD FIND SOMETHING BETTER TO DO.
COME ON! AT LEAST LET ME GET THE VIRUS. SPIDER ME UP. HOW LONG DOES THIS TAKE ANYHOW?
YOU WANT TO BE INFECTED? ARE YOU INSANE?
WAIT...

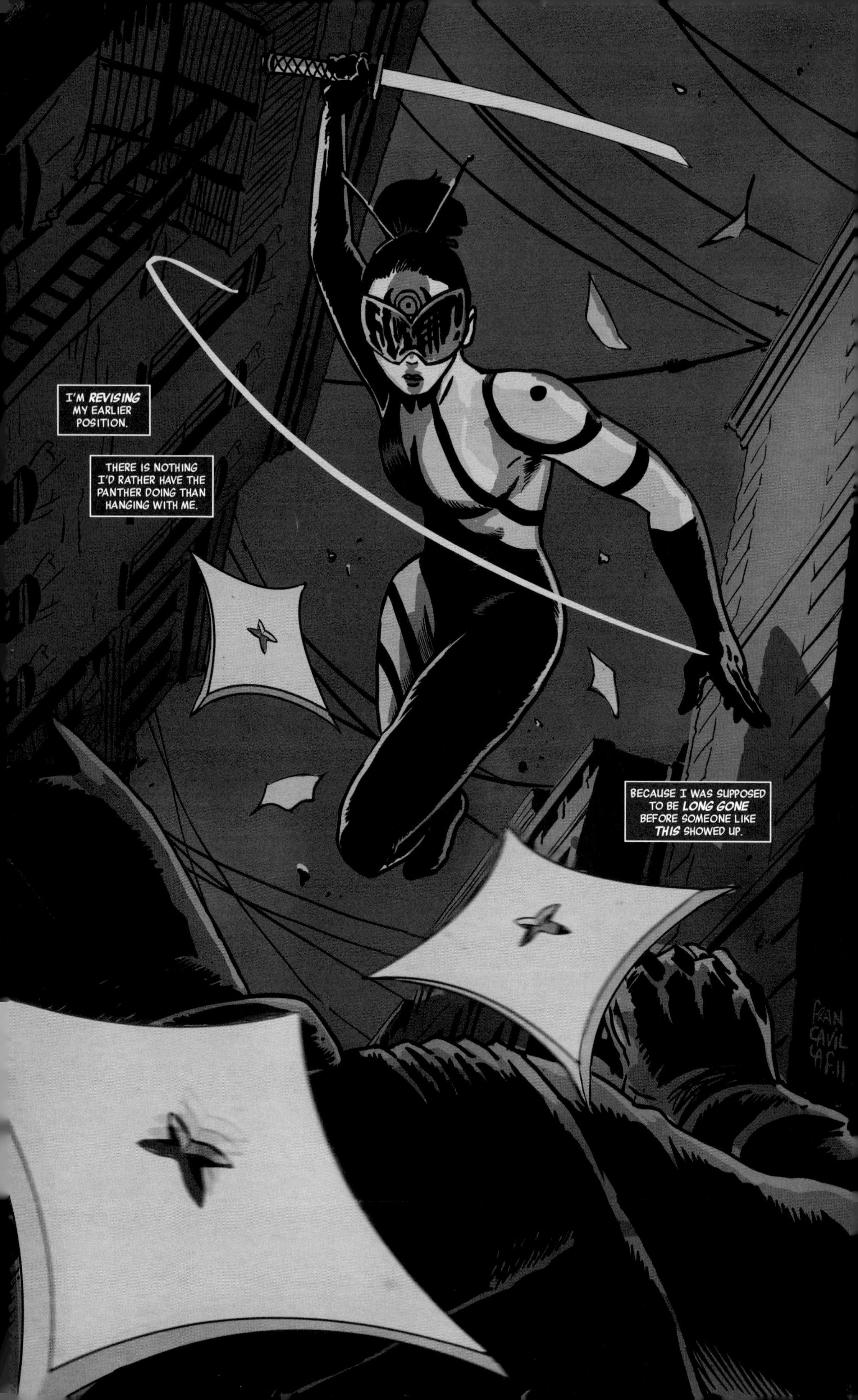
I'M REVISING MY EARLIER POSITION.
THERE IS NOTHING I'D RATHER HAVE THE PANTHER DOING THAN HANGING WITH ME.
BECAUSE I WAS SUPPOSED TO BE LONG GONE BEFORE SOMEONE LIKE THIS SHOWED UP.

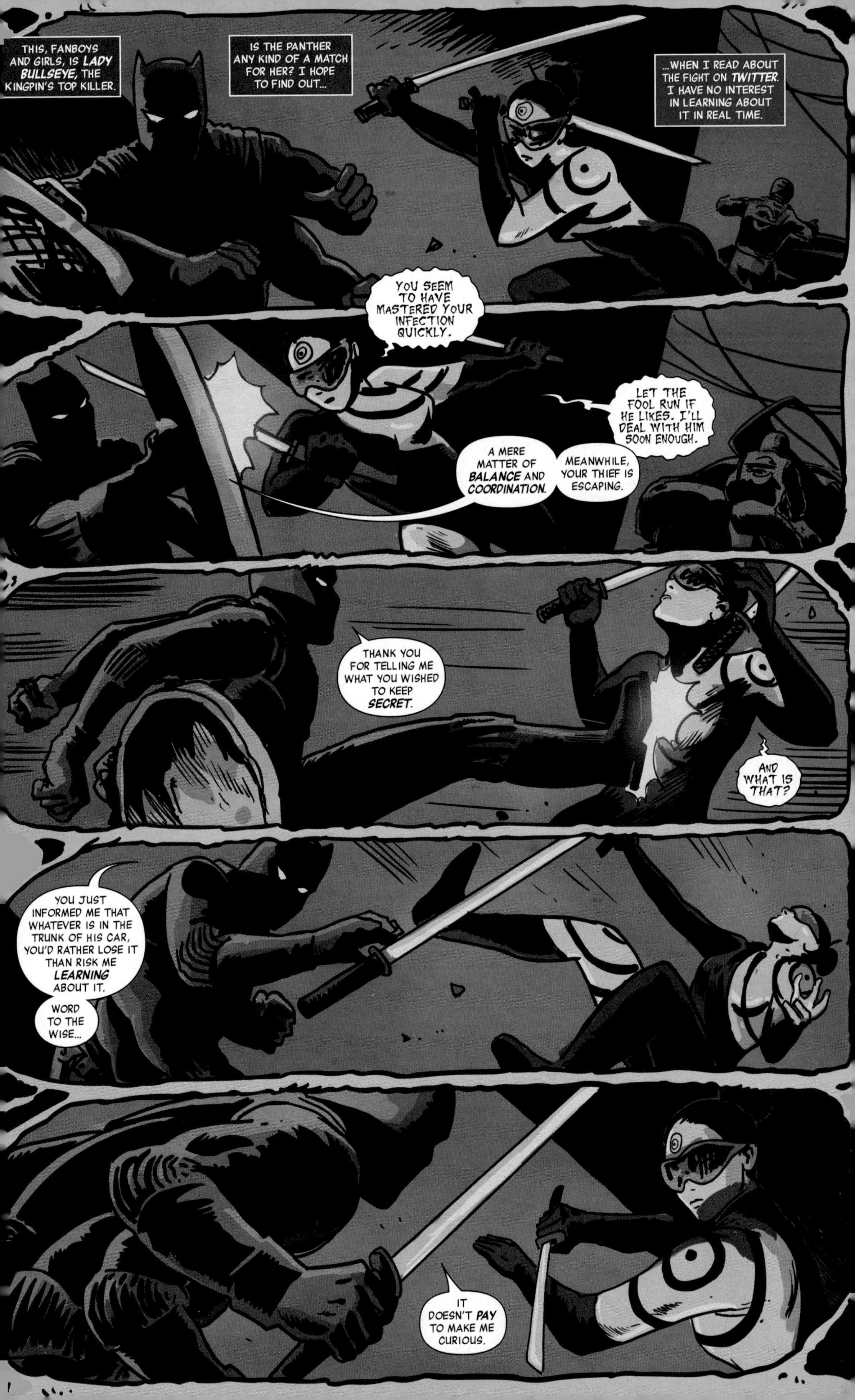
THIS, FANBOYS AND GIRLS, IS LADY BULLSEYE, THE KINGPIN'S TOP KILLER.
IS THE PANTHER ANY KIND OF A MATCH FOR HER? I HOPE TO FIND OUT...
...WHEN I READ ABOUT THE FIGHT ON TWITTER. I HAVE NO INTEREST IN LEARNING ABOUT IT IN REAL TIME.
YOU SEEM TO HAVE MASTERED YOUR INFECTION QUICKLY.
A MERE MATTER OF BALANCE AND COORDINATION.
MEANWHILE, YOUR THIEF IS ESCAPING.
LET THE FOOL RUN IF HE LIKES. I'LL DEAL WITH HIM SOON ENOUGH.
THANK YOU FOR TELLING ME WHAT YOU WISHED TO KEEP SECRET.
AND WHAT IS THAT?
YOU JUST INFORMED ME THAT WHATEVER IS IN THE TRUNK OF HIS CAR, YOU'D RATHER LOSE IT THAN RISK ME LEARNING ABOUT IT.
WORD TO THE WISE...
IT DOESN'T PAY TO MAKE ME CURIOUS.

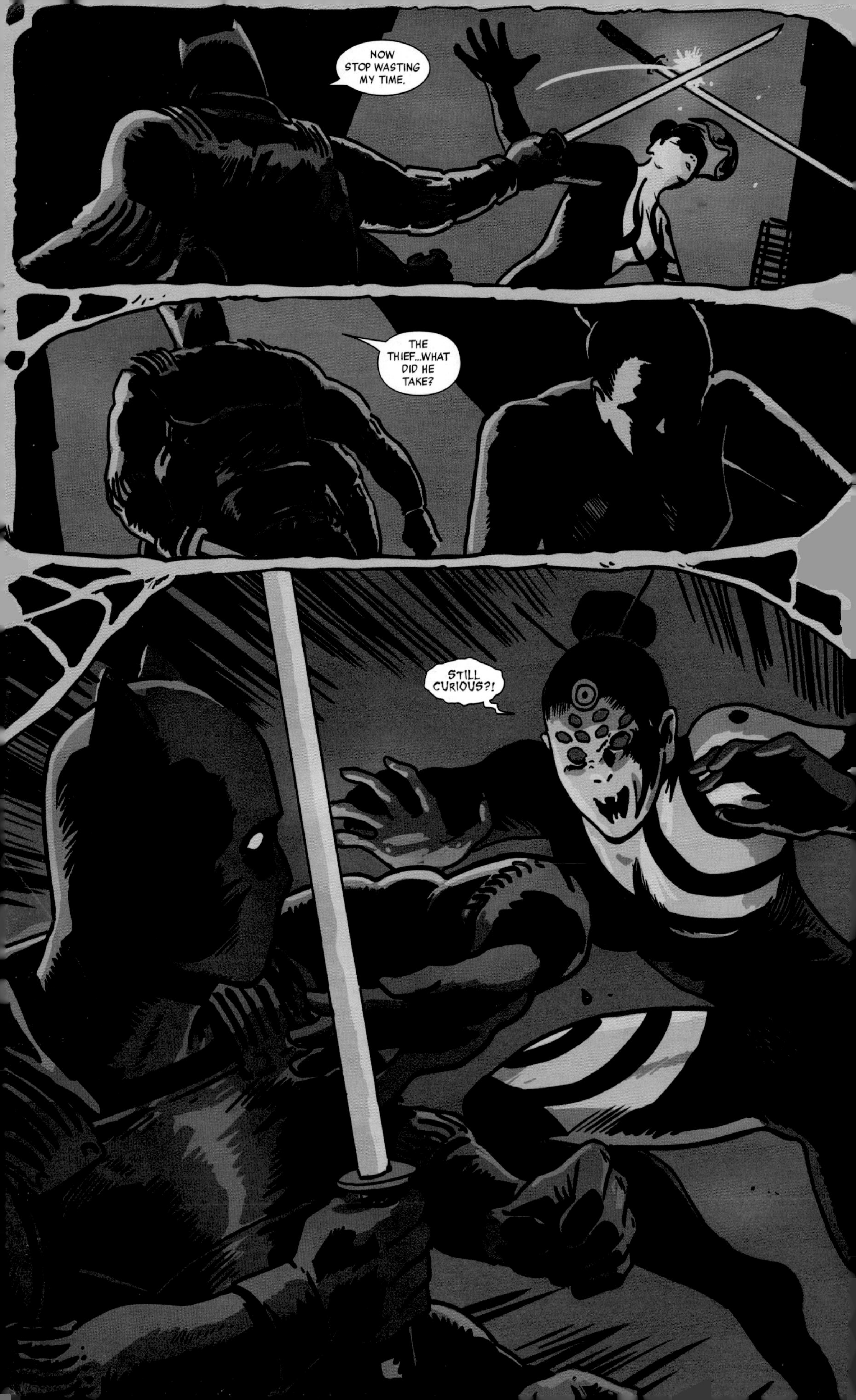
NOW STOP WASTING MY TIME.
THE THIEF...WHAT DID HE TAKE?
STILL CURIOUS?!

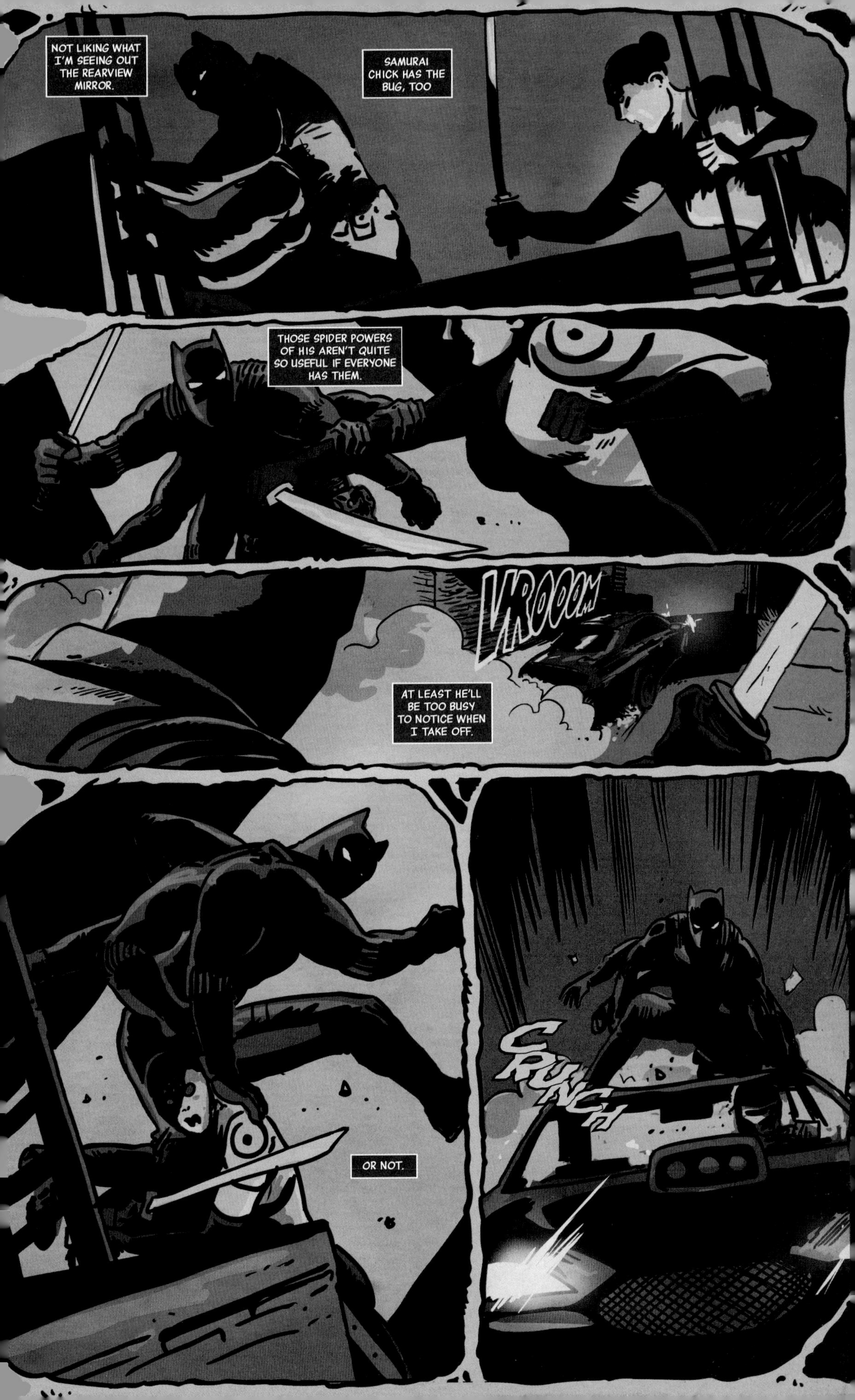
NOT LIKING WHAT I'M SEEING OUT THE REARVIEW MIRROR.
SAMURAI CHICK HAS THE BUG, TOO
THOSE SPIDER POWERS OF HIS AREN'T QUITE SO USEFUL IF EVERYONE HAS THEM.
VROOOM
AT LEAST HE'LL BE TOO BUSY TO NOTICE WHEN I TAKE OFF.
OR NOT.
CRUNCH

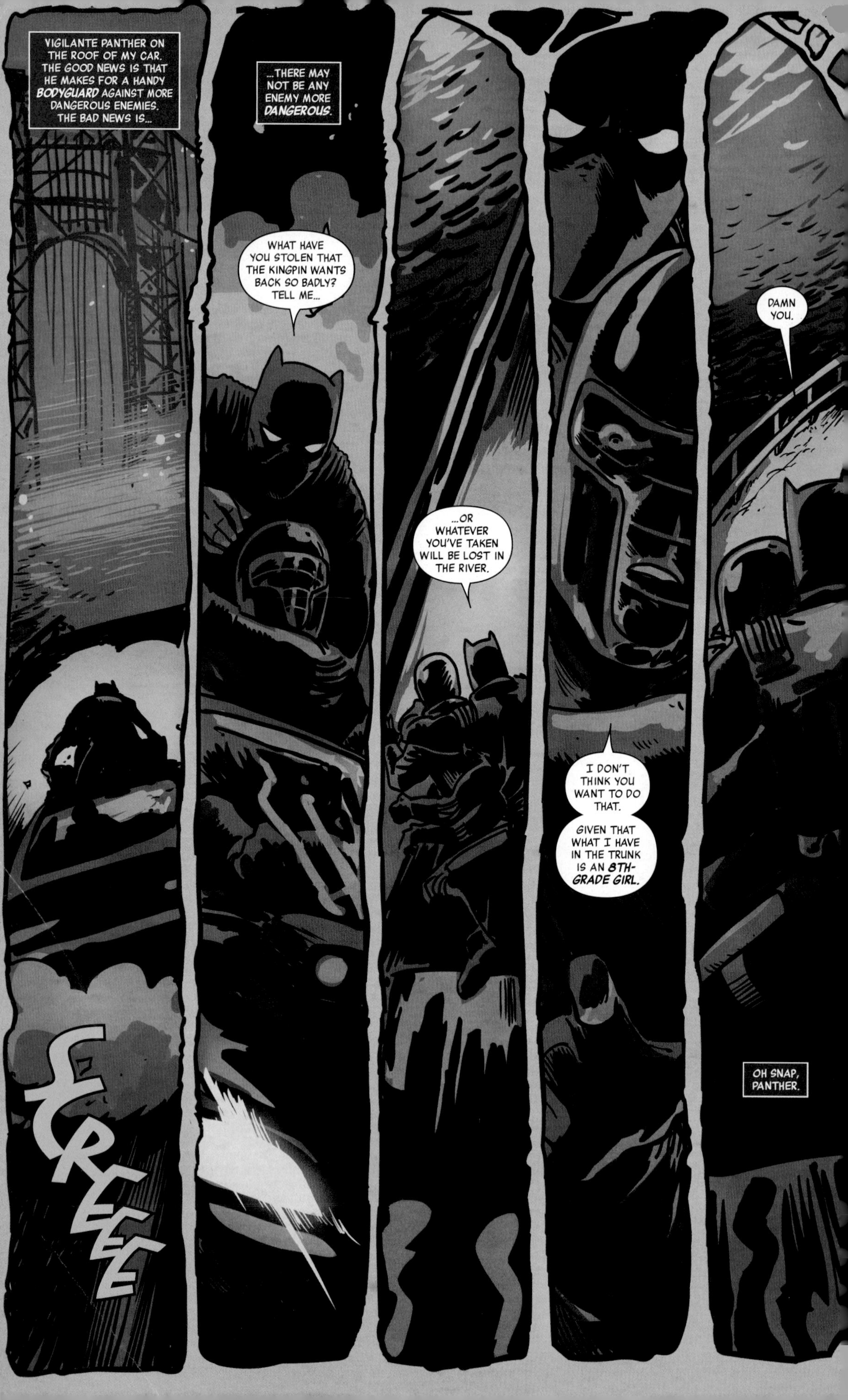
VIGILANTE PANTHER ON THE ROOF OF MY CAR. THE GOOD NEWS IS THAT HE MAKES FOR A HANDY BODYGUARD AGAINST MORE DANGEROUS ENEMIES. THE BAD NEWS IS...
SCREEE
...THERE MAY NOT BE ANY ENEMY MORE DANGEROUS.
WHAT HAVE YOU STOLEN THAT THE KINGPIN WANTS BACK SO BADLY? TELL ME...
...OR WHATEVER YOU'VE TAKEN WILL BE LOST IN THE RIVER.
I DON'T THINK YOU WANT TO DO THAT.
GIVEN THAT WHAT I HAVE IN THE TRUNK IS AN 8TH-GRADE GIRL.
DAMN YOU.
OH SNAP, PANTHER.

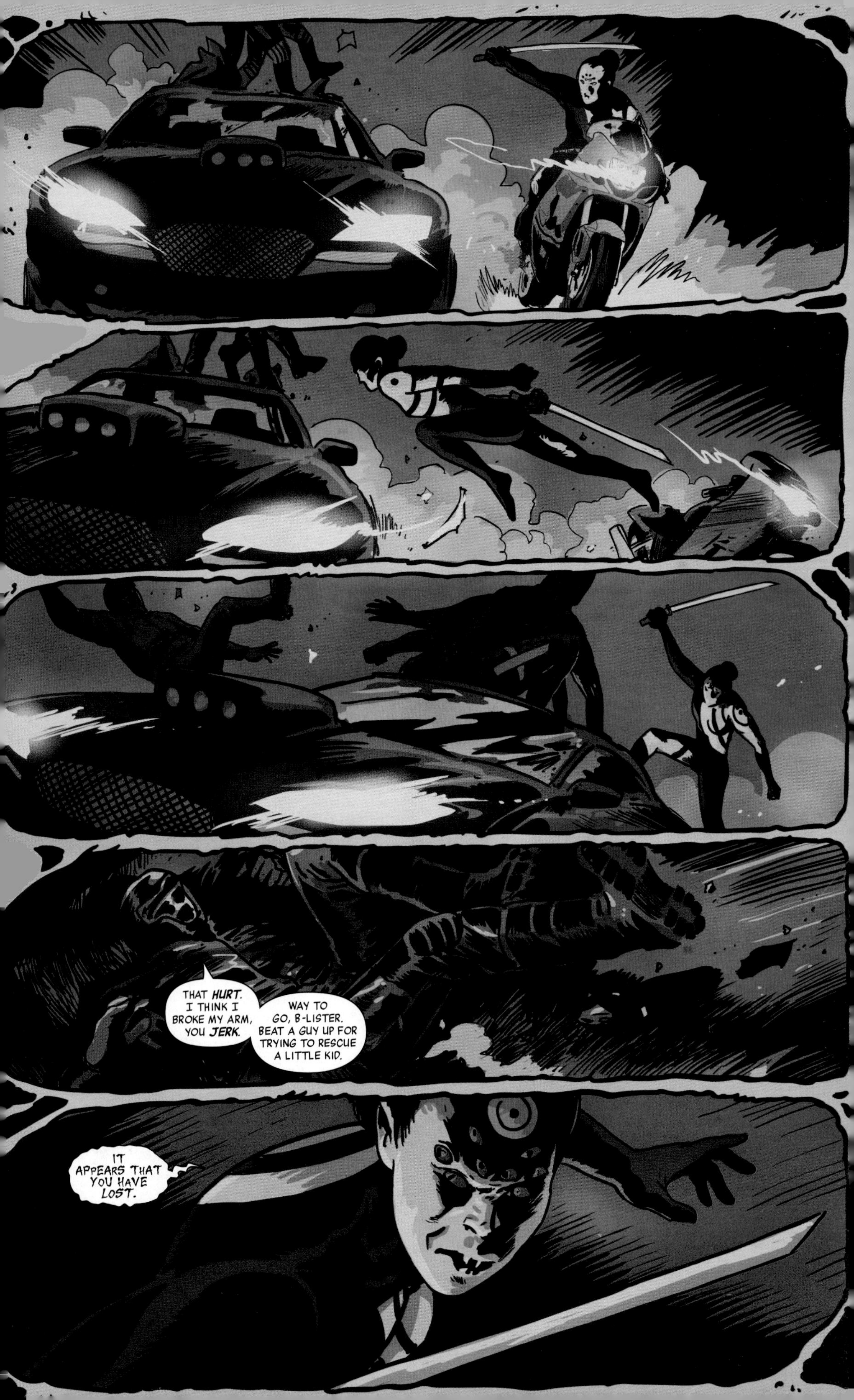
THAT HURT. I THINK I BROKE MY ARM, YOU JERK.
WAY TO GO, B-LISTER. BEAT A GUY UP FOR TRYING TO RESCUE A LITTLE KID.
IT APPEARS THAT YOU HAVE LOST.

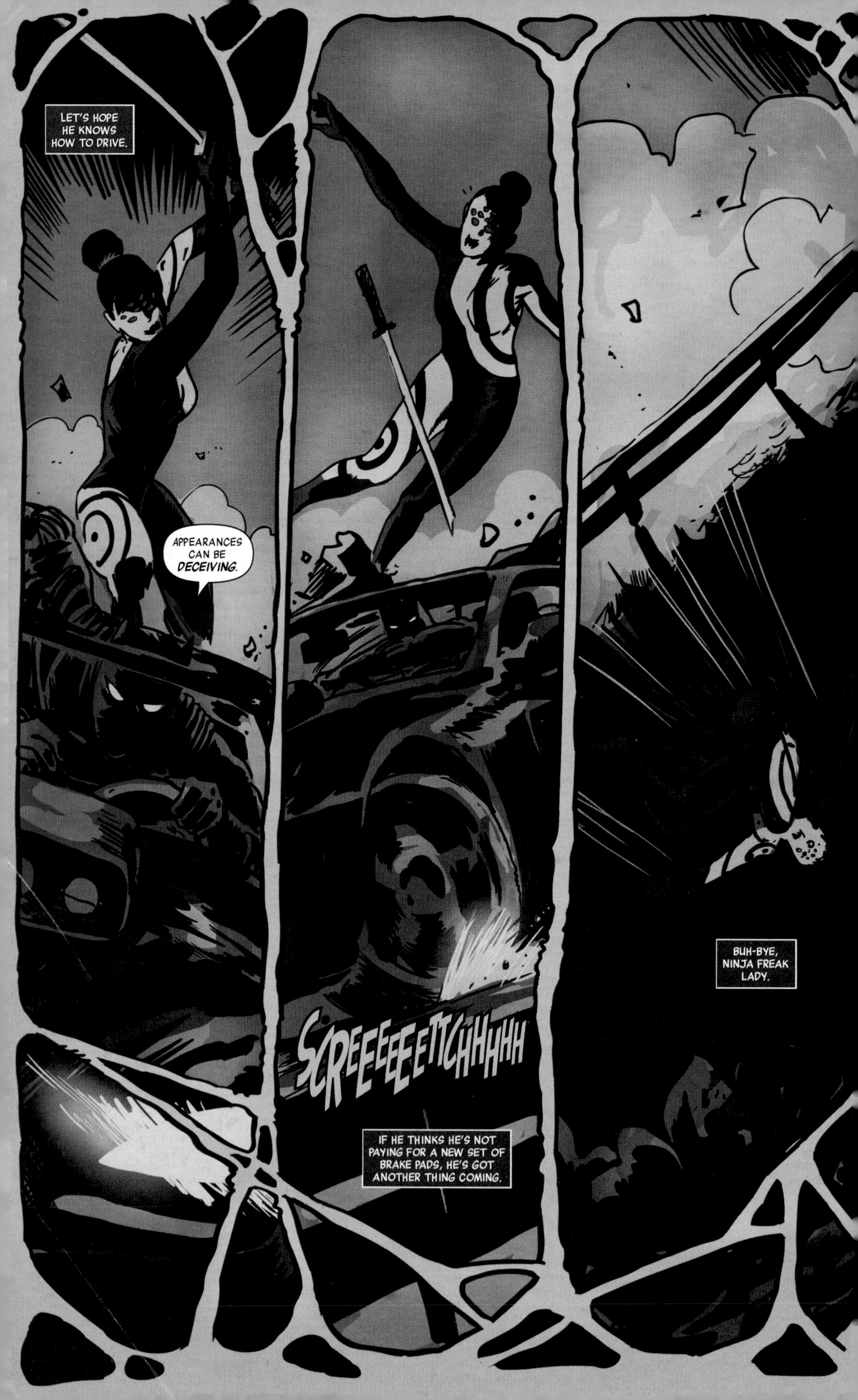
LET'S HOPE HE KNOWS HOW TO DRIVE.
APPEARANCES CAN BE *DECEIVING*.
SCREEEEEEETTCHHHHH
IF HE THINKS HE'S NOT PAYING FOR A NEW SET OF BRAKE PADS, HE'S GOT ANOTHER THING COMING.
BUH-BYE, NINJA FREAK LADY.

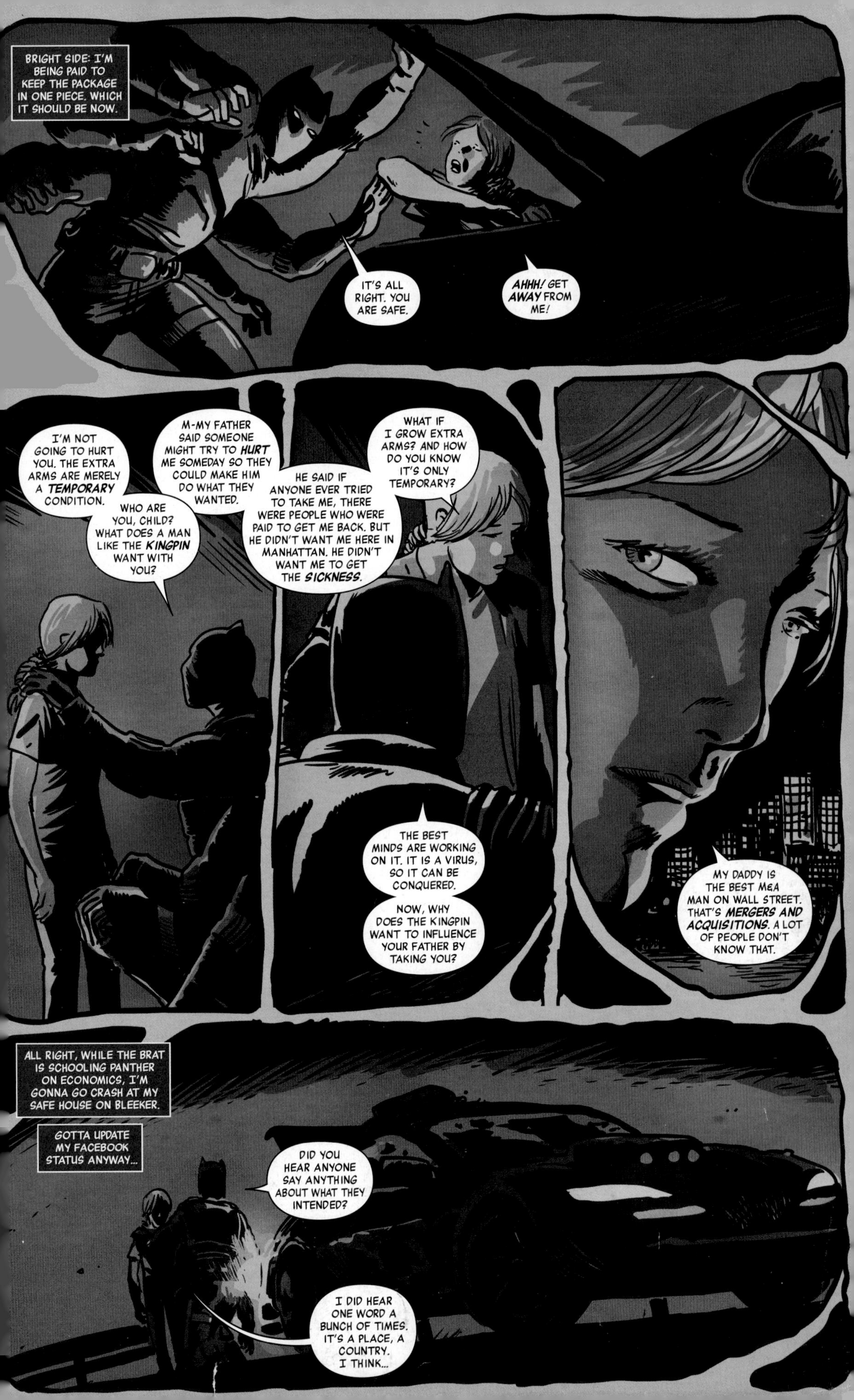
BRIGHT SIDE: I'M BEING PAID TO KEEP THE PACKAGE IN ONE PIECE. WHICH IT SHOULD BE NOW.
IT'S ALL RIGHT. YOU ARE SAFE.
AHHH! GET AWAY FROM ME!
I'M NOT GOING TO HURT YOU. THE EXTRA ARMS ARE MERELY A TEMPORARY CONDITION.
M-MY FATHER SAID SOMEONE MIGHT TRY TO HURT ME SOMEDAY SO THEY COULD MAKE HIM DO WHAT THEY WANTED.
WHO ARE YOU, CHILD? WHAT DOES A MAN LIKE THE KINGPIN WANT WITH YOU?
HE SAID IF ANYONE EVER TRIED TO TAKE ME, THERE WERE PEOPLE WHO WERE PAID TO GET ME BACK. BUT HE DIDN'T WANT ME HERE IN MANHATTAN. HE DIDN'T WANT ME TO GET THE SICKNESS.
WHAT IF I GROW EXTRA ARMS? AND HOW DO YOU KNOW IT'S ONLY TEMPORARY?
THE BEST MINDS ARE WORKING ON IT. IT IS A VIRUS, SO IT CAN BE CONQUERED.
NOW, WHY DOES THE KINGPIN WANT TO INFLUENCE YOUR FATHER BY TAKING YOU?
MY DADDY IS THE BEST M&A MAN ON WALL STREET. THAT'S MERGERS AND ACQUISITIONS. A LOT OF PEOPLE DON'T KNOW THAT.
ALL RIGHT, WHILE THE BRAT IS SCHOOLING PANTHER ON ECONOMICS, I'M GONNA GO CRASH AT MY SAFE HOUSE ON BLEEKER.
GOTTA UPDATE MY FACEBOOK STATUS ANYWAY...
DID YOU HEAR ANYONE SAY ANYTHING ABOUT WHAT THEY INTENDED?
I DID HEAR ONE WORD A BUNCH OF TIMES. IT'S A PLACE, A COUNTRY. I THINK...

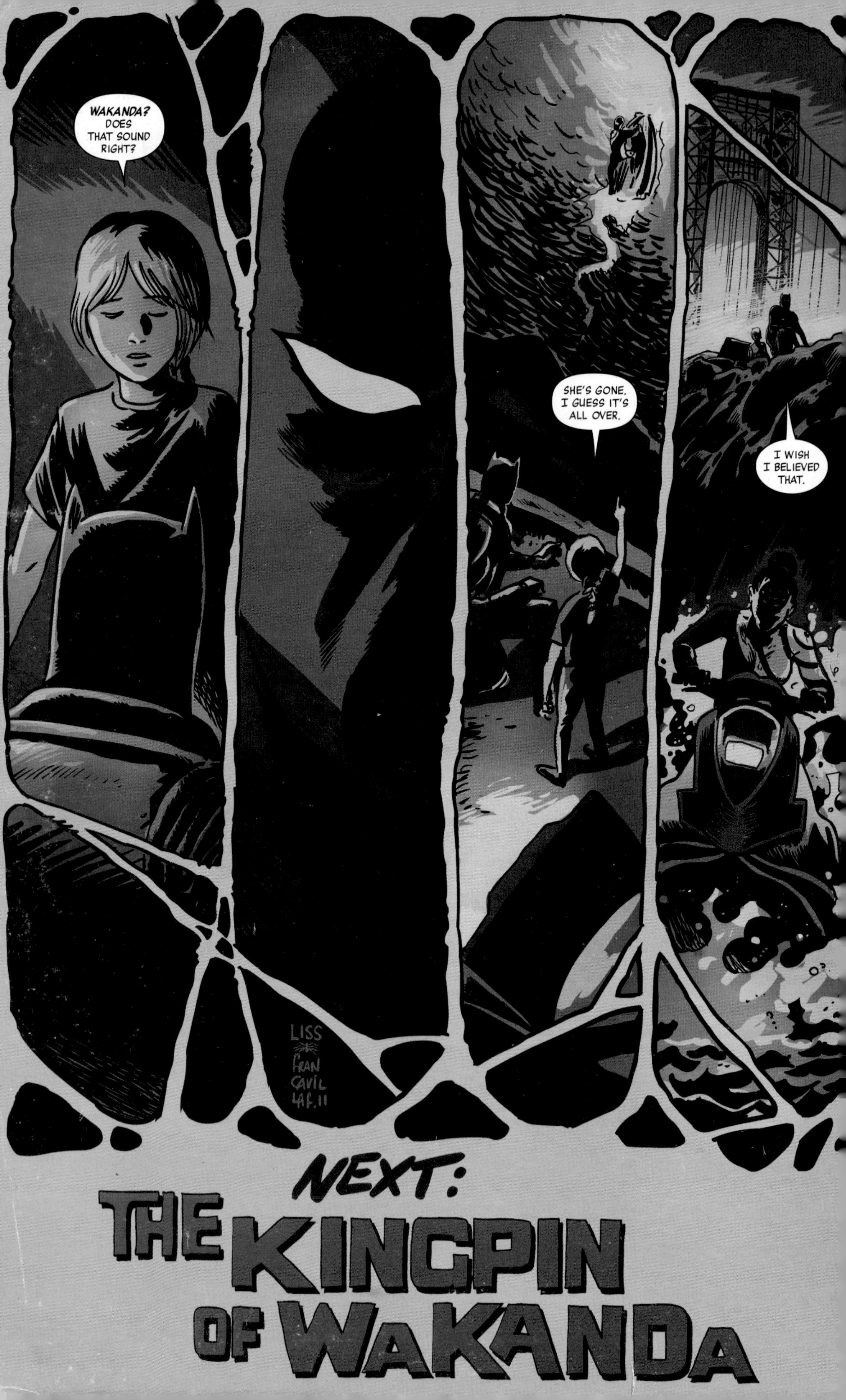
WAKANDA? DOES THAT SOUND RIGHT?
SHE'S GONE. I GUESS IT'S ALL OVER.
I WISH I BELIEVED THAT.
LISS
FRAN
CAVIL
LAF.11
NEXT:
THE KINGPIN OF WAKANDA